✣ ✣ ✣ ✣ ✣ ✣ ✣

THE ARMS DEBATE

✣ ✣ ✣ ✣ ✣ ✣ ✣

THIS BOOK HAS BEEN PREPARED UNDER THE AUSPICES OF THE
CENTER FOR INTERNATIONAL AFFAIRS, HARVARD UNIVERSITY

Created in 1958, the Center fosters advanced study of basic world
problems by scholars from various disciplines and senior officers from
many countries. The research at the Center, focusing on the processes
of change, includes studies of military-political issues, the modernizing
processes in developing countries, and the evolving position of Europe.
The research programs are supervised by Professors Robert R. Bowie
(Director of the Center), Alex Inkeles, Henry A. Kissinger, Edward S.
Mason, Thomas C. Schelling, and Raymond Vernon. A list of Center
publications will be found at the end of this volume.

❖　❖　❖　❖　❖　❖　❖

THE ARMS DEBATE

ROBERT A. LEVINE

❖　❖　❖　❖　❖　❖　❖

HARVARD UNIVERSITY PRESS
CAMBRIDGE · MASSACHUSETTS · 1963

✤　✤　✤　✤　✤

PREFACE

In reading books and articles on military policy and disarmament, I have been struck by the fact that very often when one writer summarizes another's position he summarizes that position incorrectly. I find this phenomenon most noticeable in descriptions of positions to which I happen to subscribe, as set forth in works with which I happen to disagree, but it can be found in works written from almost every point of view. I have no reason to believe that I myself am immune to the malaise of misinterpreting the arguments of others. And that explains why, in this book, I have resorted so frequently to the device of direct quotation from the source material under discussion. The chapters that follow are heavily interlaced with direct quotations of one or several paragraphs. By summarizing viewpoints in the words of their holders rather than in my own words, I hope to avoid at least the extremes of misinterpretation.

Of course this procedure too is subject to a danger—that of quoting out of context. I have, in the literal sense, always quoted out of context; it is impossible to do otherwise. I have also tried to keep the length of the volume under control by considerable use of ellipsis, removing intermediate material which is repetitive or not germane. I do not, however, believe that I have in any case cut out either context or intermediate material which would change the sense of what was said, and I am reasonably hopeful that almost all of the authors quoted would agree.

Indeed, the process of finding quotations illustrative of many viewpoints on the many subtopics of arms policy has been a highly enlightening one for me. I have frequently started out believing that a particular individual or school of thought maintained a certain position, and have set out to find an apt illustration. Then, rereading the written material produced by the individual or individuals, I have found that they did not say precisely what I had believed up until then; that the differences between what they said and what I thought they had said were subtle but distinct and important —and that what they really did say made more sense than what I had thought. One fairly well-known example of this phenomenon concerns the slogan, "Better Red than Dead." This is frequently attributed to Bertrand Russell, but Russell attributes it elsewhere and argues that it is an unfair presentation of the problem. And in fact, although Russell's views may justly be subject to criticism for other reasons, his arguments are far too complex to be dismissed simply as "Better Red than Dead." What is true of this example is true of many others less widely known. The process of not merely reading and summarizing an opponent's arguments, but actually quoting his own words, was extremely salutary to me. The reader likewise should not skip lightly over the quoted material.

But illustration by quotation runs into another danger. Most of the ideas on arms policy that are worth quoting are not written by committees, but by individuals. The purpose of this book, however, is not to classify individuals into neat pigeonholes, but instead to describe and analyze certain coherent broad viewpoints on arms policy. Although these broad tendencies can be characterized as "schools of thought," many of the individual writers who are quoted are highly eclectic, and their views, taken as a whole, do not fall into any single school of thought. And yet the schools of thought adopt ideas from these individuals as they appear useful to their general viewpoints. George Kennan, to take one example, is a highly original writer whose views span a wide range, and it would be impossible to put Kennan as an individual in any single category. Kennan's ideas on disengagement, however, have been adopted (in some cases, misinterpreted, but nonetheless adopted) by certain schools of thought on arms policy. They have been endorsed, in particular, by most of those groups who like to call themselves the "peace movement." These ideas of Kennan thus enter the arms viewpoints of this movement, and it becomes legitimate to quote Kennan to illustrate this portion of the views of these schools. But this does not make Kennan into a peace-marcher.

One additional corollary of this difference between the whole individual and his single quoted thoughts is that men change their minds over time, but their published statements remain unchanged until the paper crumbles. Were this book about individuals, account would have to be taken of how and why writers on arms policy have changed their minds. Since it is not, however, what are recorded here are statements which are still relevant to the current arms debate, even though those who made them may no longer hold precisely the same beliefs. As for the future, one cannot predict from the quotations what a writer on arms policy will say about the next problem to arise; one should be able to deduce, however, the implications of his current statements for future problems.

This book was written during a year spent as a Research Associate of the Harvard Center for International Affairs, while I was on leave from the RAND Corporation, and, in acknowledging the vast amount of help I have received from many sources, I must first thank the Center and its Director, Robert R. Bowie, for both supporting and encouraging me during the year. Both the Center and the Joint Harvard-M.I.T. Faculty Arms Control Seminar are a very fertile source of ideas on arms policy. Specific thanks are due to the Center faculty, particularly Thomas C. Schelling who gave aid, comfort and advice throughout, and Henry A. Kissinger, who provided useful comments on the draft manuscript. In addition, my fellow Research Associates at the Center deserve much credit, particularly Lawrence S. Finkelstein (who was on leave from his post as Vice President of the Carnegie Endowment for International Peace), Morton H. Halperin, James L. Richardson, M. D. Feld, and Bernhardt Lieberman, all of whom commented in painstaking detail on all or part of many drafts. Morton Halperin, in particular, should be singled out, because not only was his advice highly valuable, but also his library and his collection of clippings and reprints on military policy, the best indexed and most extensive in Cambridge, and perhaps in the country, were invaluable. Without them, the study might not have been possible at all. Much help was also given by the 1961–62 Fellows of the Center, particularly Colonel (now Brigadier General) Glenn A. Kent, USAF, and by the secretarial staff, practically all of whom worked on the manuscript at one time or another. Finally the Center Editor, Max Hall, gave the kind of assistance without which all else would have gone for naught.

In addition to my colleagues at the Harvard Center, many of my RAND colleagues provided detailed comments. Daniel Ellsberg, Allen R. Ferguson, Charles Wolf, Jr., Brownlee Haydon, Fred C. Iklé (in 1962–63 a Research Associate at the Harvard Center), Nehemiah Jordan, and James R. Schlesinger all deserve specific mention. And finally, Ernest Lefever and James E. King, Jr. of the Institute for Defense Analyses, William Fellner of Yale, and Ulric Neisser of Brandeis University were kind enough to provide comments, as was my wife Carol, who went far beyond her necessary role of supporting me emotionally, and went through the manuscript critically and in detail.

Given all of this impressive assistance, the statement that both the views expressed and the errors made are my own should be more than *pro forma*. In fact, many of the above people disagreed on various points of both substance and organization. Being a naturally stubborn sort, I frequently ignored their advice. The views, errors and blame, therefore, are *really* my own.

ROBERT A. LEVINE

Santa Monica
January 10, 1963

✤ ✤ ✤ ✤ ✤

CONTENTS

1. THE APPROACH   1

    Arms and Definitions, 5
    Arms and the Intellect, 6

2. THE LOGICAL STRUCTURE OF A POLICY POSITION   12

    The Parts of a Policy Argument, 13
      Definitions, 13
      Value Judgments, 14
      Analyses, 21
      Recommendations, 30
    Connecting the Parts: Arriving at
      Recommendations, 30
      Optimizing Mechanisms, 33
      Maximizing Mechanisms, 36
      Rationalizations and Compromises, 40

3. THE POLITICAL STRUCTURE OF THE ARMS
    POLICY DEBATE: SCHOOLS OF THOUGHT   44

4. INTRODUCTION TO THE MARGINAL
    SCHOOLS OF THOUGHT   58

5. MARGINALIST VALUE SYSTEMS   65

The Marginal Anti-War School, 70
The Marginal Anti-Communist School, 77
The "Middle" Marginal School, 82

The Balanced-Value Middle Marginalists, 85
The "Analytical" Middle Marginalists, 89
Summary, 95

6. INTRODUCTION TO MARGINALIST ANALYSES   98

7. MARGINALIST ANALYSES:
THE ANTI-WAR MARGINALISTS   104

Analysis of War, 104
Analysis of the Opponent, 110
Analysis of Power, 117
Analysis of Allies and Neutrals, 121
Analysis of Ourselves, 125

8. MARGINALIST ANALYSES: THE ANTI-COMMUNISTS   128

Analysis of the Opponent, 128
Analysis of Power, 136
Analysis of Allies and Neutrals, 141
Analysis of War, 144
Analysis of Ourselves, 153

9. MARGINALIST ANALYSES:
THE MIDDLE MARGINALISTS   154

Analysis of War, 156
Analysis of the Opponent, 185
Analysis of Power, 198
Analysis of Allies and Neutrals, 203
Analysis of Ourselves, 207

10. MARGINALIST RECOMMENDATIONS 210

    Consensus, 216
    Disagreement, 223
        Strategic Military Policy and Arms Control, 224
        United States Arms Policy in Europe, 248
        United States Arms Policy in The Rest
           of The World, 271
    Summary, 277

11. THE SYSTEMISTS 280

    The Anti-War Systemists, 282
    The Anti-Communist Systemists, 305

12. INTERPRETATIONS, IMPLICATIONS,
    AND CONCLUSIONS 313

    Why The Schools Differ, 313
    Personal Conclusions, 326
    The Intellectual and Political Processes on
        Arms Policy, 330

    ACKNOWLEDGMENTS 335
    INDEX 337

TABLES

1. Summary of values and analyses by marginal schools 212
2. Summary of recommendations by marginal schools 278

FIGURES

1. The five schools of arms policy 49
2. Values of the marginal school 96
3. The value and the analytical bases for differences of
    recommendations among the schools of arms policy 314

THE ARMS DEBATE

✦ ✦ ✦ ✦ ✦

CHAPTER 1
THE APPROACH

In recent years many clarion calls have gone out for a "great debate" over the arms policy of the United States. But a general and coherent debate has failed to materialize. There have been books, articles, and oral discussions, sometimes based on sharp disagreements over particular policies or the views of particular individuals, but these have been so diffuse that the holders of different viewpoints sometimes have not even seemed to be talking about the same things. The fact of disagreement has been obvious, but who has been disagreeing with whom over what, and why, has not been. Neither the rationale of current policies nor clear alternatives to these policies have been presented. The little debates going on have been more like the individual jousts of the Round Table knights than the final battle of Arthurian Britain (although perhaps carried out less chivalrously than either).

Much of the blame for this must be assigned to those critics of current policies who have been calling for a great debate. Their lack of understanding of what moves the makers of these policies enables the policy makers to dismiss them out of hand. But, ultimately, the failure to debate can lead to a failure of democracy, detrimental to the nation as a whole, and detrimental even to the making of the nation's arms policy. So long as things are going well, the lack of an understanding criticism is not crucial, but once they start to go badly, it can become so. The rapid growth of McCarthyism and other forms of know-nothingism during the Korean War was due not only to the fact that the war was not going well;

it was due also to the fact that the critics of military policy at the time knew little about the policy except that it was not going well. And although McCarthyism failed and the domestic witch-hunting aspects of McCarthyism receded, McCarthyism had profound effects on American arms policy. The doctrine of "massive retaliation," to take just one example, was in part a reaction to the belief that the American people would never tolerate another limited war.

The failure to make coherent the cases for both the existing policies and the possible alternatives is essentially a failure to comprehend the ramifying complexities of the subject. For one thing, there is a tendency to think of the discussion as a dialogue between "us" and "them," with "them" being everyone who doesn't agree with "us." But the differences among those put collectively on the "them" side of this putative dialogue may be at least as profound as the differences between the arbitrarily constructed sides. Thus, many advocates of multilateral disarmament tend to lump together those "arms controllers" who believe that actual arms reduction may be only a small portion of arms control and those advocates of victory in a "protracted conflict" with Communism who place little emphasis on any variety of control. And similarly, some of those who have little hope for disarmament put into a single category the advocates of negotiated multilateral disarmament, the advocates of tentative unilateral moves toward multilateral disarmament, and the all-out unilateral disarmers of various stripes.

Another reason for lack of coherence is the common inability to comprehend the interrelationships among the many parts of United States arms policy. One obvious example is the placing of disarmament (or arms control) in a separate category from "military" policy, with the implication that the one is a denial of the other. This separation of the unseparable is carried out not only by those disarmers whose free-association response to "military" is "militaristic," but also by those individuals so preoccupied by negotiation processes that they lose track of the substantive importance of what they are negotiating about. But the disarmament-military dichotomy is only a single example of this phenomenon. Perhaps an even more important case is the attempt to separate different "levels" of war. Although the possibility of strategic nuclear war between the United States and the Soviet Union is not identical to the possibility of war in Europe, the two cannot be evaluated separately. Yet there are many discussions on strategic force which, concentrating on the possibilities of accidental or self-generating nuclear exchange between the two major powers, come to solutions which ignore the role of American strategic forces in the European balance of power. And there are many discussions of war in Europe which, centering on the local military situation, ignore the importance of possible escalation to higher levels of violence. All this is not to argue that everything must be discussed chaotically and at once; organization and compartmentalization are necessary for any rational discussion. But the compartments cannot be watertight.

And, finally, perhaps the major complexity that is frequently ignored is the complexity of the logical foundations of the opposing arguments themselves. Statements on policy have three logically separable components: *recommendations* as to what should be done; *value judgments* as to what desirable effect we are trying to obtain by doing it; and *analyses* concerning what the effect of doing it will in fact be. These portions of a single argument, although they are closely intertwined in any given statement, can be distinguished from one another. But the difficulty with much of the arms debate as now carried on is that these elements are not ordinarily distinguished, and discussion thus occurs by placing in seeming opposition statements which cannot logically be opposed— for example, a recommendation confronted with an analytical statement. Thus one can hear a recommendation for increased nuclear deterrence opposed by the analytical statement that nuclear deterrence cannot prevent the spread of Communism in Southeast Asia. The analytical statement may be accurate, but, unless increased nuclear deterrence was proposed in order to stop the spread of Communism in Southeast Asia, the statement is also irrelevant.

More subtle and more common than this confrontation of the irrelevant, however, is the suppression of one of the elements—the recommendation, the value judgment, or the analysis—to the point where it is so deeply implicit that it must be ferreted out by those evaluating the argument. Thus, many arguments sharply critical of current arms policies fail to make explicit the recommendations as to what should be done, and therefore leave the hearer in doubt as to whether there is anything better available. Many arguments favoring disarmament do so on the basis of the value judgment that war is the worst of all evils, but leave the analysis of how (or whether) disarmament will reduce the danger of war so far beneath the surface that the very existence of this analysis must be deduced by the hearer. And many arguments favoring a policy of military strength depend upon sophisticated analysis of how such a policy will work in the real world, but leave so implicit the value questions of whether the primary objective of such a military policy should be to prevent war, to stem the tide of Communism, to roll back Communism, or whatever, that it takes a good deal of analysis to discover just what the arguer is aiming for.

The purpose of this book is both to analyze and to synthesize the arms debate. The "us" and the "them" in the current discussions will be analyzed into five separable "schools of thought" on arms policy. The viewpoint of each school on each major portion of policy will be analyzed into its components of value, analysis, and recommendation. By these methods it then becomes possible to synthesize—to tie together—the debate. The object is to identify the policy alternatives being offered by the various schools of thought and to understand the reasoning which lies behind these offerings. Only with such an understanding will it be possible to make coherent the many individual discussions going on, and thus to begin to create a "great debate" over the arms policy of the United States.

ARMS AND DEFINITIONS

It has frequently been noted by writers of analytical discourse that words used carelessly or with meanings other than the most common ones can provide a barrier to understanding. The usual remedy for this is to quote from Humpty Dumpty in *Through the Looking Glass* and then go on to define one's terminology precisely. In policy fields, however, often not even this is enough. The emotional connotations of certain terms remain even after the language has been redefined for exact usage. As a result, when definitions are extended to cover new cases, the extensions become frozen by political logic until the terms are used where they no longer really apply.

This book discusses the use of arms; it discusses "arms control," the placing of constraints on this use by national action or international agreement; and it discusses "disarmament," the control of arms by reducing their number. To call it a study of arms, however, is not entirely satisfactory; arms are merely the implements of war, whereas the heading which best covers the subject matter is "military policy." But "military policy" carries in some minds an emotional connotation which denies disarmament. Although I disagree strongly with those who put military policy and disarmament as necessary antitheses, I do not care to carry the disagreement to the title, and therefore this is called a book on arms. But it must be understood that arms policy is concerned with both the use of military methods and the denial of this use as alternative means of achieving national goals.

Since the prospects for domestic insurrection in the United States are small, arms policy in this country is a subdivision of foreign policy.[1] The boundary between the military and the nonmilitary aspects of foreign policy is an easy one to

[1] This does not exclude consideration of the effects of military forces on the domestic commonweal, any more than the fact that foreign economic aid is basically a portion of foreign policy excludes consideration of its effects on the domestic economy.

6] The Arms Debate

define (the military portions are those in which the creation, the use, the threat, or the denial of force play a role) but is impossible to delineate precisely in practice. Rather than trying to draw such a clear line, I shall touch on the many aspects of foreign policy tinged by the possibility of violence.

Finally, this book is centered on United States policies, although ideas from abroad are brought in. The arms policy of the United States cannot, of course, be divorced from the policies of its allies and its adversaries, but our policy is ultimately determined by our own decision makers. The actions of the United Kingdom and the ideas of Bertrand Russell are both relevant to the policies determined by these decision makers, but they are relevant only at second remove.

ARMS AND THE INTELLECT

Three sorts of discussions can be carried out on any set of policies: discussion of the substantive content of the policies; discussion of the political-administrative process by which the policies are made; and discussion of the intellectual process by which the components are devised and tied together.

The first of these, the substantive discussion, is the most common. Most of the recent work on arms policy has concerned the content of the policy and the political or military logic behind the content, making recommendations as to what this content should be. Such discussions may emphasize the political aspects of military policy, for example, such dissimilar books as Henry Kissinger's *The Necessity for Choice*[2] or Erich Fromm's *May Man Prevail?*[3] They may dwell largely on the strictly military aspects, as do Thomas Schelling and Morton Halperin in *Strategy and Arms Control.*[4] Or they may be much more abstract and theoretical, like Schelling's *The Strategy of Conflict.*[5] They may be based on the technical

[2] Henry A. Kissinger, *The Necessity for Choice* (New York: Harper, 1960).
[3] Erich Fromm, *May Man Prevail?* (Garden City: Doubleday, 1961).
[4] Thomas C. Schelling and Morton H. Halperin, *Strategy and Arms Control* (New York: Twentieth Century Fund, 1961).
[5] Thomas C. Schelling, *The Strategy of Conflict* (Cambridge, Mass.: Harvard University Press, 1960).

aspects of the effects of nuclear weapons, like *Community of Fear*, by Harrison Brown and James Real;[6] they may be moral-theological works such as Victor Gollancz' *The Devil's Repertoire*;[7] or they may even bring in disciplines not obviously applicable, as Seymour Melman does with industrial engineering in *The Peace Race*.[8] They may develop strategic recommendations from their historical antecedents, as Bernard Brodie does in *Strategy in the Missile Age*.[9] Or, finally, they may combine all approaches, as Herman Kahn tries to do in *On Thermonuclear War*.[10] But all of these works, as diverse in viewpoint as they are in disciplinary approach, have in common the fact that they discuss the substance of policy. They go from cause to effect, they criticize policies and policy trends, and they make recommendations as to what policies should be preferred. They predict, they commend, they condemn, and sometimes they scold. They touch only lightly on the processes which brought about the policies they criticize or praise, or which might bring about the policies they desire for the future. They are books about the meaty substance of policy in the tradition of John Locke and Adam Smith.

The second type of discussion, that of the policy-making process, is the subject matter of political history, starting with ancient Greece. The first normative work in the field is probably that of Machiavelli, and Machiavelli provides an ideal type of this sort of discussion. This is an analysis of "how-to" rather than "what-to." In modern terms most political journalism is of this sort, with the news columns providing descriptive matter and the editorials and columnists indulging in normative prescriptions. In recent years, some professional literature of this stripe has come into being, ranging from textbooks on public administration to specific case stud-

---

6 Harrison Brown and James Real, *Community of Fear* (Santa Barbara: Center for the Study of Democratic Institutions, 1960).

7 Victor Gollancz, *The Devil's Repertoire* (London: Gollancz, 1958).

8 Seymour Melman, *The Peace Race* (New York: Ballantine, 1961).

9 Bernard Brodie, *Strategy in the Missile Age* (Princeton: Princeton University Press, 1959).

10 Herman Kahn, *On Thermonuclear War* (Princeton: Princeton University Press, 1960).

ies. In the field of arms policy, examples are Saville Davis' article on the domestic politics of the nuclear test ban[11] and Halperin's on the Gaither Committee.[12] Certain books, such as Samuel Huntington's *The Soldier and the State*[13] and Charles Hitch and Roland McKean's *The Economics of Defense in the Nuclear Age*[14] have concentrated largely on portions of the policy-making process rather than the substantive aspects of military matters; but it is only a peculiarly bloodless work (which most of these are not) that does not get into substance at all. This sort of discussion, then, emphasizes largely the question of how we can obtain good policies, rather than what these policies should contain.

Finally, policy discussions can be concerned with the logical process of arriving at substantive content, rather than either the content itself or the political process. Such discussions are concerned with content, but, rather than agreeing, disagreeing or recommending, they investigate the intellectual bases for different sets of ideas. The questions of what is based on deduction, what is based on belief, what is based on fact, and what is based on value, are the important ones here. The attempt is to discover what fundamental concepts *really* underlie various policy recommendations, rather than what the world is *really* like. This sort of discussion is difficult because anyone holding ideas of his own does not find it easy to discuss opposing concepts in a manner which might be considered fair by his opponents; yet anyone who did not hold his own ideas on a particular subject would most likely be unacquainted with the field.[15] Nonetheless, in a field such

11 Saville R. Davis, "Recent Policy Making in the United States Government," in *Arms Control, Disarmament, and National Security*, ed. Donald G. Brennan (New York: Braziller, 1961).

12 Morton H. Halperin, "The Gaither Committee and the Policy Process," *World Politics*, 13 (April, 1961).

13 Samuel P. Huntington, *The Soldier and the State* (Cambridge, Mass.: Harvard University Press, 1959).

14 Charles J. Hitch and Roland N. McKean, *The Economics of Defense in the Nuclear Age* (Cambridge, Mass.: Harvard University Press, 1960).

15 Analysis by someone unacquainted with a field is not always a bad thing. Gunnar Myrdal was able to write his classic work on American race relations,

as that of arms policy, which has grown in little more than a decade from one studied mainly by technicians to one which is the subject of very sophisticated analysis as well as very deep emotion, such a study of the content of policy ideas can be important.

This book is such an attempt to analyze the intellectual content of ideas on arms policy. Although I try to be fair, I cannot be completely objective. I have my own point of view which can be placed among the schools of thought described in later chapters. This viewpoint, an in-between one placing primary emphasis on staying out of war, but recognizing the utility of military means in keeping both peace and national freedom, will be made more explicit as it becomes appropriate. But the point of view is not imposed to the extent of stating or implying, as would be done in a direct discussion of substance, that "This is what I believe and why I believe it; this is why my opponents are incorrect." Rather, the working hypothesis here is that since all policy recommendations, including my own, are based on value judgments concerning the way the world should be, on analyses concerning the way the world is and can be, and on logical connections between the two, some relatively objective comparison is possible. The values are treated here as matters of personal taste, and although it may be possible to prove them inconsistent with one another, it is impossible in any meaningful way to show that any single policy value is "wrong." The analyses are, in principle, either right or wrong, but except for the most elementary ones, they all concern the relative probabilities of future events, and it is difficult to argue with certainty that one possibility for the future is more or less probable than another. Even after the event, though there can be no doubt that it did occur, it may nevertheless be possible to argue that, on an a priori basis, the event was less probable than some alternative happening.

An American Dilemma, precisely because he began with a solid intellectual foundation, but with little initial knowledge and few analytical preconceptions.

It is unlikely that the holders of all viewpoints will accept my analysis as to what they believe and why they believe it. Even though values can be treated as matters of personal taste, the implicit values upon which some policies are based may, when made explicit, not be to the precise taste of those who advocate these policies. Similarly, although it is difficult to prove that any prediction is completely incorrect, some prognoses, when made explicit, seem pretty unlikely. There are, of course, plenty of unreasonable, overstated, and just plain stupid defenses of any point of view. This study attempts to use the best examples, not the worst. Nonetheless, my aspiration is less to make the holders of divergent viewpoints accept my analysis of what they believe than it is to impel them to do their own analyzing. Even the best advocates frequently fail to sit back and figure out how they got here from there.

The above may seem to imply that what is about to take place is less logical analysis than psychoanalysis. This danger can largely be avoided by concentrating on stated ideas rather than on the holders of the ideas; and, particularly, by concentrating on *the arguments by which the holders of arms-policy viewpoints try to convince others,* rather than the psychological route by which they themselves arrived at the viewpoints. In this way, it is possible to steer away from the sort of discussion which states that "X is a pacifist because he spent his childhood traveling from military post to military post and hated it." This is out of place here. What is also excluded, although the exclusion may be less obvious, is the sociological *ad hominem* type of discussion which perhaps reaches its maximum vigor in relation to American military policy in C. Wright Mills' *The Power Elite* and *The Causes of World War III.*[16] This sort of argument, which in Mills' case states that those who favor strong military policies do so because of their elite positions, is also used by those in the opposite camp who aver that many of the radical opponents

[16] C. Wright Mills, *The Power Elite* (New York: Oxford University Press, 1956); *The Causes of World War III* (New York: Simon and Schuster, 1958).

of current policy are radical precisely because they are "outs," and tend to become much more moderate if they get "in." It is also used by "red-baiters" to discredit their opponents. Although arguments of this sort need not be completely baseless, they are irrelevant to this study. It is possible to analyze ideas on their own grounds—what is stated, and on what logic and values the statements are based—and this, rather than either psychoanalysis or social analysis, is the task I have undertaken. A policy viewpoint stands on the basis of what is said by its holder, not on the basis of what the holder is or has been.

✤ ✤ ✤ ✤ ✤

CHAPTER 2

THE LOGICAL STRUCTURE
OF A POLICY POSITION

Recommendations made on matters of national policy frequently seem more simple than they actually are. Even recommendations of an extremely complex aspect are often
presented in a manner which appears to omit certain factors
which are indispensable portions of any policy recommendation. Every policy recommendation must *necessarily* rest on
value judgments as to what are the proper objects of policy;
every policy recommendation must *necessarily* rest on analysis of how the recommended steps will help attain the desired
objects. Of course it is possible to keep the value judgments
or the analysis implicit—a doctor does not have to put on the
record for each case that his policy object is to cure the pa-
tient, nor does a clergyman have to announce at each opportunity that his (theo)logical analysis leads him to the belief
that prayer will assist in attaining the explicit goal of salva-
tion. Similarly in arms policy, the goals of peace, of freedom,
and/or of national survival are implicit even in the most
cold-blooded discussions of military strategy, and the analytical belief that we can get from here to there is implicit in the
most moralistic appeal for nuclear "sanity."

The difficulty in discussions of national policy, however, is
that some recommendations are couched in terms which make
the most of analysis and leave the value judgments implicit,
while others tend to leave the analysis equally implicit by
concentrating on the values. Comparison of opposing ideas is

possible only if the constituent parts of each argument are made explicit. Then corresponding portions of opposing arguments can be compared with one another—values with values, and analyses with analyses—rather than attempting the impossible contrast between the value judgment which forms the stated basis of one position and the analytical picture of the world with which another begins. The values and analyses discussed here as the necessary constituents of a policy argument are, of course, a set of ideal types, each of which is simpler than the real-world phenomenon it is supposed to represent. These ideal-type parts can be differentiated from one another in their pure definitional forms, and they can, with more difficulty, be distinguished in substantive discourse. In most policy statements, however, the components cannot be isolated from one another for individual examination, but rather are grouped into sets of values and analyses which almost always go together. It thus becomes a chicken-and-egg proposition to decide which came first, the value or the analysis; but rather than invalidating discussion of the ideal types, this interdependence makes some sort of modeled decomposition of an argument into its components even more essential for the understanding of a complex logical process.

THE PARTS OF A POLICY ARGUMENT

Definitions

A definition is the meaning assigned to a word or phrase by its user. A user can assign any meaning he desires without violating the rules of logic, so long as he uses the definition consistently throughout, and so long as it is consistent with his other definitions. Thus an individual can, without being illogical, state that he will define the color of human blood as being green, so long as he admits that stop-lights and Soviet flags are also green, and so long as he does not call grass green. Of course it is not very convenient if one individual calls green what everyone else thinks of as being red, and convenience is the key to using definitions. I have already pointed out that although it would be closer to the dictionary definition to call this a study of military policy rather than arms policy, the two phrases have been changed by political usage in such a way that it becomes more convenient to discuss arms policy. Similarly, the terms arms control and disarmament have been used in so many different ways by so many different individuals that at this point it might be most convenient to start all over again. But nobody's definition of arms control or disarmament is *wrong* so long as it is used consistently.

Another aspect of definitional convenience is that the definition should refer simply to the object or class under discussion. Thus one may define a "unit" of eggs as being a dozen, but if he is writing a cookbook in which the recipes ordinarily use eggs singly, it is less than convenient to refer to .0833333 . . . . . units. In military policy, definitions of terms such as "limited war" run into similar sorts of difficulties, as, for example, when one needs specific terms both for wars which are limited in that they do not involve American and Soviet homelands, and wars which may involve these territories but are limited in that they avoid destruction of population centers. Again, convenience is important, but logic does not enter in, so long as consistency is maintained.

Value Judgments

Value judgments are statements (or unstated notions) of preference. It is a value judgment if I find some event preferable to another. It is an expression of a value judgment and a numerically measurable one if I would pay five cents more for a McIntosh apple than for a Delicious (although this measures the value to me of both apples and money, the one in terms of the other). The meaning and implications of value judgment are vital to the understanding of policy ideas, and it is worth recording systematically some of the major characteristics of such judgment:

1. Value judgments can be best defined as matters of personal preference which are considered by the individual holding them not to be dependent upon other value judgments. This sort of definition avoids some knotty philosophical problems as to what can be considered a true first-order value judgment. If an individual prefers a particular situation to another because the former is "good," rather than because it contributes to another situation which is a higher "good," then this preference is to him a pure value judgment. Perhaps in close argument another person could convince him that what he thought was good for its own sake was in fact dependent upon some other of his values; perhaps, once this dependence was pointed out, the individual might even change his preference scheme. In this sense, value judgments cannot be considered immutable. But in order to avoid an unnecessary discussion of the existence of true first-order value judgments, it suffices for the purpose of mundane policy analysis to state that the value portion of an argument on arms policy is that part which is considered by the arguer to be a first cause at the time he makes the argument.[1]

Within the limits discussed below, first-order personal value judgments cannot be logically challenged or called "incorrect," insofar as they are couched as first judgments, and not as logical deductions from other statements. If I state that I dislike automobiles, this is unchallengeable. If I state that I dislike automobiles because they are noisier than subways, my dislike for noise is unchallengeable, but the question of whether autos or subways are noisier is open to objective investigation. There are three major types of limitation on this unchallengeability of values. One of these, the challenge of values on grounds of ethical philosophy, is out-

[1] The economic concept of "utility" is much the same as the value concept used here. This utility concept has been frequently challenged in recent years on the grounds that personal preferences for material goods can be changed by advertising and similar mediums. It is not a denial of the logic of the challenges to state that "utility" is still a vital concept for the understanding of economics. In the same sense, first-order personal political values are useful for the understanding of conflicting ideas on arms policy.

side the scope of this book, which takes moral relativism as an operational axiom. The other two, however, the requirements of consistency and the requirements imposed by the gap between personal value judgment and social decision, require further discussion.

2. The basic requirement for consistency among value judgments by an individual is simply that the values not be self-evidently contradictory—that a preference system cannot simultaneously include both A and not-A. To this is sometimes added a second requirement called "transitivity"— that, if A is preferred to B, and B to C, then A must be preferred to C. If a person's value scheme does not violate these rules, then his preferences cannot be criticized on the basis of logic. Of course, the matter is considerably less simple in application than it may seem: many volumes of the most complicated verbal and mathematical discourse have been written discussing the implications of logical consistency for decision making.[2] The point being made here, however, is negative. An individual can claim rationality for his preference scheme only if it does not violate at least the first of these rules.

3. The requirements of logic thus rule out of rational ideologies conflicts among preferences, where these conflicts are based on an inconsistency between judgments. But *competition* among value judgments, which is in practice frequently confused with inconsistency, is emphatically *not* ruled out. It is true that if A and B are indivisible units, I cannot both prefer A to B and B to A. But if A and B are divisible, I can value both of them highly and still be willing to give up some of the one for some of the other. Thus, I value both money and apples, and am willing to surrender some cash for some apples. Apples and all the other goods for

[2] See, for a relatively simple summary, chap. 13 of R. Duncan Luce and Howard Raiffa, *Games and Decisions* (New York: Wiley, 1957), particularly pp. 297–298, which summarize J. W. Milnor's requirements for reasonable decision criteria, and show that none of the common criteria satisfies all of the requirements. The Luce-Raiffa book is the basis for most of my citations of decision theory, except where otherwise specified.

which I might spend money compete for my scarce funds. This may seem elementary, but in discussion of arms policy, this admissible sort of value competition is frequently mistaken for the nonadmissible inconsistency of preferences. An example of this is the claim that a willingness to risk war is inconsistent with a sincere desire for peace. An individual may place a high value on peace, and may at the same time place a high value on some other policy goal, the pursuit of which involves a risk of war. These values may well compete for policy emphasis, but they are not inconsistent.

4. Another sort of conflict of values is that between persons holding different ideologies. The problem of resolving conflicts among individuals in order to reach a social decision is a serious one for the making of arms policy, but it is basically a political problem which falls outside of the scope of an investigation of the intellectual bases for arms policy recommendations. This study discusses recommendations on arms policy as if they were made by single individuals (writers) to a single individual (the President) elected to represent the ideologies of the voters. This contrasts to the idea of arriving at political decisions by resolving the ideological conflicts within a large group (the electorate). In our form of representative democracy, the fact that we do elect individual decision makers rather than making national political decisions by referendum means that this individual-to-individual model of policy recommendation is not a bad description of reality. This is particularly the case for arms policy, where decisions cannot be based on simple weighing of alternative values, but also depend on analysis of information not available to the typical voter because of its highly technical and perhaps secret nature. This concept of government for the people by their chosen leaders rather than government by the people also applies particularly well to arms policy because the political impact of conflicting economic interest groups plays a smaller role here than in many other portions of national policy making.

Nor can it be said that the resolution of interpersonal value conflicts by the choice of a decision maker is antidemocratic. It has frequently been stated in recent years that Presidents are elected on the basis of their "images" rather than the issues, and it is fashionable to decry this as a perversion of democracy. But it is not a perversion of representative democracy, and indeed it may provide a way of bringing representative democracy up to date. If the general electorate is incapable of understanding all of the technical issues involved in arms policy today, the electorate is capable of choosing the candidate it likes best on the basis of his "image." And it is not unreasonable to state that the image chosen is ordinarily that one which best represents a broad consensus of the partly conflicting and mostly inarticulated value systems of the voters.

In the 1952 and 1956 elections, the Eisenhower "image" was based on much more than either the picture on the TV screen or the wiles of Madison Avenue. The image of "Ike" started among his troops in North Africa and in Europe, just as the indelible image which kept MacArthur from the presidency started basically with his troops. It was popular in some circles to state that the American people in electing Eisenhower chose a father image (usually as compared to a brother-in-law image). But they did much more than this; they elected a man whose image was that of a person of integrity, uncomplex peacefulness, mild economic conservatism, and general moderation. One might argue that this was not what America needed from 1953 to 1961, but it is difficult to argue that Eisenhower was not precisely what the United States wanted, or that his decisions (including decisions by omission) were not based on a broad consensus of the values held by the electorate in the 1950's.

Similarly, the 1960 election, although it was so close that one cannot say that the electorate clearly preferred Kennedy's image to that of Nixon, illustrates another facet of the image as representing the values. The Kennedy and Nixon images did not differ too much from one another, nor did their

values.[3] But the fact that the political conventions chose such
similar men when they could have had Senator Goldwater
(whose image implied a much "tougher" arms policy) or
Adlai Stevenson (whose image implied an arms policy considerably more oriented toward a quest for disarmament), is
in itself striking. By 1960, although the basic ideological
values of the voters had not changed from those exemplified by the Eisenhower middle of the road, their concep-
tions of the kind of person they wanted to achieve these
values in the dangerous world were changing (although Ike
undoubtedly could have been reelected were it not for the
two-term amendment). The 1960 conventions managed to
nominate two men who represented both the value consensus
of the electorate and the somewhat changed road the electorate wanted to take in achieving these values.

Obviously, this sort of thing cannot be pushed too far
without reaching either absurdity or mysticism, and it cannot
answer all questions about resolution of interpersonal ideological conflicts among the citizenry (why not Nelson Rockefeller or Lyndon Johnson?). But the important points are,
first, that conflicts of values among different persons are resolved in the United States by some sort of political process,
and, second, that American presidential politics do in fact
aid in such resolution. And if the President in some sense
represents a value consensus, then the identification of key
points of difference among different value systems and different arms recommendations bears an important relationship
to the real policy-making process on armaments.

[3] I argued in an unpublished paper written in 1960 between President
Kennedy's election and his inauguration, that, in fact, the Kennedy-Nixon
exchange in which Kennedy *sounded* as if he might be more willing than
Nixon to give up Quemoy and Matsu, implied that Kennedy as President
would be likely to follow a less aggressive arms policy than Nixon. I claimed
that this was indicated by their respective *attitudes* toward the issue even
though both were actually backing exactly the same concrete Quemoy-Matsu
policy. At that time, I was talked into removing this statement from a later
version of the paper. But, in retrospect, the fact that Kennedy as President
has actively looked for compromises with the Communists in areas such as

5. The final point to be made about value judgments is a very important one for the subsequent discussion. Such a judgment can reasonably be made at any level of concreteness. Because of this it becomes unnecessary to make a sharp distinction between ends and means. An individual is free, within the constraints of logical consistency, to attach intrinsic positive or negative value to a specific event which another individual feels has no independent interest, but only value derived from its being an instrumental means to another, more general, goal. William Fellner, for example, suggests that an individual whose preference functions imply a certain personal value associated with a certain sum of money may place less value on the same sum if it is derived from gambling. Gambling, for such an individual, has a concrete disutility not shared by others to whom the quantity of money in question is the only matter subject to personal preferences. Fellner argues that the antigambling preference can form part of a perfectly rational preference scheme.[4] It is equally important to point out, however, that another individual not sharing the antigambling preference and trying to make a decision at a roulette table would be foolish to follow policy advice based on the preferences of the nongambler.

Berlin, Laos, and even Cuba, while Nixon as titular head of the Republican party prodded him to be tougher, seems to show that I was right the first time.

[4] William Fellner, "Distortion of Subjective Probabilities as a Reaction to Uncertainty," in "Symposium: Decisions under Uncertainty," *Quarterly Journal of Economics*, 75 (November 1961). Fellner's argument is criticized, notably by Howard Raiffa in the same symposium, on the ground that while it may accurately describe decision making, it provides a bad norm for rational decision. This is still an open issue in economics, where the argument concerns business affairs. It may be reasonable to argue that if the individual is in business at all, he has no logical right to act as if business processes had a disutility for him. He should act purely rationally to maximize his profits and, if he intends to act otherwise, he should become a professor or a civil servant. Arms policy, however, is different in that there is no clearly understood set of value criteria for decisions and every citizen has a logical as well as a political right to try to convince the decision maker of the validity of his values.

This sort of difference in the concreteness of values can become extremely important to the consideration of conflicts over arms policy. If, for example, some individuals choose to place an intrinsic value on disarmament, this is as rational, per se, as other value systems which would grant to disarmament only a derived value stemming from its contribution to the more general goal of keeping the peace. But if the decision maker being advised does not place this intrinsic valuation on disarmament, then he is logically free (although, of course, not necessarily politically free) to reject recommendations which appear to be based on this value, even though the analysis connecting the particular value system and the recommendations is impeccable. If the decision maker shares, instead, the preference system giving disarmament only the value derived from keeping peace, then his consideration of disarmament measures must depend on the cogency of the analytical connection between the measures and peace. One major question in the study of the ideas behind arms recommendations is the extent to which radical arms-policy recommendations are based on unpopular value systems, and the extent to which they are based on unusual analyses but more common values. To the extent that value differences are the crux, it seems fair in a democracy to place little political weight on the unpopular recommendation. To the extent that it is the analyses which differ, however, it is necessary to consider the recommendation carefully and objectively, since the correctness of analysis should not ordinarily be subject to majority vote.

Analyses

If definitions and values cannot be called incorrect so long as they are internally consistent, two other portions of policy argument can be. These are analyses and the final output— which brings together definitions, values, and analyses—policy recommendations.

Analyses provide the connecting links which show the interactions between what should be (values) and what is, and which transform the present world of what is into the future world of what can be and what will be if. Analyses can, in general, be challenged—on the basis that a description of what is, is inaccurate, or on the basis that what is predicted will not come to pass. One type of analysis, however, cannot be challenged without changing its intrinsic nature. This is the portion of analysis which is ordinarily called "fact." A fact successfully challenged is no longer a fact.

Facts are defined here to consist of axioms, conclusions of deductive logic, and some conclusions of inductive logic. Webster defines an axiom as "a statement of self-evident truth." An observed fact can be considered a kind of axiom, which, although not literally self-evident, is evident because it has been seen. If an observation or other axiom is challenged, then it is no longer evident, and moves out of the axiomatic category, at least for the challenger. An axiom is logically rather closely allied to a value, the difference being that an axiom has no connotation of preference. If an individual refuses to accept what others consider an axiom, then the individual can build a policy system on his new set of axioms, just as non-Euclidean geometry is built on the rejection of the Euclidean axioms. But, as in the case of an individual's building policy on the basis of his own peculiar value system, those who still accept the axiom in question are logically free to reject out of hand the system built by the challenger.

Another sort of fact is a statement derived by a train of deductive logic from a definition or an axiom. Deductive logic is reasoning which goes by tautology "from given premises to their necessary conclusion." A successful challenge to a train of deductive logic can either prove that it is incorrect and thus substitute, in effect, an alternate logical train, or it can show that it is not *necessarily* correct, in which case it becomes, by definition, inductive logic, and subject to legitimate challenge. A deductive "fact" can be challenged on the basis of the assumptions (axioms or definitions) from which it stems or the logic by which it is derived. If the challenge is a good one, the deductive "fact" can no longer be considered a fact.

Finally, a quite different sort of fact is one stemming from observation by way of *inductive* logic, the logic which moves from the specific to the general. The fall of the apple was, to Newton, an observed and therefore an axiomatic fact. The law of gravity, which can be considered a set of facts, was then derived from the inductive generalization that apples and other objects would continue to move in the future according to the same rules they had observed up to that time.

For policy purposes, however, a different sort of definition, cutting across all of these classes, can be applied to the concept of fact. Operationally, about the only workable definition of a policy fact is that it is something which is agreed by all relevant persons to be a fact. Most such facts ordinarily concern the physical world. There exists, for example, remarkable agreement concerning many of the facts of radiation, nuclear testing, and nuclear warfare—and almost none concerning the policy implications of these facts.[5] Where nonphysical events are subject to enough agreement to be called facts, they are generally events of the past rather than future possibilities, and even then their policy implications are generally susceptible to a large enough variety of interpretations to make the facts themselves appear relatively trivial. It is generally agreed (at least in the United States) that the North Koreans invaded South Korea in 1950, and that this was an act of Communist military aggression. But the policy implications of even this seemingly straightforward historical fact depart rapidly from the realm of agreement when one non-Communist American analyst can write, "But to say that this invasion was an act of military aggression does not lessen its defensive overtones."[6] Indeed, fact is fact when it is agreed to be fact, and by far the largest portion of policy discussion is not agreed and therefore nonfactual.

Facts, then, form by far the smallest and least interesting portion of policy analysis. Much more important is the por-

5 See Robert A. Levine, "Facts and Morals in the Arms Debate," *World Politics*, 14 (January 1962).
6 Fred Warner Neal, *U.S. Foreign Policy and the Soviet Union* (Santa Barbara: Center for the Study of Democratic Institutions, 1961), p. 20.

tion of analysis based on inexact inductive logic. The bulk of all policy argument is contained in this category. Inductive logic which generalizes that "these causes have had these effects before, and therefore they are likely to have them again," is by its nature imperfect. There is no *necessary* reason why the effects will occur again, it just seems likely that they will. Even what were termed above "inductive facts" are factual only to the extent that the operational definition of "agreed facts" applies to them. In cases such as Newton's apple it is very likely that history will repeat. The kind of history which is relevant to policy analysis, however, almost always has too many personal and other variables to repeat itself exactly. Inductive policy analysis is thus concerned with isolating from the infinity of events occurring before or simultaneously with an occasion of interest, those which were relevant to the particular occasion; and with estimating which of these events are likely to recur.

Once relevant events have been isolated, the predictive portion of inductive analysis becomes, in a broad sense, statistical. That is, given a set of causes, there is a range of possible effects, rather than a single predetermined outcome. It is possible to argue philosophically that, were it possible to isolate all causal events in the real world, there would be no statistical answers—all effects would be determinate. This argument may or may not be valid, but for policy purposes it is irrelevant, since it is not possible to isolate all causes. Some events, such as President Eisenhower's heart attack, are completely unexpected; others, such as President Kennedy's narrow election, make it difficult to believe that precise prediction of important political events is possible. Rather than predicting determined events, then, inductive analysis predicts most likely results or ranges of results, always with some statistical chance that the actual result will even be outside the predicted range. The results of inductive analysis are frequently expressible in terms of probabilities—that there is a 75 per cent chance that certain events will occur as a result of the known set of causes, or at least that the events are more likely than other events. The efforts of inductive-statistical analysis should be twofold: to narrow down the range of uncertainty by discovering as many of the relevant causes as is economically and otherwise feasible; and to ensure that the remaining residual chances of error are unbiased, in that any excluded causal events are believed likely to cancel one another out rather than all biasing the answers in one direction.

The results of inductive policy analysis are initially untested. The analysis predicts future chains of events, and cannot be tested until the relevant futures come to pass.[7] Given this constraint of initial untestability, inductive predictions can be divided into three categories: predictions which will be testable in practice; those which are testable in principle, but probably will not be in practice; and those which cannot be tested in any case.

Predictions which can be realistically tested are unconditional and, for the most part, simple, such as "it will rain tomorrow," or "there will be a thermonuclear war within five years." Because of the multiplicity of causes and the statistical nature of inductive prediction, it is either a careless or a cocksure policy analyst who is willing to go on record with a testable inductive generalization.

Much more common is the conditional prediction which is in principle subject to test, but in practice can be tested only when the conditions are fulfilled. The favorite Latin phrase of economists is *ceteris paribus*—all other things being equal. All other things seldom are. Nonetheless, because testable propositions in a field such as arms policy are almost

7 Analytical futures can be future time periods from the instantaneous to the infinite, and identifying the future for which predictions are being made is ordinarily an important portion of the analysis. The rate of discount which should be applied to future time periods (how much more important the near future should be considered than the distant future) is a function both of ideology, which can value near and distant events, and analysis which can differentiate between the degree of certainty attached to near and distant futures. The value aspect of the discount rate can be illustrated by the dispute over the effects of nuclear testing on future generations; the analytical aspect by the dispute over the imminence of war.

always naïve, conditional propositions form the bulk of inductive policy analysis. Statements take the form, "if this action is taken, this event will result."

The third category, however, contains the most precise inductive propositions, which are even more qualified than this—so qualified that they cannot be tested even in principle. These are statements such as "If this action is taken, there is a 75 per cent chance that this result will follow." If the action is in fact taken, the result will either follow or not; and without replication of the type carried out in statistical experimentation in the laboratory, there will be no *ex post* way of testing the *ex ante* probabilities. In the real world of policy, this sort of repetition of precisely controlled conditions is impossible even in principle. Yet, when untestable but quantified predictions can be made, they give the most useful advice to the decision maker, since they provide him with more information than any of the others.

At any rate, the important portion of policy analysis concerns itself not with agreed facts, whether observed, axiomatic, or deduced, but with inductive statistical generalization. The idea that almost all useful policy results are uncertain is basic to the discussion of policy differences. As has been argued above, values differ, and the differences are for the most part beyond worldly debate. If all analyses were either deductive and certain or uncertain but testable, it would only be necessary to trace the logical conclusions of value judgments, and let some political process choose the determinate policy results of a majority set of values. In fact, the uncertainty of the real future leads analyses to differ, and the necessary task is to distinguish the differing inductive analyses as well as the differing value systems upon which different arms policy recommendations are based.

Recommendations

Values and analyses, then, are the two portions of the logical train which leads to policy recommendations. Recommendations are sometimes defined broadly to include desires, hopes, and goals, but a narrower definition is closer to ordinary usage. I define a policy recommendation as a statement suggesting that some *action* be taken by some individual or corporate *actor* whom the maker of the statement believes capable of taking that action. The identity of the actor may be only implied, but unless he exists there is no recommendation. Thus I exclude from the category of recommendations general statements about things which the maker of the statements would like to have happen, but which he does not have the slightest idea how to bring to pass.

Policy recommendations, like analyses, are open to logical dispute. They can, of course, be questioned on the basis of the challengeable inductive logic which is a necessary part of the reasoning leading up to the recommendation. In addition, because of the intervention of the imperfect logic between values and recommendations, it is not always clear what implicit value judgments are contained in policy recommendations. The recommendations can thus also be questioned on the basis that these implicit values differ from those of the actor to whom the recommendation is addressed. A personal distaste for gambling is not challengeable on a personal basis, but it is reasonable for a progambling adviser to inform the bettor at the roulette table that he is in danger of taking advice from an antigambling man whose unexpressed preference scheme he does not happen to share.[8]

Policy recommendations have a number of features important to the subsequent discussion of the content of specific policy ideas. Recommendations can be *unconditional* or they can be *conditional* to any degree. An unconditional recommendation is generally worded in one of two ways. It can say to the policy actor, "Do this now, without waiting for any intervening steps"; or it can say, "After taking specified

[8] In practice, this investigation of implicit values must be sharply distinguished from the questioning of personal motives discussed in relation to C. Wright Mills and others in Chapter 1. With the possible exception of the Communist party, membership in an organized group or societal "class" does not ordinarily imply automatic predetermination of the policy values of an individual. Communist party members in the United States in 1962 are

first steps, take the subsequent steps no matter how the first steps turn out." Conditional recommendations shade off from this last statement. Recommendations for sequential measures are conditional if they conceive of any outcomes of the first steps which will preclude taking the next ones, and they become more conditional as the recommender enlarges the set of early outcomes which may obstruct the taking of the later steps. Unconditional recommendations can be made for long as well as short future time periods (unilateral disarmament is thought of by some of its advocates as a long-run unconditional recommendation), but once the possibility of preclusive early outcomes is admitted, conditional recommendations are likely to be *more* conditional the further in the future is their execution. For a distant future, there is a large number of intermediate outcomes which may possibly intervene. Indeed, at some stage, very conditional or very far-distant desires should be excluded completely from the recommendation category. A statement, for example, that if Russia and China disarm unilaterally we should follow suit is hardly a recommendation.

In any case, discussion of policy must focus primarily on the unconditional end of the scale—recommendations for current action and those for future action which are predicated on few, if any, uncertain intermediate outcomes. What distinguishes the schools of arms policy is their attitude toward these relatively unconditional recommendations. If we set enough previous conditions, all schools might "recommend" the same utopia.

These relatively unconditional recommendations, then, can be further divided between those aimed at *marginal* change and those that are *systemic*.

Unconditional *marginal* recommendations are those which advise the policy shaper to make only small changes in exist-

---

rare enough to have no significant effect on policy debate, and the ideas of all of the individuals and schools of thought mentioned, whatever their outlook on arms policy, are treated here purely on the basis of what they say and have said—not who they are.

ing policies.[9] An individual can, of course, make his recommendations in a chain, with the later, more drastic, ones conditioned upon the success of the earlier. But if nothing but the initial, less drastic recommendations in the chain are made unconditionally, then the chain can be considered to be made up of marginal recommendations.

Were the later actions recommended regardless of the results of the initial marginal ones, however, this would be something else again, since the unconditional recommendations would encompass drastic as well as marginal changes to current policies. The name given here to such large unconditional recommendations is *systemic* recommendations because the changes involved are on so large a scale that they pervade entire military or political systems; they may, in fact, effectively mean the scrapping of old systems and the adoption of new.[10] A simple arms-policy example of the difference between marginal and systemic recommendations is given by the difference between proposals for the unilateral abandonment of the testing of nuclear weapons and those for the unilateral abandonment of the weapons themselves. Abandonment of nuclear testing may or may not be a good idea;

[9] The concept of "marginal change" is taken largely from the idea of "incrementalism," suggested by Robert Dahl and Charles Lindblom in *Politics, Economics and Welfare* (New York: Harper, 1953), pp. 82 *et seq.* The use of the concept here, however, does not follow their theory in all details.

[10] The use of the word "systemic," here, has two antecedents in modern social science. One is in the method of systems analysis by which the attempt is made to analyze a proposal in its total environment, rather than in isolation, and then to compare different systems. This method is widely used in the analysis of military equipment, and somewhat less widely in military strategy. Systems analysis is not incompatible with purely marginal recommendation if the new system recommended is only marginally different from the old, and *systems analyses of military strategy do not typically come up with recommendations for systemic changes in this strategy.* For the best description of systems analysis see Herman Kahn and Irwin Mann, *Techniques of Systems Analysis* (Santa Monica: The RAND Corporation, RM-1829–1, revised June 1957). In addition, Robert Strausz-Hupé, William R. Kintner, and Stefan T. Possony refer in their book *A Forward Strategy for America* (New York: Harper, 1961) to the "systemic" revolution now engulfing the underdeveloped areas of the world. Although this usage is more limited than that here, this "systemic" revolution provides one good example of systemic change as defined here.

in any case a recommendation for such abandonment is only marginal. We have in the past gone for a number of years without testing and we could presumably do so again without any very fundamental change in our military strategy. Our strategy is, however, based on the existence and the possible use of nuclear weapons; to abandon such weapons entirely would mean an entirely new system of world-wide strategy and an unconditional recommendation for their unilateral scrapping would thus be systemic.

It is ordinarily easier to get marginal recommendations accepted by American decision makers than systemic ones. This might lead to a presumption on the part of those who try to change national policy that they should look to marginal change before systemic, but not all of those who make arms recommendations follow this precept. The types of recommendations made by different schools of thought on arms policy are among the major distinguishing characteristics of these schools discussed below. As a generalization which has a number of exceptions, extreme schools of thought on arms policy tend more than moderate ones to concentrate on recommendations which are difficult to put over; indeed, this is precisely what makes them extreme. They tend to argue in relation to their difficult-to-sell recommendations: "Without this, holocaust." Neither extremists nor moderates have yet come to grips with implications of the gloomy possibility that certain recommendations may be both necessary and impossible. It is not logically excluded that holocaust is unavoidable.

CONNECTING THE PARTS: ARRIVING AT RECOMMENDATIONS

Fritz Machlup, in a discussion of decision making in business, wrote:

What sort of considerations are behind the routine decision of the driver of an automobile to overtake a truck proceeding ahead of him at slower speed? What factors influence his decision?

Assume that he is faced with the alternative of either slowing down and staying behind the truck or of passing it before a car which is approaching from the opposite direction will have reached the spot. As an experienced driver he somehow takes into account (a) the speed at which the truck is going, (b) the remaining distance between himself and the truck, (c) the speed at which he is proceeding, (d) the possible acceleration of his speed, (e) the distance between him and the car approaching from the opposite direction, (f) the speed at which that car is approaching; and probably also the condition of the road (concrete or dirt, wet or dry, straight or winding, level or uphill), the degree of visibility (light or dark, clear or foggy), the condition of the tires and brakes of his car, and—let us hope—his own condition (fresh or tired, sober or alcoholized) permitting him to judge the enumerated factors.

Clearly the driver of the automobile will not "measure" the variables; he will not "calculate" the time needed for the vehicles to cover the estimated distances at the estimated rates of speed; and, of course, none of the "estimates" will be expressed in numerical values. Even so, without measurements, numerical estimates or calculations, he will in a routine way do the indicated "sizing up" of the total situation. He will not break it down into its elements. Yet a "theory of overtaking" would have to include all these elements (and perhaps others besides) and would have to state how changes in any of the factors were likely to affect the decisions or actions of the driver. The "extreme difficulty of calculating," the fact that "it would be utterly impractical" to attempt to work out and ascertain the exact magnitudes of the variables which the theorist alleges to be significant, show, merely, that the *explanation* of an action must often include steps of reasoning which the acting individual himself does not *consciously* perform (because the action has become routine) and which perhaps he would never be *able* to perform in scientific exactness (because such exactness is not necessary in everyday life).[11]

These paragraphs are part of a strong defense of the economic theories of marginalism as being an accurate descrip-

11 Fritz Machlup, "Marginal Analysis and Empirical Research," *American Economic Review*, 36 (September 1946).

tion of rational decision making in business, even though the description might not be recognizable to the business decision makers themselves. In similar wise, the mechanisms of policy recommendation discussed here may not provide recognizable descriptions of the way in which recommendations are reached, yet it is argued that the descriptions are accurate in outline. Just as every policy recommendation must explicitly or implicitly be based on values and analyses, every such recommendation must contain some system of connections among the parts of the argument. The picture I draw here might be termed "descriptive-normative." Although no normative claim is made that one system is better than another, the "optimizing" mechanisms discussed below are used by many theorists as a norm for many purposes, and in any case they provide a standard case to which other systems can be compared. And, in the spirit of the above quotation, even though the description of these mechanisms may not be familiar to observers of the making of real arms policies, it nonetheless does purport to show the way in which many decision makers and recommendation makers think and hope they operate.

To connect their values and analyses into coherent chains of logic and thus to come up with recommendations, different individuals operate in many different ways, but systems of choice among recommendations can be divided into two groups according to two contrasting ideal types. Some people *optimize* in order to arrive at policy recommendations; some *maximize*.[12] Optimizing systems of choice attempt to resolve

12 The following discussion is based very generally on the existing body of decision theory, the formalized theory of choice. But to lay out enough of the formal theory for the treatment to satisfy a decision theorist would confuse the lay reader far more than is necessary, and thus both the language and the precise logic of decision theory are avoided. In general "optimization" as discussed here covers methods of decision making under uncertainty, like that of Savage, which are adapted from the model of decision making when the risks are known. "Maximization" covers those systems such as minimax, maximin, and maximax, which concentrate on extreme values. The use of the optimization-maximization terminology in this context was suggested by Thomas Schelling.

conflicts among competing values by weighing the relative subjective importance of the values, measuring analytically the relative objective probabilities of their fulfillment by different policies, and then arriving at a policy recommendation which provides a "best" combination of value fulfillments. Maximizing systems concentrate on a few noncompeting values and, without having to resolve any conflicts, choose policies which are best in relation to these values.[13]

Because those who make decisions on arms policy in the United States ordinarily take into account conflicting values, they typically use optimizing systems. Many of the makers of arms recommendations, however, are maximizers, and the distinguishing characteristics of the two modes of choice may thus become quite important.

Optimizing Mechanisms

The simplest optimizing mechanism is one which starts by assigning relative value weights to various policy outcomes and by computing the probabilities of these outcomes stemming from alternative policies which might be adopted. If such values can be meaningfully assigned, and if such probabilities can be computed in the sense that the probability of a toss of a fair coin turning up heads twice in a row can be computed, then the policy which should be chosen can be computed by straightforward arithmetic.

All that need be done is to sum, over all possible future results of a given policy, the products of the numerical probability of each result and the numerical value assigned by the decision maker to this result. If this is done separately for the alternative policies which might be adopted, the policy providing the highest sum of products is the one which will bring the decision maker the highest expected fulfillment of his value system.

[13] The word "maximization" is used in economics to denote the standard decision-making system *for business*. This is done on the assumption that profits are the single criterion for making business decisions. With only one criterion, maximization and optimization are equivalents.

It is sometimes argued that if one can meet the stringent requirements for ability to compute probabilities and to assign relative values, this simple optimizing system is the most "rational" one. Insofar as this system is used as a definition of rationality, it is, of course, impossible to disagree. But, since systems of the maximizing type as well can be made compatible with the requirements of logical consistency, it becomes inconvenient to identify optimization and rationality by definition.

The chief advantage of the optimizing mechanism is that, used under the postulated conditions, it is mathematically most likely to give its user the highest fulfillment of his values in the long run. A gambler using this system by multiplying probabilities by dollars will make more (or lose less) by using this mechanism than by using any other. In addition, the optimizing mechanism has the features, which appeal to the intuition, of utilizing information on *all* the relevant alternative future outcomes—not just the best or worst ones used by many of the other systems discussed below—and of weighting these futures according to the probability that they will come to pass. It seems reasonable to count the more likely results of a policy choice more heavily than those which are less likely.

There are two major difficulties with using the simple optimizing system. One of these is that policy is determined in a real world in which the probabilities of different outcomes are much less certain than the probability that heads will come up in the toss of a fair coin; the other is that arms policy leads to a variety of qualitatively different outcomes much more difficult to compare than the monetary outcomes of gambling or business policy.

The first problem, that of probabilities which are at best imprecise, can usually be circumvented, but circumvention may also weaken the advantage attributed to simple optimization of giving a mathematical promise of highest possible value fulfillment. A mathematically-minded analyst could *force* his inductive analysis to yield relative probabilities of future outcomes, perhaps even relative probabilities stated as exact numbers. The decision maker or recommender could then use these numerical probabilities just as the more precise coin-toss probabilities are used in the simple case. But this is not the way arms (or any other) policy is actually made. In the real world, the relative probabilities themselves are always highly uncertain. This contrasts to the coin example, where, even though it is impossible to predict surely the outcome of any individual toss, one can state accurately the relative chances of different outcomes. Because of this lack of sure knowledge as to even the relative chances of the outcomes of an arms policy, counting on a particular set of probabilities may give anything but the highest long-run value fulfillment. It is also important to note, however, that use of these uncertain probabilities may still provide a better chance of value fulfillment than any *other* system which has yet been devised for this uncertain world.

But in any case, it is at least possible to overcome these uncertainties, albeit in a very imprecise way. The second difficulty, that of the quantitative comparison of qualitatively different outcomes, cannot be bypassed by similar mechanical means. The use of monetary examples may be satisfactory for monetary or business problems, but such examples cannot be applied very simply to arms policy, and this makes the use of optimizing systems for military choices considerably more difficult. Money is both readily measurable and homogeneous. Optimizing systems used for economic choice need not assume that personal value is directly proportional to quantity of money—if I want an automobile, the first $500 which enables me to buy a used Ford may mean a lot more to me than the additional $4500 I need for a new Cadillac—but the transformation from dollars to personal value is relatively easy to make. Values in arms policy are much more difficult to quantify, although the basic difficulty is not the alleged cold-bloodedness which, it is sometimes argued, is associated with putting numbers into the picture of nuclear war. If avoiding human death is a major reason for desiring to avoid such war, then estimating the number of such deaths must be relevant. But a personal value system can make avoiding the first 10,000 deaths the value equivalent of avoiding the next 10,000,000, exactly as the first $500 is more important than the next $4500 to the car buyer.

This aspect of quantification is thus not the basic problem. The difficulty arises not in comparing numbers of deaths, but in the numerical comparison of policy outcomes which are completely dissimilar from one another. If peace is quantified by number of deaths avoided, how do we quantify the values associated with freedom? Working with a statistic like "x degrees of liberty preserved for y Berliners" would be sticky at best. The matter is much different from monetary comparison.

None of this is intended to imply, however, that value judgments on arms policy cannot be compared. The fact that arms decisions are made means that such comparisons and even *ad hoc* measurements are carried out, at least implicitly. Choice almost always implies comparison of values. But the difficulties with making the value measurements necessary for the precise application of the simple optimizing mechanism, together with the difficulties involved in estimating exact probabilities of future events, can leave some doubt that this is the proper method of choice.

Maximizing Mechanisms

Maximization was not specifically designed to overcome the faults of optimization, but rather, like optimization, it is a description of the way some people arrive at policy choices. If optimization attempts to resolve competition among values, maximization looks for policies which provide the highest fulfillment of a relatively small number of noncompeting values. Ordinarily, the same policies will best fulfill all of the values held by a maximizer.

Maximizers, therefore, need not indulge in the same sort of complex probability-value calculus that optimizers use. Although the maximizer must estimate which policy will most probably be best in relation to his key values, this is a relatively simple task compared to estimating the probabilities of a wide range of future outcomes of a large number of alternative policies, as must be done for optimization. Similarly, instead of having to weigh the relative values of many possible outcomes (not only which is more valuable than which, but also how many times as valuable), as is necessary for optimization, maximizing systems need only to distinguish which is the single worst outcome, which the single best, or some similar variant. Answers for maximizers are frequently straightforward and obvious, which they can never be for optimizers who attempt to find policies which will be preferable over mixed sets of values and probabilities.

This characteristic simplicity gives the maximizing systems a certain appeal for decision making in the imprecise real world. The fact that they lay no claim to highest long-run fulfillment of values, however, and the fact that they make almost no use of probability information, even in a world where such information is available, if inexact, detracts considerably from this appeal. As R. Duncan Luce and Howard Raiffa state (in italics), "They focus so strongly on the best and worst states of nature that often they do not permit one to gather negative information about the plausibility of such states, no matter how slight the cost."[14]

The most familiar of the maximizing systems, and the ones that are probably most applicable to arms-policy recommendations, are those in which the value to be maximized is the avoidance of the worst possible outcome. Such a mechanism, applied to a gambling situation for which there is possibility of loss as well as gain, for example, would say "Don't bet!" since not betting ensures that the worst result is zero, whereas the worst result of any gambling policy incurs some liability of financial loss. *This is true no matter what the odds.*

The best-known example of such a no-loss precept on arms policy is the statement, "Better Red than Dead."[15] The state-

14 Luce and Raiffa, p. 316.
15 This statement, usually attributed to Bertrand Russell, is credited by him to some "West German friends of peace." *Has Man a Future?* (New

ment implies first, that deadness is worse than redness, and second, that the policy which should be chosen is the one for which deadness is impossible and the worst result available is redness. Lacking a policy which will guarantee not being dead, at least take that policy where the chance of remaining alive is greater than for any other policy. This interpretation, perhaps more realistic, implies attention to probabilities to the extent that the chooser must be sure that he is really choosing the highest probability of being not-dead, but this is something about which the users of the decision system are almost always inherently sure. Beyond this, the question of how little the policy may decrease the probability of deadness or how much it may increase the probability of redness is absolutely irrelevant. Those who oppose "Better Red than Dead," by boldly proclaiming "Better Dead than Red," are, of course, using the same sort of reasoning, albeit with a reversed value system.

No-loss maximizing mechanisms are sometimes called conservative, because, like the "Don't bet" precept, they concentrate entirely on worst possibilities and pay no attention either to gains which may be obtainable or to losses of any value other than the primary one. But, as the red-and-dead example indicates, they can be conservative in a manner so extreme that conservatism loses definition. The extreme nature of such maximizing systems can be demonstrated by showing how a particular type of *optimization* can be forced to give consistent maximizing answers. The simple optimizing system of multiplying probabilities by values and summing the products will do this if the value system applied is one which gives the avoidance of the particular *Götterdämmerung* an infinite value-weight. The product of any positive probability number and infinity will always be infinity, and the resulting infinite-value policy will be the same as the maximizing choice.

York: Simon and Schuster, 1962), p. 89. In fact the statement is shunned now by most pacifists, including Russell. They believe analytically that they can avoid this stark choice between values.

On this basis, a statement such as, "Well, I place a high value on liberty, but I think that avoiding war is always overriding" (i.e., the value of avoiding war is infinite) can be shown to be inconsistent for the comparison between liberty and peace. As the value of avoiding war approaches infinity, all other values approach zero relative to peace, and all policies are evaluated on this criterion alone, no matter what the effect on liberty. Only if analysis shows that two policies give the same likelihood of being able to avoid war, does one even consider liberty.[16] In this sense, then, relative to the infinite value placed on peace, liberty is as nothing, and the statement of a high value placed on liberty is incorrect. This is true even though liberty may be weighed very heavily as compared to all other values aside from peace (e.g., material comfort).

A maximizing system even more extreme than no-loss is one which pays attention only to the best possible outcome, again ignoring probabilities. It states that the choice should always be that policy which gives a chance at a value pay-off higher than given by any other policy. The multiple rocks and shoals nature of arms policy being what it is, this is obviously much less applicable than no-loss. It would be a rash recommender indeed who would ignore *both* Scylla and Charybdis while chasing highest values. Nonetheless, echoes of this can be heard in some extreme policies. The search for "total victory over Communism," or for that golden commonwealth which will be available when the world disarms down to sticks and stones, are such ideas.

Because they are by their nature extreme and because they throw away available estimates of probabilities, the maximizing mechanisms seem intuitively less reasonable to most people than does the simple optimizing system. Conservatism in regard to such high stakes as peace and freedom, however,

16 The sort of decision system which pays attention to secondary values only if two actions provide exactly the same pay-off in primary values is known as lexicographic. In the lexicographic process of arranging words alphabetically, it makes no difference what the second letters are unless the first letters are the same.

does give some appeal to the no-loss maximizing mechanism. This is particularly true because real-world probabilities are just never very sure.

Rationalizations and Compromises

The competing pulls of optimization and maximization have led to two sorts of attempts to find a way out. One of these is the rationalization, the use of an extreme system under the guise (and probably in the honest belief), that the user is being less extreme. The other is the search for a real compromise between the criteria of conservatism in the face of extreme danger and the quest for over-all high fulfillment of values.

Perhaps the chief rationalization used by those drawn to the extreme maximizing mode of choice consists of assigning *not-quite-infinite* value to the prize goals they wish to maximize. (The converse of this, claiming absolute value for some objective of national policy, but not really meaning it, appears in rhetoric, particularly mass-meeting rhetoric, but not ordinarily in reasoned argument. It may sound good if shouted, but it is a difficult way to convince people who have a chance to think.)

It takes a brave man to admit to the extremism of infinity, and many of those inclined toward maximization will shy away from the absolute nature of "Better Red than Dead" or the reverse. Rather than giving the single chosen goal an infinite value relative to all others, the more common attitude is to make it nearly infinite—that is, to decide "Better Red" in all policy issues as they come up, but not to go far enough in theory or in their own minds to say, "This, always and inevitably, above all." This mode of thought is ordinarily accompanied by policy analysis which tries to make it possible to arrive at the same recommendations by the simple optimizing mechanism. The correlation of value and analysis makes characterization of a school of thought relatively easy, but investigation of the sources of the thought rather difficult. A possible psychological explanation of "almost-infinity" is provided by Nehemiah Jordan in his theory of "psychological certainty." Jordan claims that even though in a logical sense one may be aware of certain probabilities, one is psychologically able to act as if these probabilities were absolutely nonexistent. He takes as an example the actions of Californians who live near the San Andreas earth fault, but act without regard to the chances of an earthquake.[17] In the same way, some arms-policy maximizers may claim to place both a probability and a value on certain policy goals other than the ones on which their recommendations concentrate, but they may nonetheless act in any specific situation as if these other goals did not exist.

Aside from rationalizations, the quest for no-loss conservatism without abandoning probability can lead to some attempts at real compromise which assign to avoiding the worst outcomes an added but still less-than-absolute weight. One such system is suggested by Daniel Ellsberg.[18] The Ellsberg method is a complicated one, which takes account of the analyst's or decision maker's best guess as to the set of uncertain relative probabilities, his guess at another set of probabilities which can be characterized as the most pessimistic set which still appears to be reasonable, and his confidence that his "best guess" is a good guess. But despite the complexity, it is possible, by this method or similar ones, to construct decision systems with built-in conservatism which do not omit available information but use what can be estimated about probabilities. Such conservatism abandons the basic advantage of the simplest version of the optimizing system in giving highest long-run expected value; but in any case the fact that less than complete confidence is placed on the best-guess probabilities implies that less than complete confidence is placed on the ability of best-guess to provide highest expected value.

Finally, one mode of decision making cuts all of the

17 Nehemiah Jordan, *Decision-Making under Uncertainty and Problem Solving: A Gestalt Theoretical Viewpoint* (Santa Monica: The RAND Corporation P-2156, December 1, 1960).

18 Daniel Ellsberg, "Risk, Ambiguity, and the Savage Axioms," in "Symposium: Decisions under Uncertainty," *Quarterly Journal of Economics*, 75:664 (November 1961).

Gordian knots discussed above. Most frequently it is used as a rationalization for a decision already made; but if its conditions are fulfilled it is a perfectly good method. This is the use of *dominance*. Dominance is achieved in logic when a particular policy provides higher values than any alternative for some of the possible futures, and provides no lower values for any of them.[19] Then there is no need to consider probabilities and no need to use arithmetic. The preferred policy is at least as good as any alternative, no matter what future transpires and no matter what decision system is used.

In practice, of course, dominant policies guaranteed to be no worse than any alternative under any condition, are rather hard to come by if there are more than a very few policies to choose among. It is, however, frequently possible to *eliminate* a policy by the use of dominance. A particular course of action is dominated, and thus can be eliminated, if any other policy can be found which is better on some counts and no worse on any. But, for purposes of finding a best policy, rather than eliminating a worst, the most that can ordinarily be done is to discover something which will be greatly preferable for some criteria, and only a little more harmful for others. Such policies, however, are politically far less weighty than truly dominant ones, since anyone whose value system happens to put most weight on the slightly downgraded possibilities can claim that *he* still feels the policy to be unfavorable. An action, for example, which greatly strengthens the United States militarily vis-à-vis the Soviet Union, but makes war slightly more likely, may seem favorable to a large number of people. Those who place the highest value on a peaceful future, however, and care little about who has what power still will not be convinced.[20] Since the major use of domi-

---

[19] Actually, what is defined here is weak dominance. Strong dominance occurs when the policy is better for every possible future. For present purposes it is sufficient to discuss weak dominance.

[20] Kahn and Mann, p. 68, argue that those favoring the criterion which was only slightly downgraded *should* be convinced. This may be true when the alternative criteria are similar and quantifiable. It is difficult to see why they should be convinced in the more general case discussed here.

nance for choosing best policies is to convince everybody that the policy is good, almost-dominance leaves a large loophole for opponents. As a result, what is usually claimed, by both moderates and extremists, is actual dominance. That is why the use of dominance has been listed among the rationalizations commonly resorted to by the schools of thought on arms policy.

C H A P T E R   3

THE POLITICAL STRUCTURE
OF THE ARMS POLICY DEBATE:
SCHOOLS OF THOUGHT

What makes the study of ideas on arms policy interesting from a political as compared to a logical standpoint is that policy recommendations do not ordinarily come singly, but rather in closely correlated groups. Conditional recommendations are correlated with unconditional ones, and the unconditional recommendations that bring the major disagreements over policy are correlated with one another. Enough similarity exists among the grouped arms policy ideas of various individuals or political groups to warrant the use of the phrase, "school of thought." The schools will be classified on the basis of their unconditional recommendations for arms policy. Although such a classification necessarily entails some oversimplification, it can help to make coherent the differences of opinion among a very large number of individuals.

Taxonomy, the science of classification, is almost as easy to abuse as it is to use. Any objects or phenomena can be divided into classes. Even items as homogeneous as the grains of sand on a beach can be classified, if in no other way, by "the first 5,000 I pick up," the second 5,000, and so forth. But, for the classification to be useful, the boundary lines between the classes must be less arbitrary. They should, ordinarily, be natural bounds, outlining categories which have both internal coherence and external divergence. The schools of thought on arms policy outlined here are not completely clear-cut; no taxonomy of real social phenomena can avoid borderline cases. A school of thought is an ideal type rather than a precise real-world category, and since makers of arms recommendations are real people rather than ideal types, many of them will not fit into the categories in all particulars. Some individuals will adhere to a school on most of their recommendations but diverge on some specific issues; some will be close to the borderline and be more difficult to classify precisely; a few may be assignable to a particular school on the basis of the unconditional recommendations which provide the sole basis of this classification but will *sound* more like the members of another school in terms of their long-run, not-now-achievable goals. Since the major purpose here is to describe broad viewpoints rather than to pinpoint individuals, such ambiguities are not crucial. For the schools of thought outlined below, the precepts of similarity of recommendation within the classes and difference among them are fulfilled, and this suffices as an initial justification for the particular scheme.

The traditional mode of characterizing policy schools has been, since the French Chamber first seated its deputies that way, along a continuum from left to right. The major schools of thought on arms policy might be listed in the standard manner without doing violence either to their philosophies or to the ordinary political concepts of left and right as applied to these policies. A twofold mode of classification, however, illustrates some points not brought out by the simple continuum. Under this scheme, one categorization is according to major *purpose* of unconditional arms recommendations; the other is according to the *degree of change* implied by these recommendations.

By the first criterion, major purpose of recommendation, arms-policy schools in the United States can be grouped into three classes: (1) those whose main objective, apparent both in their recommendations and in the reasoning by which these recommendations are reached, is to decrease the probability of war, particularly thermonuclear war; (2) those whose primary objective is to stem and/or reverse the advance of Communism; and (3) those, in some sense in the middle, who can be best characterized by the fact that they do not fit comfortably into either of the other two groups because their recommendations do not appear to put one of these two objectives clearly above the other. It is important to note that this classification does not imply that any school need be impelled *solely* by a single objective (and it should be emphasized that exceedingly few makers of arms recommendations are either *pro*-war or *pro*-Communist). Rather, the first group, corresponding somewhat to the traditional left, is relatively more concerned with avoiding war, but may nonetheless feel the importance of anti-Communist considerations; the "right" group sees Communism as the main current menace, but may also feel a danger of war; and the "middle" contains a wide variety of mixtures of the two. The three classes according to this simplified categorization should be labeled primarily anti-war, primarily anti-Communist, and "middle." For purposes of exposition, the word "primarily" is hereafter dropped, but it should be understood throughout.

The second mode of classification, according to the degree of change recommended unconditionally, may help to clarify somewhat the meanings of the first mode. As already pointed out, recommendations can be either *marginal* or *systemic*. Marginal recommendations are for small incremental changes in existing processes and mechanisms, while systemic ones are for large variations affecting entire systems. The common political term for those who recommend changes in whole systems is "radical," an adjective which, like "systemic" can be applied to those favoring drastic moves to the political right as well as to the left. In order to avoid any invidious connotations, however, the word used here will be "systemic," except when the political implications of radicalism become germane.

The three-by-two classification creates six schools of thought on arms policy—marginal and systemic schools in each of the anti-war, anti-Communist, and middle-road categories. Defining the marginal schools presents few problems; they include all of those individuals whose unconditional recommendations on arms policy are for no more than marginal change, with the three specific schools being characterized by the direction of these relatively small changes. Similarly, the systemic anti-war school is not difficult to define; systemism is the presentation of greater-than-marginal recommendations and the members of this school make such recommendations with the purpose of avoiding war. Anti-Communist systemism presents one problem: among those who base their political thought primarily on anti-Communism are some who oppose military expenditures because they believe the real Communist threat to be an internal one which will be exacerbated by federal expenditures even on armaments. These individuals are excluded from this discussion and the systemic anti-Communist school includes only those who make systemic recommendations for the use of military power to stem external Communist threats.

Systemic middle-roadism, however, may appear to be a contradiction in terms. This is not necessarily true, using the definitions set forth. The "middle" is merely the place in which anti-war and anti-Communist motives are well mixed, while the systemic nature of a recommendation concerns distance rather than direction of movement. These two definitions are not inherently contradictory, but, for reasons which have more to do with the temperament of the analysts involved than the requirements of logic, the systemic-middle group is almost empty. A rather impressionistic illustration of the temperamental difficulties of a systemic middle of the road lies in the observation that political rallies of the radical left are inspired by folk singers, and rallies of the radical right by American Legion fife-and-drum corps. It is difficult to think of music to inspire the radical middle, although the Republican and Democratic parties try every four years without notable success. Further word, possibly the last word, on the radical middle can be found in Jules Feiffer's *New Re-*

public cartoon, in which the spokesman for the radical middle concludes his television interview by saying "Bold times call for bold answers. Within reason. In a manner of speaking. More or less. On the other hand . . ."[1]

Because the systemic-middle grouping is empty, even though logically imaginable, it can be eliminated from the analysis. With this omission, then, it would become possible to list the five schools of arms policy from traditional left to traditional right—the systemic anti-war school, the marginal anti-war school, the center, the marginal anti-Communist school, and the systemic anti-Communists[2] rather than using the twofold direction-and-distance classification. The linear listing, however, conceals the key point that the two extreme schools are distinguished from the three central ones by a different criterion from the one that distinguishes the central groups from one another. It has often been remarked that policy schools fall more naturally into a circle or a "horseshoe" like that of Figure 1, than into a straight line, and that *the ends are in many ways closer to one another than they are to the middle.* This similarity of right and left systemists has perhaps been best described by Arthur M. Schlesinger, Jr., in discussing not the 1960's but the 1930's:

Radicalism, like conservatism, thus ended in the domain of either-or. The contradictions of actuality, which so stimulated the pragmatists of Washington, only violated the proprieties and offended the illusions of the ideologists. [John] Dewey and [Harold] Laski wholly agreed with Herbert Hoover and Ogden Mills that one must have either capitalism or socialism; any combination of the two was impossible. The protagonists on both sides saw themselves as hardheaded realists. But in fact they were all unconscious Platonists, considering abstractions the ultimate reality.[3]

[1] *The New Republic*, January 22, 1962, p. 19.
[2] To clear up any ambiguity, I consider myself in the center, although close to the marginal anti-war school. (The boundary is blurred.) I believe that this is an accurate characterization of my own arms ideas, although it has been pointed out to me that one *always* considers oneself to be in the middle.
[3] Arthur M. Schlesinger, Jr., *The Age of Roosevelt*, Vol. III: *The Politics of Upheaval* (Boston: Houghton Mifflin, 1960), p. 176.

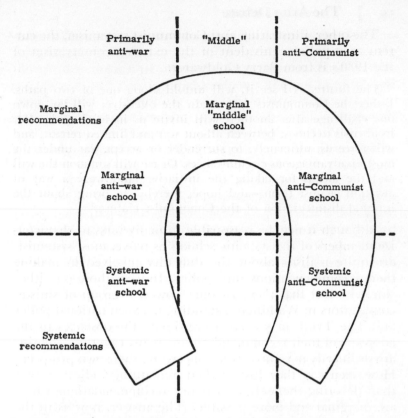

Primarily
anti–war

"Middle"

Primarily
anti–Communist

Marginal
recommendations

Marginal
"middle"
school

Marginal
anti–war
school

Marginal
anti–Communist
school

Systemic
anti–war
school

Systemic
anti–Communist
school

Systemic
recommendations

FIGURE 1: The five schools of arms policy

Schlesinger's description is almost directly applicable to the arms controversies of today. This is well shown by the contrast of the following two quotations. The first, representing anti-war radicalism, is from Bertrand Russell: "There is no conclusion possible in this march towards insane death except to turn right round and march, instead, towards sanity and life. Our present courses lead inevitably, sooner or later, to the extinction of the human species. We are not *doomed* to persist in the race towards disaster. Human volitions have caused it, and human volitions can arrest it."[4]

4 Bertrand Russell, *Common Sense and Nuclear Warfare* (New York: Simon and Schuster, 1959), pp. 27–28.

The other, illustrating anti-Communist systemism, the current arms-policy equivalent of the extreme conservatism of the 1930's is from Barry Goldwater:

The future, as I see it, will unfold along one of two paths. Either the Communists will retain the offensive; will lay down one challenge after another; will invite us in local crisis after local crisis to choose between all-out war and limited retreat; and will force us, ultimately, to surrender or accept war under the most disadvantageous circumstances. Or *we* will summon the will and the means for taking the initiative, and wage a war of attrition against them—and hope, thereby, to bring about the internal disintegration of the Communist empire.[5]

Although it may be reasonable in many ways to characterize members of the systemic schools as naïve, most systemists are quite realistic about the difficulty involved in making their recommendations into policy. Indeed, those on either side who feel that there is some powerful group of sinister conspirators in Washington standing between national policy and The Truth may even overestimate the obstacles to the adoption of their recommendations. In any case the systemists are ordinarily not unrealistic concerning their own prospects. How then can they justify their remaining radical, rather than devoting themselves to policy recommendations which are marginal and more possible? The answer, now as in the 1930's, lies in what Schlesinger calls "the domain of either-or." For one to be enthusiastic about the close-to-impossible, he must be convinced that it is close to necessary. "Either this or holocaust." Unless we turn around, we get extinction of the species, in Lord Russell's term. *Either* we are forced to the wall, *or* we must bring about the disintegration of the Communist empire, in Senator Goldwater's.

Russell's beliefs, in fact, can be used to provide another sort of evidence that the arrangement of the schools of arms policy around a horseshoe, with the ends closer to one another than to the middle, gives a more accurate picture than the simple

[5] Barry Goldwater, *The Conscience of a Conservative* (New York: Hillman, 1960), pp. 126–127.

left-to-right continuum. Because he is systemic in style and mode of thought, Russell was able to change his recommendations from anti-Communist systemism (preventive war) to anti-war systemism (unilateral disarmament) without ever passing through the middle at all. The constant factor was his belief in drastic solutions, the solutions which provide the definitional distinction between systemism and marginalism. And what is true of Russell's right-to-left movement is also true of the left-to-right motion of some American systemists, such as James Burnham, who at an earlier date moved from left-radical criticism of society to right-radical criticism without passing through the center.

Systemists are thus distinguished from marginalists by their journey through the "domain of either-or" in quest of the thoroughgoing solutions they believe to be the only possible answers to the overwhelming problems of the real world. Systemism and marginalism are easy to distinguish by definition, and in the case of some systemists like Russell and Goldwater, the definitional distinction is easy to apply. For other recommendation makers nearer the border between the two types of thought, however, the application of the definition is more difficult, and categorization must be tentative. Although the classification of individuals is not important, the reasons for the difficulty throw further light on the important difference between systemism and marginalism.

The precise definitional distinction between the two categories is that, whereas the systemists make unconditional systemic recommendations, the marginalists confine their unconditional recommendations to suggestions for marginal change. It does not follow, however, that because the marginalists make no systemic recommendations, the systemists make no marginal ones. Many marginal recommendations are jointly espoused by marginalists and systemists alike. And the basic problem is that the existence of these joint marginal recommendations frequently leads to confusion between the marginalists who stop with the marginal proposals and the systemists who go far beyond.

It is possible to differentiate between the marginal and the systemic attitudes to joint marginal recommendations (although the distinction is, of course, not as clear-cut as that between their contrasting attitudes to systemic proposals). The basic difference on the jointly espoused marginal recommendations is that the marginalists, much more than the systemists, evaluate the proposed measures on the basis of their specific favorable and unfavorable effects on their near-term policy values. Those marginalists who may be interested in certain measures as steps toward long-run systemic change make the second steps conditional upon the success of the first. The systemists, however, are interested in these common recommendations less on the basis of their specific effects on the world than on account of their help in moving toward the long-run systemic goals. Whatever the outcome of the first, marginal, steps, they want to continue quickly *and unconditionally* to the next moves toward their ultimate objectives. The systemists may expend much energy and emotion in promoting their marginal recommendations, but these are nonetheless distinctly subordinate, intellectually, to the systemic changes.

An excellent example of the difference in marginalist and systemist approaches to a jointly espoused marginal recommendation can be found in the 1961–1962 debate over the marginal issue of whether the West should resume atmospheric nuclear testing after the initial Soviet breaking of the moratorium. The issue was to many people a difficult one, with marginalists coming down reluctantly on both sides. A *New Republic* editorial, for instance, presented a brief but detailed discussion of five possible weapons developments, and then stated that:

A discussion of the specific reasons advanced for atmospheric testing shows, in short, that while significant military use could be made of the findings gained from tests, there are not at this time overriding security reasons for a test resumption. Weighed against psychological and political factors on the side of continuing to abstain and thus to underscore the Soviet violation of the moratorium, the military reasons so far publicly apparent are unconvincing. However, what has been left out of the discussion so far is an unknown—the fear that the Russians, through their latest series of tests, may have come upon something which our nuclear scientists have not conceived of and which could only be discovered through continued nuclear testing. In the long run, if the Soviets continue to explode large numbers of nuclear weapons, the US may have no choice but to resume testing in order to insure against some now unimaginable breakthrough.[6]

In other words, all things considered, don't test now, but we must necessarily consider all things. This is the essence of a marginal policy recommendation. Contrast it to the writing of Kingsley Martin of the British *New Statesman,* also against tests, but from a systemic viewpoint, who starts by reviewing the technical controversy over one of the five possible weapons developments listed by *The New Republic* (the anti-missile missile). He then goes on to say of the arguments which he has mentioned, arguments on both sides similar in tone to that of *The New Republic,* that "it is incredibly macabre to have to listen to speeches and arguments of this kind—all of them hopelessly insincere—while we sit contemplating fall-out and the now almost certain acceleration of the arms race."[7]

It seems fair to state that although Martin's policy recommendation is the same as that of *The New Republic,* it is a corollary of his strong systemic prodisarmament viewpoint, and could not be changed by any new or unknown factors. And what is true of the difference between the joint anti-war marginalist and systemist recommendation not to test is equally true of the recommendation jointly espoused by other marginalists and by anti-Communist systemists not to stop testing. Just as *The New Republic* opposed resumption conditionally, while Martin opposed it unconditionally, the following two statements imply the same vote for test re-

6 *The New Republic,* November 13, 1961, pp. 4–5.
7 Kingsley Martin, the *New Statesman,* November 10, 1961, p. 679.

sumption but for different reasons. The first is by Edward Teller, a very strong advocate of nuclear testing, but not a maker of systemic recommendations:

The crux of the test ban is the question of control. It is a long-standing and well-founded position of our government that disarmament must not be unilateral and that disarmament must be subject to reliable verification . . .

At the present time no world-wide system of control exists, and it will be several years before such a system could be put into effect . . .

Thus it is clear that several years must pass before any world-wide inspection system can be put into effect. In the meantime there is no objective evidence that the Russians have actually stopped nuclear tests . . .

. . . the Russians could make decisive one-sided progress if we agreed to an unenforceable test ban.[8]

Thus, don't stop testing—for the reason that the Russians can violate an agreement with impunity. One can conceive of arrangements which would satisfy Teller and cause him at least to accept a test ban. Senator Goldwater, however, feels more strongly, as did Kingsley Martin. Goldwater writes:

Therefore, the only excuse for suspending tests is that our forbearance somehow contributes to peace. And my answer is that I am unable to see how peace is brought any nearer by a policy that may reduce our relative military strength. Such a policy makes sense only under the assumption that Communist leaders have given up their plan for world revolution and will settle for peaceful coexistence—an assumption that we make at the risk of losing our national life.

If our objective is victory over Communism we must achieve superiority in all of the weapons—military as well as political and economic—that may be useful in reaching that goal.[9]

It is fairly safe to say that Senator Goldwater could find no conditions of inspection which might satisfy him.

[8] Edward Teller, "The Feasibility of Arms Control and the Principle of Openness," in *Arms Control, Disarmament, and National Security,* ed. Donald G. Brennan (New York: Braziller, 1961), pp. 125–131.

[9] Goldwater, *The Conscience of a Conservative,* p. 113.

This type of difference between the marginal and the systemic approaches to jointly espoused marginal recommendations becomes both crucial and delicate on the anti-war side, where it cuts through a politically coherent but intellectually bifurcated movement based on the "Unilateral Initiatives" theories of psychologist Charles E. Osgood. Osgood advocates trying to break through the stalemate on negotiated disarmament by having the United States unilaterally take small "tension-reducing" steps with the explicit purpose of inducing Soviet reciprocation and thus starting a chain reaction which would end with a stable disarmed world.[10] The basis of the scheme is that "in the present climate of fear and distrust it is hard to see how bilateral commitments of any significance can be reached,"[11] but that this fear and distrust can be dissipated by unilateral acts of good will.

The crucial question about unilateral initiatives is, what are the actual steps recommended? It is the substantive content of the specific unilateral measures recommended for action *without previous conditions* which distinguishes the systemists from the marginalists. If the first steps are in themselves systemic, the recommender is obviously a systemist; the same is true if the first steps are merely marginal, but it is recommended unconditionally that we go on to further systemic measures, *regardless of whether the first steps are successful* in inducing Soviet reciprocation, reducing tensions, and the like. If neither of these is the case, i.e., if only marginal recommendations for first steps are made, and if further steps are conditioned on the success of the first, then the recommender can be classed as a marginalist (although, if faced with the failure of his suggested unilateral initiatives, he might *then* opt for systemism).

And those who consider themselves advocates of unilateral initiatives fall into both the marginal and systemic groups

10 A detailed but succinct exposition of this is to be found in Charles E. Osgood, "Reciprocal Initiatives," in *The Liberal Papers*, ed. James Roosevelt (Garden City: Doubleday, 1962). Copyright © 1962 by James Roosevelt. This quotation and all subsequent quotations are reprinted with the permission of Doubleday & Company, Inc.

11 *Ibid.*, p. 179.

defined in this manner. On the marginal side, Professor
Amitai Etzioni of Columbia advocates what he calls Gradualism. "Gradualism is based on a sequence of stages: we cannot
emphasize this too strongly. The later phases are activated
only after earlier ones have been successfully completed."[12]
And Etzioni's suggestions for early measures are basically
marginal: propaganda shifts, increased attempts at controlling nuclear accidents, increased exchanges with the Soviet
Union, and so forth. His recommendations may be good or
bad, practical or impractical; furthermore, he is not clear as
to whether, if these marginal recommendations did not work,
he would then go systemic. He writes, "Even if Gradualism
should fail, the other two major alternatives, the more extreme and more dangerous policies of unilateralism and an
accelerated arms race . . . will still be available,"[13] but, not
expecting the failure of Gradualism, he does not say which
of the other alternatives he would then choose. Nonetheless,
on the basis of his current recommendations, Etzioni is
clearly a marginalist.

Contrast Etzioni's approach to that of Mulford Sibley in a
pamphlet entitled *Unilateral Initiatives and Disarmament,*
who writes:

> . . . unilateral initiatives and eventually unilateral disarma-
> ment are ways of seeking a more effective defense than military
> weapons can any longer provide.

> . . . while the program would be carried out in phases, its
> basic premises and logic would be made public from the very
> beginning. Thus it would be necessary to make it clear that the
> United States had repudiated deterrence and intended to disarm.

> . . . If . . . preliminary agreements were not forthcoming
> within a reasonable period (six months, for example,) the gov-
> ernment would proceed with its planned unilateralist policy.

[12] Amitai Etzioni, *The Hard Way to Peace: A New Strategy* (New York:
Collier, 1962), p. 94.
[13] *Ibid.*, p. 108.

. . . once launched there would be no hope for success apart from a continuing determination to see things out to the finish and never go back to the prison house of nuclear deterrence.[14]

Sibley's unilateral initiatives are clearly a mere technique to assist in achieving his unconditional recommendation for the extreme arms-policy systemism of complete unilateral disarmament. He would, of course, prefer the Russians to disarm in step with us, but this is not an essential condition.

Precise classification of particular individuals into particular schools of thought, however, is not important. The discussions quoted are for the purpose of illustrating the difference between marginalism and systemism, rather than for pinning people down. So far as any given maker of recommendations is concerned, the categorization can be of the "if the shoe fits," variety. A systemist makes unconditional systemic recommendations; a marginalist does not. The categories are ideal types, and the boundary between them would be blurred even without the existence of concepts like "unilateral initiatives," which means different things to different men. It is the real distinction between the idealized categories which makes it possible to discuss separately the marginal and the systemic views on the substantive matter of arms policy.

[14] Mulford Sibley, *Unilateral Initiatives and Disarmament* (Philadelphia: American Friends Service Committee, 1962), pp. 19–28.

✣ ✣ ✣ ✣ ✣

C H A P T E R 4

INTRODUCTION TO
THE MARGINAL SCHOOLS
OF THOUGHT

Throughout the political history of the United States, the fundamental differences which distinguish marginalism from systemism have remained remarkably constant. On both domestic and foreign issues, the marginalists have used the optimizing mechanisms of choice described above to reconcile competing policy values, while makers of systemic recommendations have remained in the "domain of either-or," choosing policies through maximizing mechanisms based on single values.

And throughout the controversies of history, it has almost always been the optimizing marginalists who have been in the decision-making positions of authority. Regardless of the relative political strength of one systemic group or another, the systemists have never been in or even close to power. One rough index of this is the fact that in American presidential elections, never has the runner-up, let alone the winner, been an advocate of unconditional systemic change in the important policies of the time.[1] The reason for this continued marginalist dominance is not difficult to explain. In order to be chosen as decision makers in a socially heterogeneous

---

[1] One possible exception to the rule that decision makers are not systemists is Woodrow Wilson's advocacy of abrupt change from traditional American isolationism. This advocacy was notably unsuccessful.

but stable democracy, individuals and parties must of necessity balance competing ideological and political considerations. When the main competing groups in a democracy
become polar, separated only by a small middle group, as has
sometimes been the case in France; or when the marginal
ideals clash with a harsh and systematically different objective
reality, as was true in Germany in 1932, revolution rather
than democratic change is likely to provide the solution.

In the United States of the 1960's, neither of these stresses
is present. The extreme groups on arms (or any other) policy
are separated by a heavily predominant middle majority;
and, whatever the view of the systemists, this majority is far
from the belief that the objective reality of either the arms
race or world Communism requires revolutionary change.
America's elected and appointed decision makers are, therefore, optimizing marginalists. On arms policy they must
balance many competing considerations, particularly the
avoidance of war and the avoidance of Communist advance
by military action or the threat of such action. Given these
competing values, it is impossible for them to use maximizing systems, since maximizing the chances of avoiding one
danger might also maximize the risks of running into the
other.

The marginalist category, then, includes almost all of those
who actually make the decisions on the arms policies of the
United States. (There are anti-Communist systemists such as
Senator Goldwater in Congress, and in the military. It is
more difficult to think of anti-Communist systemists in high
civilian executive posts in the Kennedy administration, and
it is equally difficult to think of anti-war systemists anywhere
in the upper reaches of government.) Probably the majority
of those in nonofficial positions who make arms-policy recommendations in books, articles, and lectures are also marginalists, although the balance with the systemists is more nearly
equal than within the government itself.

The group of marginalists in and out of government who
take an active interest in arms policy is a widely, even wildly,

divergent one. Its members have in common the definitional characteristic that their unconditional recommendations for policy change are no more than marginal; in addition most of them have in common the fact that they arrive at these recommendations by optimizing mechanisms which attempt to reconcile competing policy values. But these general similarities among marginalists are coupled with wide differences over specific recommendations, values, and analyses. It is on the basis of their different *recommendations* that the marginalists are divided into the three schools called anti-war, anti-Communist, and "middle."

This classification on the basis of recommendations alone, however, recalls the admonition of the late great economist, Joseph Schumpeter, when he discussed the "Cultural Indeterminateness of Socialism." Schumpeter warned that although many people associate Socialism with various cultural and political concomitants—some think it to be "warlike and nationalist," others to be "peaceful and internationalist," for example—none of these characteristics has any necessary connection with the economic and sociological bases of Socialism as such. Rather, Socialism is a "cultural Proteus," adaptable to many different intellectual and political climes.[2]

Similarly, the division of individuals into schools according to their unconditional arms *recommendations* can divide persons who on matters such as long-run policy goals are quite congenial, or it can unite individuals who, in terms of general cultural and political outlook may be, at best, uncomfortable bedfellows. The recommendations are protean: those who agree on arms recommendations may agree on nothing else, not even on the political values upon which they base the recommendations. Indeed, different individuals arrive at similar recommendations on the basis of quite different trains of logic, and although it is the similar recommendations rather than the different logic which classifies them into schools, the details can lead to a good deal of con-

2 Joseph A. Schumpeter, *Capitalism, Socialism, and Democracy* (New York: Harper, 3rd ed., 1950), pp. 170–171.

fusion. Because of this, although both the recommendations and the values and analyses which comprise the logic leading up to them are thoroughly gone into below, it is useful to pause at the outset in order to characterize briefly the three schools and the differences among and within them.

1. The anti-war marginalists are defined by the fact that their recommendations are clearly designed for one major purpose—to avoid war, particularly thermonuclear war. The recommended arms policies hedge against the danger of Communism, but this is a hedge, and not a primary purpose. Although the school is thus defined by a range of recommendations all of which are primarily anti-war, the individuals making the recommendations tend to fall into two groups. On the more moderate end of the range, that farthest from systemism, are those individuals, many of whom are now in government, who are optimizers by nature, but optimizers who are most worried about war, and whose recommendations reflect this. The writings of individuals such as Presidential Science Adviser Jerome Wiesner, United Nations Ambassador Adlai Stevenson, and former Undersecretary of State Chester Bowles exemplify this moderate tendency among anti-war marginalists. In addition to these, however, the other group of anti-war marginalists consists of some who, although attracted to anti-war *systemism* reject it as being intellectually insufficient or politically impossible. Even after rejecting systemism, they search for marginal changes which, if they work out, will make politically possible ultimate systemic difference. Many of the ideas of marginalist adherents to "Unilateral Initiatives," such as Amitai Etzioni and Arthur Waskow, fall into this category. The marginal anti-war school provides an excellent example of the importance of Schumpeter's warning: the two wings of the school seem to attach quite different emotional-cultural connotations to what they are saying, but their arms recommendations are just not very different.

2. The anti-Communist marginalists also design their recommendations for one primary purpose—the ultimate defeat

of Communism, world-wide. Their recommendations hedge against the worst kinds of war, and strive in any case for the lowest levels of violence, but these are hedges rather than aims. For various institutional reasons, the marginal anti-Communists form more of a single coherent grouping than do either the anti-war or the middle marginalists. Most of them are gathered around the Foreign Policy Research Institute of the University of Pennsylvania, and the names Robert Strausz-Hupé, William Kintner, James Dougherty, Alvin Cottrell, and Stefan Possony, all of whom are or have been associated with the Institute are the familiar ones. Because these gentlemen tend to write in groups of three or four, it is difficult to say whether there are many differences of opinion among them.

3. The middle marginalists form the largest and most heterogeneous group, and include most of those responsible for current American arms policies. "Middle" recommendations are those which appear not to aim primarily at either preventing war or preventing Communist advance, but rather try to do both at the same time. Such a definition includes a wide variety of recommendations, going from the arbitrarily drawn border with anti-war marginalism on the one side to the arbitrarily drawn border with anti-Communist marginalism on the other, and the single title of "middle marginalist" conceals a great deal of difference of opinion. But even among those who may agree on particular subsets of middle marginal recommendations, two trains of thought exist. These start out from quite different bases of values considered relevant to arms policy, but come together through policy analysis to similar middle recommendations. On the one hand, some middle marginalists come up with recommendations which are balanced between anti-war and anti-Communist directions simply because their values are balanced that way. Writers such as Sidney Hook and Ernest Lefever are middle marginalists because they see no reason to assign significantly greater weight to avoidance of either war or Communism. On the other hand, there are those who do assign much

greater value weight to avoidance of war, but because their analysis tells them that the Soviet Union is an enemy and the best way to avoid war is to treat her as such, come up with recommendations similar to those which put more explicit value on anti-Communism as such. Representative are Edward Teller and Thomas Schelling. Most middle marginalists, however, fall between these poles of balanced values and "anti-war analysis," and although the polar cases must be treated separately in the discussion of marginalist values, they can be treated as belonging to a single range of analyses and recommendations.

The three marginal schools, then, are not three widely separated monoliths, but rather are three intricate and arbitrarily bounded subsections of a complex continuum. It is easier to define the differences among the schools and to characterize them by some of their internal features than it is to draw precise boundaries between them. But in spite of the arbitrary nature of the boundaries, it remains possible and useful to distinguish the schools from one another. (The difficulties with any arbitrary division of the United States into regions do not obscure the agreed facts that New York is in the East, Los Angeles in the Far West, and Chicago in the Midwest. This classification is generally accepted even by those who might argue about the categories in which Cleveland and Denver should be placed. And the problem of the separate trains of thought within each of the three schools might be likened to the problem of deciding whether Baltimore is north or south, after having agreed that it is east.)

At any rate, in order to understand the bases of policy disputes among marginalists, more than definition is needed. It is necessary to understand the differently weighted value judgments and the different probability pictures of the world which enter the optimized policy recommendations of the three schools. The range of marginal recommendations is so wide that they cannot be simply listed, but must be described in detail; the range of value judgments and probability analyses that enter the optimizing mechanisms is so large that in order to discover how the schools arrive at their varying recommendations, these judgments and analyses must be described in detail.

What is presented here is neither a complete portrait of the major marginal schools of thought nor a complete survey of the literature, but a set of schematic diagrams of the various areas of arms policy, showing approximately where each school is in relation to the others and how it got there. Why it arrived there—the historical and psychological background of the value judgments and the evidence for the analyses—is omitted. As a result, it will be impossible to draw any conclusions about which of the competing marginal analyses and recommendations is "right." Where there is consensus among the different marginalists, the implication is that there may well be good reason for the agreement, but where there is no consensus the solution to the substantive policy issue must be left open.

The objective of this investigation of arms-policy marginalism, then, is to answer these questions:

What are the values, analyses, and recommendations of the three marginalist schools of arms policy?

On which matters is there consensus and on which disagreement?

What are the implications of these agreements and disagreements for choice by decision makers among alternative policies?

✣　✣　✣　✣　✣

CHAPTER 5

MARGINALIST VALUE SYSTEMS

Values and analyses are not always easy to separate from one another. Although values about what should be are distinguishable conceptually from analyses about what is and can be, such distinctions are difficult to draw in practice. The use of the simple optimizing mechanism of choice implies not only that the chooser can estimate the probabilities and weigh his values, but also that someone observing the chooser can follow his calculations without too much trouble (if the chooser cooperates). But the problem with separating values and analyses within the logical processes leading to recommendations in the real world of arms policy is that the value and probability factors which enter the multiplication for a given outcome of a given policy are not separately observable. Perhaps the makers of recommendations should explicitly separate that which they consider first-order value judgment from that which they believe to be deductible from the rest of the argument, but ordinarily they do not do so. Rather, the product of the value-times-probability multiplication, the over-all "importance" attached to that outcome, is all that can be extracted directly from most arms arguments. It is almost as difficult to guess the components of this product as it would be if a quizmaster were to say "twelve" and challenge a contestant to guess whether he meant two times six or three times four.[1]

---

[1] In the simpler problems provided by certain well-designed experiments in economics, it has been possible to accomplish some factoring of this type. See William Fellner, "Distortion of Subjective Probabilities as a Reaction to Uncertainty," *Quarterly Journal of Economics*, 75 (November 1961).

Thus if a maker of recommendations says that he believes thermonuclear war to be a greater "danger" than Communism, for example, he may mean that his value system is such that, if forced to choose, he would rather be Red than dead; or he may mean that his probability analysis leads him to believe that thermonuclear war is just around the corner, whereas Communist world domination is in any case a long way away. Most likely he means both, and each depends on the other.

All that can be observed directly, except in those rare cases when individuals consciously separate their subjective and their objective views, however, is the product of value and probability—the "importance" of thermonuclear war for the determination of arms policy as compared to the "importance" of Communism in the example given. A particular policy outcome may be considered important because both its value and its probability are significant, or it may be important because its value is so high that even multiplying this value by a low probability results in a high product. An example of this high-value low-probability high-product case is provided by one common view of thermonuclear war: even though such war is thought by some people to be quite improbable, the value of avoiding it is so high that it is important to their arms-policy calculations. In addition, a third case, a high "importance" product of the multiplication of a low value and a high probability, is logically possible, but it is difficult to think of real examples; if an individual "cares" little, subjectively, he is not very likely to worry about the objective probability of an outcome.

But because of the difficulty in separating the medium-value medium-probability cases from the high-value low-probability cases among the policy outcomes considered "important" by the various makers of arms recommendations, one caveat is necessary in listing the values of the marginal schools. All of the values listed for each school are likely to be significant for that school, even if separated from their accompanying probabilities. But some outcomes (value-probability products) which appear relatively *less* important than others may actually give this appearance because they are considered objectively improbable, rather than being considered subjectively less valuable. In the limit, some of the schools omit certain values from their systems because they consider the relevant outcomes to be analytically improbable, even though they would be considered quite important if likely. The omission by some of the possible danger of domestic Fascism as a consideration relevant to arms policy provides a case in point. Fascism may be considered abhorrent on a value basis, but so very unlikely as to be unimportant for arms policy.

The values relevant to arms policy can be grouped into four general categories: peace, freedom, power, and time. *Peace* and *freedom* are the traditional liberal moral values, but in spite of their seeming simplicity, they are very complicated concepts, and the different schools of thought vary widely on how they interpret these familiar words. *Power* may or may not be moral, but it certainly is considered relevant by some makers of arms recommendations. These first three categories are parallel to and compete with one another; indeed, the major differences among the marginal schools of arms policy are based primarily upon this competition and secondarily upon the competition of the various detailed values within each of the categories. The fourth general category, *time,* however, rather than competing with the other three, is applied across the board to each and all of the others.

Peace can be simply defined as the absence of war, but the apparent simplicity conceals a number of complexities. Many people put some value on complete absence of war, but nonetheless believe (on the basis of analysis rather than value judgment) that war of some sort will always be with us, and they therefore want to meliorate the terror of the wars they expect. And because terror may in itself deter war, efforts for absolute peace and for melioration can compete. Most marginalists put value both on decreasing the likelihood of war and on melioration of those wars which do occur; but the different schools differ widely on how to weight these two competing values against one another. And to complicate the picture further, some also consider important a third "peaceful" value: the refusal to kill or threaten to kill, even to preserve the peace.

Freedom is even more complex. To begin with, freedom can be threatened by Communism, but it also can be threatened from the "right," by Fascism, reaction, or militarism at home or abroad. The different schools put quite different values on avoiding the different threats. And even under each of the two subheadings of threats to freedom from the "left" and threats from the "right," there come individual competing values. A person can worry about the forceful advance of Communism, or about its advance by peaceful persuasion. Furthermore, some, but not all, of the makers of recommendations on arms policy put great weight on forcing Communist retreat as compared to preventing advance. And so far as "reactionary" threats to freedom are concerned, an individual can value democratic government abroad, he can be against imperialism, valuing indigenous government abroad regardless of whether it is democratic or not, or he can value both with varying relative weights. Furthermore, one can worry about reaction and about military power within the United States too, and can put the value of avoiding these dangers into competition with all of the other values associated with freedom, as well as those relevant to peace.

Power valued for its own sake must be clearly distinguished from power as a tool to aid in the achievement of other values. Power as a value is sometimes omitted from polite policy discussion because those who put most weight on peace and freedom consider power less "moral" and therefore less relevant than the other two. But it is the power of one's nation to control its own destiny and to influence the rest of the world which is relevant to argument over arms policy, rather than the drive for personal power, which, because it is selfish, might really be immoral in the most commonly accepted sense. Personal drives for power or wealth might be *politically* relevant to arms policy, but since nobody expressly argues from the premise of his own desire for power, they are irrelevant to the logic of policy dispute. And a desire to see one's nation powerful in the world is as impersonal and is considered by some at least to be as valuable in its own right as is any other policy value. Patriotism and nationalism have moved as many spirits as have peace and freedom. Power values of this nature are as complex as are the values in the other categories. One can value United States power to control its own future; one can also put weight on United States power outside of its own borders. In "third" areas of the world, one can value those nations which back us up internationally or one can value equally all who do not oppose us (or one might not care at all). Considerations like this relate power-as-a-value to power-as-a-tool. And as values they compete with one another and they may also compete with peace and freedom. Or, conversely, analysis of power-as-a-tool can lead to conclusions by which power values reinforce one or both of the other categories.

Finally, value judgments associated with *time*, rather than competing with any of the other three categories, cut across all of them. Whatever a person's peace, freedom, and power values, he can look at them on a short- or a long-run time basis, and this decision is in part a matter of value judgment. To take an analogous example from the economics of borrowing, lending, and saving, most individuals put considerable value on the possession of money. But some want this value desperately in the short run, others are more willing to wait. In economics, the interest rate adjusts these short- and long-run time preferences. One person might need $100 so badly in the present that he is willing to pay back the $100 plus $200 interest a year later. Someone else might also rather have the $100 in the present than later, but he may value the present over the future only 6 per cent per annum's worth. And a third person might value the future over the present and save his money, obtaining interest if he can, but saving it, even in a mattress if necessary. Similar time preferences are brought to bear on the values relevant to arms policy. Some individuals evaluate alternative policies almost entirely on the basis of present effects. (This is in part a question of analysis which says the present time is the dangerous one; but it is in part a question of value.) Some may consider the present the most important, but may also weigh the next decade. And some makers of recommendations are so oriented toward long-run "goals" that they consider this long-run effect almost entirely and worry little about this year (although everyone gives at least lip service to all time periods).

Peace, freedom, and perhaps *power,* then, are weighed against one another whenever a marginalist considers policy recommendations. Within each of these three general categories and that of *time* as well, individual values compete with each other. It is on the basis of the different weights assigned to these different categories and individual judgments that the value systems of the three marginal schools of arms policy differ from one another. The contrasts can be best seen if the two ends of the marginal spectrum, the anti-war school and the anti-Communists, are described first. The "middle" school in its various aspects can then be differentiated from the ends and described in all of its multivalued complexity.

THE MARGINAL ANTI-WAR SCHOOL

The members of the marginal anti-war school all share a value system which emphasizes the importance of peace as the major goal for arms policy, but they come to this belief from two starting points. On the one hand, there are those who begin with the optimizer's belief that no problem is simple but feel that in the modern age the first task of arms policy is the prevention of nuclear war. Taking account of all the complexities, they come up with marginal anti-war recommendations. Presidential Scientific Adviser Jerome Wiesner wrote, before he entered the Kennedy administration:

Mankind's almost universal desire is to halt the frightening arms race and to provide, by rule of law, the security now sought so futilely from nuclear armaments and ballistic missiles. While the goal is clearly visible, the course is not . . .

Though the writer believes in the importance of eliminating all military power from the arsenals of independent nations as rapidly as is feasible, he also believes that it will be extremely difficult to achieve this goal in one mighty agreement and that it may be necessary to reach it through a series of steps, in which the total available military force is successively reduced.[2]

This viewpoint is marginalism because it recognizes the necessity for small steps and because the author, in working toward his goals within the Eisenhower administration as well as President Kennedy's, has necessarily realized the competing values and difficulties. But it is anti-war marginalism because within the constraints of this competition, the aim is to "halt the frightening arms race."

On the other hand, some anti-war marginalists arrive at marginal recommendations because, although initially attracted to anti-war systemism, they recognize either its intellectual limitations or the political limitations on the adoption of systemic policy changes, and thus become optimizing marginalists. Persons such as these, who have moved into anti-war marginalism on the basis of a conscious rejection of the appeals of systemism, tend to remain more extreme than the others like Wiesner who are basically optimizers. Both sorts of individuals fall under our definition of marginalism, however, in that their unconditional recommendations for arms-policy changes are no greater than marginal. The more extreme group includes those of the "unilateral initiatives" advocates who, like Etzioni, are, by their recommendations, marginalists and not systemists. Their approach is put by Anatol Rapoport and J. David Singer:

As long as the national policy maker sees the peace worker as either blind to the constraints under which the policy maker must operate or in uncompromising opposition to the demands placed upon him, the policy maker has little choice but to dismiss the peace worker as naïve or as dangerous.

2 Jerome B. Wiesner, "Comprehensive Arms Limitation Systems," in *Arms Control, Disarmament, and National Security,* ed. Donald G. Brennan (New York: Braziller, 1961), p. 198.

. . . if the American peace movement, now enjoying a dynamism which has hitherto escaped it, is to play an effective role in slowing down and perhaps reversing the gruesome race toward destruction, its members should go through a certain amount of soul searching. We must give up simplistic notions about the forces which operate upon the policy makers and must give clear expression to a revised image of the world.[3]

This might be paraphrased, "Abandon systemism, all ye who wish to affect the real policy process."

In any case, both the anti-war optimizers and the optimizing anti-war men are close together on their values as well as on their recommendations, closer perhaps than their different styles might indicate. The basic value judgment is that the greatest policy weight must be put on peace. This does not mean that freedom is unimportant in any absolute sense. It is very important, *but it is not what arms policy is all about.* The members of the marginal anti-war school reject such systemic recommendations as unilateral disarmament because they recognize the constraint provided by the need to prevent the erosion of freedom. But when looking for *positive* arms recommendations to push, any possible favorable effect on freedom is secondary to the major search for an end to international violence. Walter Millis expresses the attitude: "The liberal or rational attitude toward military policy must find its deepest foundation in an appreciation not simply of the costs and cruelties of war but of the essential irrelevance of the military problem to most of the real issues of the world we inhabit."[4] To the anti-war marginalist, freedom is important but is among those "real issues" for which military power is irrelevant. The value of the third category, power, is not even considered great enough to make it a "real issue."

Within the class of anti-war values, the marginal anti-war

[3] Anatol Rapoport and J. David Singer, "An Alternative to Slogans," *The Nation*, March 24, 1962, pp. 249–251.

[4] Walter Millis, "A Liberal Military-Defense Policy," in *The Liberal Papers*, ed. James Roosevelt (Garden City: Doubleday, 1962), p. 114. Copyright © 1962 by James Roosevelt.

school puts more weight on decreasing the likelihood of war than on meliorating it if it does come. Wiesner writes: "Many advocates of controlled mutual-deterrent systems derive considerable comfort from the fact that thus to limit the size of strategic nuclear forces will limit the damage that would occur if a war started in spite of our best efforts. While it is clearly true that a smaller force can do less damage, I am unable to get any real comfort from the fact that only one hundred bombs (instead of one thousand or ten thousand) could fall on our country and on Russia. In either case the possible scale of suffering and damage is beyond my comprehension."[5] For like reasons, many anti-war marginalists oppose civil defense. They argue that even such a minor melioration of the terrors of nuclear war may make its coming more likely. They would rather go all out for avoiding nuclear war between the United States and the Soviet Union than take what they believe analytically to be the chance that "insuring" against such war may actually hasten its arrival. Similarly, whereas some other makers of arms recommendations try to meliorate war by channeling conflict toward "limited" wars, the anti-war marginalists fear the "escalation" of such little wars into big ones, and they generate small interest in meliorative substitution of "limited" war for the larger variety. And, also within the value category of peace, the marginal anti-war school puts some additional weight on not-killing and not threatening to kill. As marginalists they see a necessity for the implied threats of deterrence (for the members nearest the boundary with systemic pacifism, only the short-run necessity), but they would prefer some other way. This not-killing value, however, is less weighty than that given to no-war.

Though the anti-war marginalists' primary concern is with peace, the value they put on freedom is small only by comparison with the other. But within the freedom category it is probable that they give more weight to avoiding right-wing than Communist threats; at least it can be stated certainly

5 Wiesner, p. 223.

that they give more weight to avoiding threats from the right than does any of the other marginal schools. Some of them are quite worried about threats to liberty *within* the United States, particularly those who feel they might stem from the military. Arthur Waskow, for example, writes, "And since our aim is to protect our society not merely against foreign tyranny but against tyranny of any sort, the kind of deterrence we adopt must also protect liberty against domestic usurpation, against any groups that would abolish the free play of electoral and social disagreement in order to impose their own views of national interest and national security."[6] Coupled with an analytical belief that the power of military forces in American life is increasing rapidly, this worry becomes a specific fear of the "garrison state."

And what is true at home is also true abroad; most of the members of the anti-war school (like many others who, however, consider such matters analytically less relevant to arms policy) abhor Franco's Spain and Salazar's Portugal, look askance at military dictatorships in South Korea and Pakistan, and have their doubts about close civilian control in South Vietnam. In addition to opposing Fascist or military governments, they are anti-imperialist as well. This feeling is coupled to analytical belief that colonialism can generate violent anti-colonialism, anti-Americanism and even Communism through a dialectical process, but nonetheless for anti-war marginalists there is an important residual component of pure value judgment. The value is coupled to a humanitarian value, germane to arms policy only via budgetary competition, which holds that we have a moral duty to help raise living standards in poor sections of the world. Many anti-war marginalists feel strongly enough about imperialism that they are inclined to find much positive value in the left-but-not-Communist dictatorial regimes which have succeeded colonialism in some countries. Indeed, for some members of the

---

[6] Arthur I. Waskow, *The Limits of Defense* (Garden City: Doubleday, 1962), p. 11.

school, their opposition to both imperialism and indigenous tyranny abroad is so strong that they would prefer the United States to withdraw backing from right-wing regimes like those of South Korea and South Vietnam even at the cost of allowing Communist take-over of these countries.

Although it might seem reasonable, at least on a simplistic basis, to value the avoidance of threats to freedom from the left about equally with avoidance of those from the right, the emotional overtones of Fascism and imperialism associated with the latter make them more obnoxious to some anti-war marginalists than Communist threats. Nonetheless, the marginal anti-war school does put value on resistance to Communism, and many members of the school probably value such resistance at least as highly as resistance against the right. The anti-war marginalists pay relatively more attention than do the other groups to stopping the peaceful advance of Communism as compared to the forcible advance, but this can be deceptive. On the basis of their *analytical* world view, they see the peaceful advance as the greatest danger; on a *value* basis there is no doubt that they dislike Communist rape more than seduction. But as suggested above, their arms policies are designed to hedge rather than to militate against Communist aggression. Forcing the Communists to retreat is not among their values.

Similarly, their power values are almost nonexistent. They are not interested in "prevailing" in any thermonuclear war which might occur because they feel that prevail or not our free institutions would be irrevocably gone. They are not interested in questions such as "who is to be boss" in the world, independently of whether the boss is an advocate of freedom. If anything, they have a value judgment *against* the use of force, allied to value of not-killing and the anti-military feelings. In third areas of the world, they would prefer countries to be non-Communist, but primarily for liberation reasons; they are not particularly interested in anti-Communism abroad.

Finally, the time preferences of the marginal anti-war school give great weight to the future. They think of world peace as much in the long-run as in the next-year sense. Many of them are "goal-oriented"; they are interested in permanent peace through general and complete disarmament and/or world government. This future-orientation is particularly true of those who are very near the border with systemic pacifism. Many of these individuals apparently give *greater* weight to long-run solutions than to the next-year effects of their recommendations. Etzioni, for example, rejects what he calls "preventive arms control schemes," because they "just trim the arms race of some of its most irrational and dangerous side effects—the dangers of accidental and suicidal war— leaving the arms race itself to continue in its fatal course."[7] A focus on the short run would find the lessening of irrational and dangerous side effects a highly desirable outcome. In part, however, the focus on the long run is not pure value judgment; it is also based on an analytical assumption that any measure which aims for peace in the long run will necessarily also help to keep the peace in the near future. Waskow argues that "only by using means that are clearly peaceful in themselves can the long-range aim of peace be achieved in the modern world."[8] So far as values are concerned, this analytical assumption means that long and short runs can be made equivalent, without competition between time values and without greater "preference" being put on either.

Neither equivalence between the long and short runs nor valuing the future more than the present, however, is characteristic of all the members of the marginal anti-war school. The more moderate individuals see such ultimate solutions as general disarmament and world government as being desirable but very long run. But they too are interested in working toward a degree of arms reduction and international détente beyond what is possible "next year."

7 Amitai Etzioni, *The Hard Way to Peace: A New Strategy* (New York: Collier, 1962), p. 127.
8 Waskow, p. 117.

THE MARGINAL ANTI-COMMUNIST SCHOOL

In contrast with the anti-war marginalists who for some purposes fall into two subgroups according to whether they are primarily anti-war or marginalist, and in contrast with the middle marginalists who are heterogeneous in the extreme, the marginal anti-Communist school is relatively unified. Indeed, they themselves have some consciousness of being a coherent grouping. The idea that we are engaged in a "protracted conflict" with Communism was brought to prominence in 1959 by Robert Strausz-Hupé, William Kintner, James Dougherty, and Alvin Cottrell of the Foreign Policy Research Institute of the University of Pennsylvania, in their book, *Protracted Conflict*.[9] Since then, much of the work of the school has come from or been related in some way to the Institute. Strausz-Hupé, Kintner, and Stefan Possony in 1961 followed up the first book with *A Forward Strategy for America*,[10] in a real sense the Bible of the school, which gives a more complete exposition of the problem and the proposed solutions. In addition, the Institute publishes a quarterly journal, *Orbis*, which contains many articles representative of the marginal anti-Communist school, as well as many which are not.[11]

[9] Robert Strausz-Hupé, William R. Kintner, James E. Dougherty, and Alvin J. Cottrell, *Protracted Conflict* (New York: Harper, 1959).

[10] Robert Strausz-Hupé, William R. Kintner, and Stefan T. Possony, *A Forward Strategy for America* (New York: Harper, 1961).

[11] This greater unity and coherence of the marginal anti-Communists brings up one small problem in the utilization of sources for this book. Although there is no reason to believe that the anti-Communist school is the smallest of the marginal groups, the range of source material on the ideas of the school is apparently smaller, because almost everything seems to come from one center. To a great extent this narrowness of range is more apparent than real, however. *A Forward Strategy for America*, for example, has only three authors on record, but the authors in their preface give credit to eleven other individuals who have made major contributions to specific chapters. Evidently, with only slight permutations, the book could have been a symposium, as is another source of marginal anti-Communist material, *American Strategy for the Nuclear Age* (Garden City: Doubleday, 1960), edited by Walter F. Hahn, the editor of *Orbis*, and John C. Neff. *Orbis* itself, of course, carries articles by many authors.

Because of this greater coherence of the anti-Communist marginalists, their values (and their analyses and recommendations as well) are not difficult to identify. In many ways these values provide a mirror image of those of the marginal anti-war school—looking much the same, but with everything reversed. Whereas the anti-war group puts its greatest weight on peace but also gives considerable importance to freedom, the marginal anti-Communists give clear precedence to freedom, although hedging against the worst varieties of war. It is difficult to state how much of this is value and how much analysis; faced with a stark value choice between substantial devastation of the United States and enslavement, different members of the marginal anti-Communist school might opt differently. But the school as a whole gives by far the greatest value-analytical "importance" to opposing Communism, and in terms of value alone, at least gives greater weight to this opposition than do any of the other marginal schools. Strausz-Hupé, Kintner, and Possony write in *A Forward Strategy:*

Unless and until the U.S. discards strategic concepts that are passive or, at best, reactive, our choice will be confined to two equally disastrous alternatives: (1) to keep on living in a fool's paradise and to let ourselves be drained slowly of our strength or (2) to risk the holocaust of nuclear destruction . . . It has been argued throughout these pages that the main goal of the U.S. should be—for its own sake and the sake of mankind—the extension of freedom . . . Our efforts should be always harnessed to the pursuit of prudent measures; toward limiting, but not shrinking from, risk; and toward the positive, the creative, solution.[12]

They want to be prudent and they recognize that the danger of thermonuclear holocaust must constrain their recommendations, but the primary goal is "the extension of freedom."

[12] Robert Strausz-Hupé, William R. Kintner, and Stefan T. Possony, *A Forward Strategy for America*, pp. 400–401. Copyright © 1961 by Robert Strausz-Hupé, William R. Kintner, and Stefan T. Possony. This quotation and all subsequent quotations from this book are reprinted with the permission of Harper & Row, Publishers, Incorporated.

And because they view the world in terms of a struggle between the West and the Communists, freedom and the third value category, power, overlap analytically, although freedom is the more important in value terms.

The *"extension* of freedom," however, provides the key. Their aim is not merely stemming the tide of Communism, it is reversing it and finally winning. Unlike *systemic* anti-Communists, they are in no hurry; they do not have Hamlet's desire "to take arms against a sea of troubles, and by opposing end them," the more so because the Danish prince's next two words are "to die." But ultimate victory is the direction in which they want to move. The immediate task, however, is stopping the advance of Communism. Unlike the anti-war school, they draw no distinction between peaceful and forcible Communist advance—both are Communism. The question of the particular form the advance takes is of little interest, and the proper way to stem it is a matter of tactics rather than values.

Possible threats to freedom from the right are of no interest to the anti-Communists. So far as a domestic "garrison state" is concerned, they are not interested. The only question is that of efficiency in the struggle with Communism. Possony criticizes the Kennedy-McNamara Department of Defense, for example, by saying that ". . . the sound notion of civilian control has been inflated to a point where we would need supermen as defense secretaries. Yet we are getting civilians without strategic experience. We are forcing them to tackle life-and-death problems which they have been unable to assimilate or solve creatively.[13] And their lack of interest in right-wing threats abroad is indicated by the fact that *A Forward Strategy for America* makes no references to such anti-war school bugaboos as Franco, Chiang, or Salazar (but one reference to Batista in a discussion of Castro), no reference to Fascism, and a number of references to imperialism, all of which are designed to show that modern imperialism is Soviet

[15] Stefan T. Possony, "Aerospace Power: The Decisive Weapon," review in *Orbis*, 6:139 (Spring 1962).

imperialism. In part, this lack of interest in the right wing abroad is based on analytical belief that it is unimportant to the main issue; in part it is value judgment.

Power, however, does interest the anti-Communists. American power is, of course, closely linked to free power, but power and freedom are distinguishable. Freedom is the primary value, but the question of who is to rule the world has great interest beyond that derived from freedom. Strausz-Hupé, Kintner, and Possony open with the words: "The greatness of a nation lies neither in the abundance of its possessions nor in the strength of its arms. A people finds greatness in its response to the historical challenge—by how it manages to harness its strivings to the aspirations of the age. Thus, to be great is to fulfill a promise that surpasses the national interest . . . Rome and Britain attained, within the limits of the techniques of their day, predominant power—military, political and economic. Each wedded power to a noble idea of community. Greatness lies in the creative use of power and not in its denial."[14] This is an idealistic view of power, but power it is, and not merely in the name of freedom. The marginal anti-Communist school wants the West to organize the world. They prefer their foreign countries, whether in Europe or in the "underdeveloped" areas to be anti-Communist, rather than being merely non-Communist neutrals, which would satisfy the requirements of freedom. And they want the United States to "prevail" in any war. While analytically some of them disagree with the anti-war school's belief that freedom cannot survive a thermonuclear war, they want to prevail, free or not.

Indeed, although the anti-Communist school gives considerable absolute weight to peaceful values, these are evaluated quite differently from those of the anti-war group. The anti-Communists feel as a matter of analysis that in the "protracted conflict" with Communism there is no chance of avoiding war of some sort; rather the aim must be to melio-

[14] *A Forward Strategy for America*, p. 1. Copyright © 1961 by Robert Strausz-Hupé, William R. Kintner, and Stefan T. Possony.

rate it. They want to design our forces to keep the inevitable war from being thermonuclear; they want to design our defenses against thermonuclear war to keep it from being the ultimate holocaust. They want war to be nonthermonuclear, if possible, and their interest in fighting guerrilla wars preceded by several years the interest shown by most other military analysts. They feel such wars are inevitable in the world power struggle between freedom and Communism; they feel that such wars are preferable to thermonuclear war. But they do not wish to avoid even thermonuclear war at *all* costs.

Finally, the time preferences of the anti-Communist marginalists are similar to those of the anti-war group. The specific values to which the time preferences are applied are reversed, but time operates in a similar way. Like their opposite numbers, the marginal anti-Communists are goal-oriented. They want to win the next battle with Communism, but they are also very much concerned with finding the road to final victory.

The more moderate members of this school see this victory as being in the very long run and worry more about the immediate battle. Unlike the more extreme *anti-war* marginalists, however, those *anti-Communist* marginalists who are extreme in that they are close to the boundary with systemism do not go very far in elevating the long-run goal over the short-run objective. The main reason for this difference between the value judgments of the two sets of "extreme" marginalists lies in a difference in the direction in which they feel called upon to use an analytical assumption they hold in common. Both groups tend to assume an equivalence in the short- and long-run effects of arms policies. The anti-war marginalists are not hard put to show that their recommendations go in the desired *long-run* direction (e.g., a single disarmament step is a move toward long-run general disarmament) and they assume that they therefore must be right for the short run as well. The anti-Communists, on the other hand, can demonstrate relatively easily the *short-run* anti-Communism of their proposals, and thus use the same analytical assumption of equivalence to maintain a belief that the same steps move toward the long-run goal. An example here would be the endorsement of one of the gamier anti-Communist leaders in the underdeveloped world. There is little difficulty in arguing that these gentlemen will be more likely to halt the short-run spread of Communism in these areas than some of the left-wing "neutral" alternatives, and it then becomes easy to assume that backing the anti-Communists will aid in stopping the long-run Communist advance. This analytical assumption, which makes it possible to suppress a possible value conflict between the long and short time periods, works for the anti-Communists against the raising of the long run over the short, and there is thus less tendency among the more extreme individuals of this persuasion to subordinate immediate effects over "goals" than is apparent among their anti-war opposite numbers.

In any case, however, one identifying characteristic of the anti-Communist marginalists is a dedication to ultimate victory over Communism which is considerably greater than that of the other marginal schools.

THE "MIDDLE" MARGINAL SCHOOL

Of those who actually make the decisions on American arms policy or who make their recommendations from within the decision-making apparatus, the majority are probably middle marginalists. How large a majority depends, of course, on where the lines between the marginal groups are drawn, but given the blurred boundaries which suffice for demarcation of the major schools, it seems clear that more of those who are closest to the seats of power are in the "middle" than anywhere else.

But the middle marginal school is a heterogeneous one. Although in terms of recommendations it can be characterized as a grouping intermediate between the anti-war and anti-Communist marginalists, these recommendations can stem from one or the other (or, ordinarily, some combination of both) of two trains of logic. These two lines of thought start with two different value systems, although the values of most individual middle marginalists come between the two poles. One of these ideal types of middle-marginal thought bases intermediate recommendations simply on an intermediate set of values and analyses, which does not give significantly greater prominence to either of the twin threats of war and Communism. Those who reason this way do not deny that they are taking more risk of war than would be accepted by the primarily anti-war school, and more risk of Communist advance than would be accepted by the anti-Communist group. Perhaps the typical exponent of this sort of reasoning is the philosopher turned policy analyst who starts his thought with values about where he wants to go, and attempts to apply these values to the world as he sees it. Because he finds that his values are balanced he is not a systemist, but his value-oriented sort of logic makes it easy for him to debate with systemists. The middle marginalist, Sidney Hook, in arguing with anti-war systemist Erich Fromm writes: "Intelligent fear is aware that not only is there a danger of nuclear holocaust, *there is also as great a danger of a Communist takeover and destruction of free society.* Hysterical fear runs thoughtlessly from the jaws of one danger into the jaws of another. Intelligent fear, as well as dedication to our moral values, should motivate us in a quest for a world of peace *and* freedom."[15]

The other train of thought which arrives at middle-marginal recommendations does not begin with values and aims. It starts with a complex analysis of a complex world, and this world picture dominates the reasoning leading to recommendations. Many (but by no means all) of those who reason in this way consider avoidance of thermonuclear war as the primary object of arms policy, as do the members of the marginal anti-war school. But based upon their analytical view of the world, they believe that *in order to avoid such war* it is necessary to stop Communism. Reasoning in this way, they need not consider the question of whether the use of arms

15 Sidney Hook, "Escape from Reality," *The New Leader,* May 29, 1961, p. 12.

is justifiable to defend the value of freedom as such; arms are needed to prevent thermonuclear war and that is enough justification. The road to peace thus runs through deterrence and balanced strength rather than through disarmament and balanced weakness, as is argued by both the marginal and the systemic anti-war groups. These middle marginalists believe that because of the way the world really is, the recommendations of the marginal anti-war school are badly designed and will fail to prevent thermonuclear war. Typical here is Thomas Schelling, who, in the course of a lengthy analysis in opposition to total disarmament, builds his case on the contention that disarmament is a faulty road to peace, and stays entirely away from possible arguments that disarmament is a dangerous road leading to Communist world domination. He ends his discourse by saying that "disarmament may make some of our military problems more manageable. It will not make them disappear."[16]

Very few members of the middle-marginal school base their recommendations entirely either on closely balanced values or an analysis of the realistic road to peace. More typical of the middle marginalists than either polar type of reasoning is Herman Kahn's use of both value bases:

It is easy to write graphically and persuasively of the dangers of the arms race, nuclear and otherwise . . . Yet the question remains unanswered: Why do nations in general, our own in particular, continue to play such a dangerous and pointless game?

Here we hit on the nub of the matter: the game is indeed dangerous, but not pointless, since not to play it (even to reduce forces or submit to arms control) can also be dangerous: a Pearl Harbor or a Munich is all too possible. If we examine the whole range of possibilities, . . . we discover that there are no pleasant, safe, or even unambiguously moral positions for the individual, for a nation, or for civilization.[17]

[16] Thomas C. Schelling, *The Stability of Total Disarmament*, Institute for Defense Analyses, Special Study Group, Study Memorandum no. 1 (Washington, October 6, 1961), p. 51.

[17] Herman Kahn, "The Arms Race and Some of Its Hazards," in *Arms Control, Disarmament, and National Security*, p. 89.

The reference to Munich represents the balanced-value portion of the middle-marginal reasoning, the value for which we may have to risk war; but the reference to Pearl Harbor indicates that Kahn also plays his "game" because he thinks that it may be the best way to avoid surprise attack and thermonuclear war itself.

In any case, to get to the middle one must necessarily utilize a complex structure of logic. Some base it one way, some the other; most rest their reasoning on the twin bases of avoiding Munich *and* Pearl Harbor. But all of these "middle" trains of thought arrive at sets of arms recommendations intermediate between those directed primarily against war and those directed primarily against Communism. Because it is on these recommendations that the classification and nomenclature of the schools is based, there is only one "middle" marginal school. This middle is a single school in terms of its recommendations, and it is also a single school in terms of its analyses of the way the world is and can be. Not every middle marginalist recommends exactly the same policies or analyzes the world in the same way, but the differences within the school are smaller than the differences between the middle marginalists and the other schools. It is only in terms of values—the world as it should be—that the middle is spread between two substantially different poles, the "balanced-value" middle exemplified by Hook, and the "analytical" middle of Schelling. In describing these two polar tendencies among middle-marginal values, no implication is intended that most of the makers of recommendations are at the poles; most, in fact, fall between. Rather, the implication is that the line between the ends is smooth and straight enough that its entire range can be deduced from the two points.

The Balanced-Value Middle Marginalists

The distinctive value basis of balanced-value middle marginalism is perhaps best expressed by Ernest Lefever:

President Kennedy has it within his power to end the cold war. Two equally dramatic and effective paths are open to him to accomplish this purpose. He can end the cold war by capitulating to Communist demands in Berlin, in Laos, and on the disarmament dialogue, or he can end it by starting a hot war.

As long as Mr. Kennedy and the American people regard these alternatives as morally wrong and politically unwise, which I hope will be a long time, we will have to adjust to the perils and the pitfalls of a not-so-peaceful coexistence.[18]

This differs from anti-war marginalism by its unwillingness to "capitulate" to any Soviet demands; the anti-war marginalists would not call it capitulation, but many of them would be willing to make unilateral accommodations (marginal ones) on these issues. It differs from anti-Communist marginalism in that it accepts coexistence, even "not-so-peaceful coexistence." And it also differs from "analytical" middle marginalism in that the "analysts" would not admit that such small capitulations as giving up Berlin could end the cold war.

Most important, the Lefever statement, like Sidney Hook's sentences, reflects the difficulty in granting preponderance to the values of either peace or freedom. No marginalist gives either sort of value absolute priority—to do so ordinarily leads to systemism—but the middle marginalists of this subschool come to the closest balance between the two.

Similarly, within the peaceful category, the balanced-value middle is reluctant to put either reduction in the probability of war or melioration of war above the other. They are clearly against war; they are clearly for its melioration if it should occur. The two values are weighted closely enough to one another that it is difficult to make a guess on the basis of values alone as to what policy recommendation will emerge from the optimizing process. Most middle marginalists favor some civil defense, for example, but for many this is based on an analysis that civil defense does not appreciably increase the probability of war, rather than on a value system which subordinates avoidance to melioration. On subtler issues than civil defense (e.g., to what extent should offensive and defensive strategic war plans be based on deterrence of any nuclear war; to what extent on melioration of war if it should occur) the middle is split every which way. And on the third value under the heading of peace, that of not-killing, those balanced-value middle marginalists who consider it at all do so only after all of the other problems have been dealt with.

Within the category of freedom, the dominant theme again is balance. The anti-Communist values balance not only with those in opposition to war, but also with those in opposition to reactionary threats, although the middle marginalists consider possible right-wing threats to be analytically less relevant than those of Communism. Nonetheless there is some concern with domestic militarism, as expressed by President Eisenhower's farewell warning against the "military-industrial complex." There is distaste for extreme right-wing regimes abroad, although their acceptance or rejection is largely dependent upon analysis of their effect on the larger problems of war and Communism. Similarly, the balanced-value marginal feeling about imperialism is conditioned both by value judgment and analysis. According to Hook: "All the economic aid in the world will not win us friends and allies unless the United States regains for itself its reputation as an anti-imperialist power . . . It is our *ideas,* the common ideas of the free world, the heritage of the Atlantic democracies and their allies, which can inspire a continuing offensive against Communism all along the line."[19] Other middle marginalists might analyze the situation differently and subordinate the anti-imperialist value in order to maintain solidarity with Europe; the range of middle-marginal recommendations can include both of these. And similarly, while middle marginalism has little interest in forcing Communist retreat (except, perhaps, as a tactical measure to avoid further advance), the question of whether to concentrate on stopping the peaceful or the forcible advance depends much more on analysis of what the real problem is than on value judgment. Most

[19] Sidney Hook, *Political Power and Personal Freedom* (New York: Criterion, 1959), pp. 428–429.

balanced-value middle marginalists probably share with the anti-war school a greater abhorrence for aggression than for peaceful Communist penetration, but the effect of this value depends on its analytical relevance.

Whereas the anti-war school possesses a positive distaste for power as such and the anti-Communist school has some enthusiasm for power for its own sake, the balanced-value middle is interested in power, but the interest is not based on first order value judgment. Rather it is derived from other values. Lefever writes:

The drama of world politics is an intense, unending and universal struggle of power and purpose among men and nations . . . National power can be used to support policies which contribute to greater justice, peace and security; or it can be made the instrument of injustice, aggression and exploitation . . . The significant moral difference between the governments of two nations has nothing to do with the quantity of power each possesses; it has everything to do with the quality of the purposes to which the power of each is committed, the appropriateness of the means employed to pursue this purpose, and the effect of these means on persons at home and abroad.[20]

From this may flow a need for the United States to win wars, *if* analytically such victory will serve the ethical purposes of power; from it may flow a desirability of Western organization of the world, *if* this will serve the interests of peace and freedom. From it flows a division of nations in third areas between those it is hoped will be positively anti-Communist and others for which the desire is merely non-Communism, depending on what serves long-run "moral" interests.

Finally, in their time preferences, the balanced-value middle marginalists are less future-oriented than either the anti-war or anti-Communist marginalist schools. The dilemma is

[20] Ernest W. Lefever, *Ethics and United States Foreign Policy*, pp. 5–8. Copyright © 1957 by The World Publishing Company. A Living Age Book, published by Meridian Books, The World Publishing Company. This quotation and all subsequent quotations from this book are reprinted by permission of The World Publishing Company.

put by Lawrence Finkelstein: "The point . . . is not that world order will never be achieved. It is that the road will be long and difficult and that we are very far from having established the conditions in which we can expect to achieve the end we seek. To me, it is more important to learn to live successfully with the problems of today and the near future than to rest our hopes on our ability to eliminate them . . . If we devote too much energy to the long range goals, the result may be to divert essential effort from the tasks that confront us now."[21] The implication that the long range and the present may well clash differs from the analytical assumption of the anti-war and anti-Communist marginalists that policies designed for one time period will also help in the other. Finkelstein assumes that conflict does exist, and by giving greater emphasis to the present without wholly sacrificing the long-run search for world order, he tries for a "balanced" resolution of the differences.

The "Analytical" Middle Marginalists

By characterizing the other polar tendency in middle-marginal thought as "analytical," no implication is intended that the rest of the schools are "emotional"; all are analytical to a greater or lesser degree. What distinguishes the "analytical" middle marginalists, however, is that, whether for reasons of temperament or roles as "technicians," their thought tends to *start* with where we are and where we might get to rather than with value judgments about where we want to be. They avoid conceding, as did Lefever, that it may be necessary to risk one value to gain another and they thus treat their recommendations as being close to dominant—best for at least one value and no worse for any. Thus Kahn writes that the important thing is "avoiding disaster and buying time, without specifying the use of this time . . . The practical job of finding a path may be more difficult than the job of design-

21 Lawrence S. Finkelstein, *Defence, Disarmament and World Order*, Canadian Institute of International Affairs, "Behind the Headlines" series, vol. XXII, no. 1 (September 1962), p. 10.

ing the goal."[22] This statement, in addition to having some interesting time-preference implications, also suggests that a *single* type of solution is needed for avoiding disasters of all kinds—is, in other words, dominant. Kahn's coupling of Pearl Harbor and Munich, quoted above, has a similar implication.

This concentration on analyses leading to recommendations which are dominant over the range of values, however, means that the specific values upon which the "analytical" middle marginalists base their arguments are difficult to ferret out. This is particularly the case because the "analysts" seldom explicitly set forth their values in print. And in any case the values of the "analysts" are less clear and more amorphous than those of the balanced-value "philosophers." Nonetheless, policy values do exist, indeed logically must exist, in the reasoning of those makers of recommendations who are primarily students of the world as it is, as well as in the reasoning of those who concentrate primarily on the world as it might become.

The key *analytical* belief of the analytical subschool is that the best way to stay out of thermonuclear war is by the use of Western power to keep Communist ambitions from getting out of hand. This combination by analysis of all three major value categories—peace, protection of freedom from Communist incursions, and power—means that the priorities among the three are not as straightforward as those of the other schools. Yet it is reasonably clear that as an objective of arms policy, peace is above the rest. According to Henry Kissinger: "There is no doubt that the avoidance of war must be a primary goal of all responsible statesmen. The desirability of maintaining peace cannot be the subject of either intellectual or partisan political controversy in the free world. The only reasonable issue is how best to achieve this objective . . . We cannot have war. But we have had to learn painfully that peace is something more than the absence of war. Solving the problem of peaceful change is essential; but we must be care-

[22] Herman Kahn, *On Thermonuclear War* (Princeton: Princeton University Press, 1960), p. 7.

ful not to deny its complexity."[23] Much more so than among the balanced-value middle marginalists, the peaceful values are first. But the quest for peace can lead through tortuous byways. The concentration on a search for *dominant* solutions to the problems of peace, freedom, and power, diminishes the operational significance within the optimizing mechanism of the value priority placed on peace.

Within the category of peaceful values, however, the "analysts," like the balanced-value "philosophers," give predominance neither to decreasing the likelihood of war nor to its melioration. They feel, with Schelling, that "war cannot be made impossible . . . Short of universal brain surgery, nothing can erase the memory of weapons and how to build them."[24] Because of this it is necessary to meliorate—to reduce the level of violence in the all-out thermonuclear variety Kahn calls "spasm" war[25] to "controlled" nuclear war; to weight the probabilities against nuclear war as compared to nonnuclear. But the hopelessness of completely abolishing war does not mean that its likelihood cannot be reduced. Many middlemarginal "analysts" have hopes of very significant reductions. Indeed, steps to reduce the over-all likelihood of any kind of war, together with meliorative measures to make the residual wars less terrible, might even make the most violent wars almost impossible. But if so, this is to be done by melioration as well as by measures of direct prevention, and conflicts between reduced likelihood and such melioration are to be resolved analytically for each proposed measure. And in this complex calculus of peace and war, any weight put on the third "peaceful" value of not-killing disappears.

The concentration on the problems of war and peace by those nearest the "analytical" end of the middle-marginal scale means that the other categories of value become some-

23 Henry A. Kissinger, *The Necessity for Choice*, pp. 169–171. Copyright © 1960, 1961 by Henry A. Kissinger. This quotation and all subsequent quotations from this book are reprinted with the permission of Harper & Row, Publishers, Incorporated, and Chatto & Windus Limited, Publishers.

24 Thomas C. Schelling, "The Future of Arms Control," *Operations Research*, 9:722 (September–October 1961).

25 Kahn, *On Thermonuclear War*, p. 308.

what obscure. Freedom may be given a high value in the abstract, but it is analytically less relevant to arms policy than are the peaceful values. In this the "analysts" are like the anti-war marginalists; but unlike the value-oriented anti-war school, the "analysts" are much less concerned with the inner competition among the values subsumed under the heading of freedom. Thus they are more interested in the anti-Communist freedom values than in the threats coming from the right wing, but their greater interest does not imply a value judgment that Communism is worse than Fascism. Communism, they feel, is part of the military problem, the right wing is not; from 1941 to 1945 Fascism was the problem, Communism was not.

The "analysts" have little feeling, either value or analytical, about "right-wing" domestic threats to liberty. Most of the military personnel who give thought to general arms policy fall into this "analytical" middle category, and they obviously are not likely to be *anti*-militarist. The civilian analysts of this subschool, in sharp distinction to the more extreme anti-war marginalists, want to associate the military planners with the quest for stable peace. "The cooperation of the military services in an arms control enterprise is likely to be critical to its success; and the morale and the understanding of the military services, in an arms control environment, will still be essential to the nation's security,"[26] according to Schelling and Morton Halperin.

The intricacies of Fascism, militarism, and imperialism abroad are of little interest to the analytical middle, because they are felt to be of little relevance to the war-and-peace problem. To the extent they are shown analytically to be relevant, however, they may become important, and latent values may come into play. *Probably at this point the "analyst" is forced to consider his value system in enough detail that he begins to move toward balanced-value middle marginalism.* The same can be said of the "analysts' " views on the competi-

26 Thomas C. Schelling and Morton H. Halperin, *Strategy and Arms Control* (New York: Twentieth Century Fund, 1961), p. 138.

tion of values between the prevention of forcible and peaceful Communist advance. Prevention of forcible advance is analytically a part of the problem of preventing war which might stem from Communist overreaching; prevention of peaceable advance is to them a problem largely beyond the range of arms policy. But if it becomes necessary to compare these two on a value basis, the "analyst" is likely to start moving away from the pole of pure analysis.

On the values within the power category, paradoxically, the "analysts" put little weight. This is paradoxical because military power is the tool and the substance with which they work in their analyses. But unlike the anti-Communist marginalists, they have little tendency to be bemused by power for its own sake. The "pure" analyst cares little, for example, about the degree of backing we get from non-Communist or from anti-Communist nations in third areas, except as they affect the basic questions of war and peace. He may care about "prevailing" in a war—in large measure, "prevailing" is espoused either as a means of meliorating war damage to the United States or as a hope of preserving American freedom, but in part it is a first-order value judgment held by some analysts. The general attitude of the "analysts," however, is similar to that of Lefever: wanting to use power for moral ends. But, unlike Lefever, there is among them little moral calculation; the calculus of the "analysts" is almost entirely analytical, designed to bring power considerations to bear on the major moral values in the category of peace.

Finally, the analytical middle marginalists have the shortest time horizons of any group, giving the greatest relative weight to the present as compared to the future. The typical time periods they consider in making current recommendations are the fiscal year for which budget planning is now commencing or the operational period of the weapon system now being researched. The "analysts" do have longer-run goals which they weigh in the evaluation of policy recommendations, but these goals are much less ultimate than those of the anti-war or anti-Communist marginalists. The unity of Western Europe is a typical nonimmediate objective of the analytical middle. This is considerably shorter-run than world government, the comparable goal espoused by many members of the anti-war school and some balanced-value middle marginalists.

In addition, however, the analytical middle marginalists do give one very important reverse twist to their time preferences. Although they do emphasize the short run, they mean next year and not tomorrow in any literal sense. This becomes obvious in questions of immediate appeasement of Soviet desires; they remember that the Munich conference postponed World War II for approximately eleven months, and they reject appeasement because analytically they believe it acts against their single major value which they hold in common with Prime Minister Neville Chamberlain, "peace for our time." If the anti-war and anti-Communist marginalists both make their short- and long-run time values compatible by means of analytical assumption, the middle "analysts" define their prime short-run value by an analysis which concludes that the Munich experience is relevant for today.

In any case, the most important and the most relevant time preference of the "analysts" is that they are willing to go further than Finkelstein in sacrificing the future to the present whenever these compete. With Kahn, they want to buy time. With respect to what is probably the most important case in point, the competition between short-run stability through arms control on the one hand, and the long-run "goal" of general and complete disarmament on the other, Schelling is willing to admit more than most of his fellow proponents of arms control in proclaiming that the short and the long may be incompatible when he says that ". . . by far the most frequent argument raised in favor of particular limited measures of arms control, perhaps the most widely persuasive, is that these limited measures are at least 'steps toward' the goal of ultimate disarmament. We have not faced up to the implications of the anomaly that 'measures to safeguard against surprise attack' are designed to preserve a nuclear striking power, and are not easily construed as just another 'step toward' ultimate disarmament."[27] With this analysis many of the marginal anti-war opponents of putting the major stress on immediate control would agree. The difference is over values—the "analysts" will almost always opt for short-run stability, for "next year's" fulfillment of their major goal of keeping the peace.

SUMMARY

The marginal schools of arms policy, then, differ in the values which they put into the optimizing mechanism to weigh the possible outcomes of alternative policies; they differ in the relative weights they assign to these values; and they differ in the relevance they believe these values have to the making of arms recommendations. The differences are complicated, and they are summarized in Figure 2. Because marginalist recommendations depend as much on relevancy and relative weight of the different values as on selection and omission of values, any summary must go beyond listing, and indicate relative importance. The values of the four schools and subschools are illustrated in Figure 2 with four different comparative weights, as shown in the legend. The categories of value and individual values are listed vertically; the schools and subschools, horizontally. Horizontal readings to discover whether one school weights a particular value more highly than another school are not very meaningful; as has been suggested above, interpersonal comparisons are seldom meaningful. The more interesting aspect of Figure 2 is in the vertical readings—comparing the values for each group, and only then comparing entire columns for the four schools and subschools. From this it is possible to get some impression of the value differences among the marginalists. But the wording, "some impression," is important; Figure 2 is meant to be impressionistic and not definitive. It gives some idea as to how the schools differ and it shows why it is impossible to present a simple continuum of value from anti-war

[27] Thomas C. Schelling, "Reciprocal Measures for Arms Stabilization," in *Arms Control, Disarmament, and National Security*, p. 168.

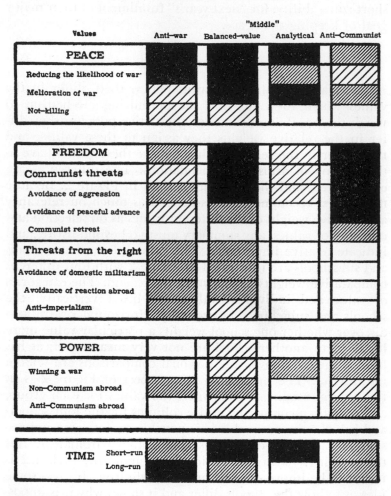

FIGURE 2: Values of the marginal schools

to anti-Communist. To go beyond this would be presumptuous in the extreme.

Figure 2, then, shows that the *anti-war* marginalist school centers its values about peace, although maintaining more or less interest in practically all of the freedom values espoused by the other groups. Conversely, the center of gravity of the *anti-Communist* marginalists' values is clearly located at avoidance of Communist encroachments on freedom, and, while they care little about possible encroachments from the "right," their anti-Communist values are both tempered by a desire for peace and reinforced by a desire for national power. Both of the "extreme" marginalist schools give more time-weight to the long-run than do the two subschools in the "middle."

These two polar tendencies among the values of the *middle* marginalists are very unlike one another. The "balanced-value" subschool really represents a balance between the anti-war and the anti-Communist marginalists—balancing peace and freedom, coming close to balancing Communist and reactionary threats to freedom (although giving the former analytical precedence as to relevance), and paying some attention to power. *The values that the "analysts," consider relevant to arms policy, however, resemble a less developed version of the anti-war marginalists more than they do those of the balanced-value middle,* and this has important bearing on the debate between the anti-war and middle-marginal schools. The "analysts' " main interest is in peace—particularly in avoiding the worst wars; they are interested in freedom and power as analytically relevant; other values which they might possess are considered analytically irrelevant to arms policy. On the basis of these values, quite similar to those of the anti-war group, they come to recommendations which are substantially different. Different values, then, do not suffice for explaining the different recommendations of the three marginal schools. It is necessary to turn to analyses—the world as the marginalists think it is and can be made to be.

✣ ✣ ✣ ✣ ✣

CHAPTER 6

INTRODUCTION TO
MARGINALIST ANALYSES

The identification of marginalist value systems has been complicated by the fact that the logical separability of value judgments and probability analyses from one another cannot be readily translated into the real world of arms policy. All that can be observed directly from most current writings on arms policy is the "importance" product of value-times-probability. Certain future outcomes are thus omitted from the optimizing calculations of some individuals because of their estimated low probabilities, even though they may actually be given a high value in the abstract—a value which is not visible to the observer because a large value times a zero probability is still zero.

Similar difficulties arise in the investigation of marginalist analyses. In principle, the analytically estimated probability that a particular outcome will stem from a given policy should be independent of the positive or negative value attached to that outcome; in practice, this is seldom the case. The basic problem is the apparent tendency on the part of many makers of recommendations to concentrate on the "best" or the "worst" possible policy outcomes. In the case of arms recommendations it is ordinarily the worst which is relevant, because thermonuclear war and Communist takeover are drastic enough to draw attention away from most Utopias. And "worst," like "best," is a value term. Optimizing marginalists do not think *exclusively* of these worst results—if they did so they would rapidly become maximizing systemists—but they are bemused enough by Apocalypse for the negative value of the most drastic outcomes to have an effect on their probability estimates. For this reason, the probabilities of worst outcomes may frequently be estimated to be higher than would be the case were these analytical estimates actually independent of value judgments.

None of this is particularly or necessarily irrational. As pointed out in the discussion of the attempts to allow for "conservatism" while optimizing, real-world probability estimates are so very uncertain that there is a warrant for giving extra weight to the outcome Daniel Ellsberg calls "the worst expectation that might appear reasonable," with reasonable being defined as having a significant probability.[1] But although this is not irrational, it at least makes it necessary to precede this discussion of marginalist probability analyses with a caveat corresponding to that given for the discussion of values: Any policy outcome estimated analytically by a maker of marginal recommendations to have a significant probability would most likely be significant even if the estimate could be completely independent of the recommender's values; *but some outcomes with apparently high probability estimates might be gaged much lower if his values did not lead the recommender to profound worry about "what if" it did happen.*

The analysis relevant to the making of arms policy, however, is much more than the abstract estimation of the probabilities of future outcomes of alternative policies. In principle it is only these estimates for the future which enter the optimizing mechanisms of choice; what is past is past. But in practice, of course, probabilities are calculated on the basis of inductive reasoning which generalizes from the past and present. Indeed, the bases of history and current observation with which most inductive policy analyses start are so predominant in most analytical discourse that a categorization of

[1] Daniel Ellsberg, "Risk, Ambiguity, and the Savage Axioms," *Quarterly Journal of Economics*, 75:664 (November 1961).

these provides the most convenient breakdown for the investigation of the analytical world views and predictions of the marginal schools.

The five headings under which arms-policy analysis is discussed here are *war,* our *opponents, power, allied and neutral countries,* and *ourselves.* These are not mutually exclusive— they overlap, but utilization of the headings makes it easier to follow complex analyses of a complex world and to compare the different pictures of this world held by the different schools.

The analysis of *war* obviously has a close relationship to the value category of peace. The value put on avoiding a thermonuclear war is partly dependent upon the analytical picture of what such a war in the future will look like. The value put on avoiding a smaller war is related to both the picture of such a war and the estimate of the likelihood that it will lead to a larger war. The analysis of war is composed of the answers to questions of this nature. How likely is it that wars will start with each of alternative trains of events? How probable do the different sorts of wars then become? What will they look like once they start? These questions are answered quite differently by the members of the different marginal schools.

Similarly, the analysis of our *opponents,* the Soviet Union, China (and perhaps other Communist nations), is related to the value put on avoiding Communist threats to freedom. How likely is the Soviet Union to threaten us? Is their object our total defeat or are they becoming defensive and interested mainly in consolidating their own *status quo?* Will they respond favorably to friendly gestures on our part or are they more likely to take advantage of such gestures? Are there forces within the Soviet Union we should encourage? What about encouragement of Russia as against China (or vice versa)?

Whatever the Soviets' current objectives and ours, how are these objectives best achieved in the current world? The third heading of analysis, that of *power,* covers questions of such a "how to" character. What are the uses of military power, economic power, political power? What about less tangible instruments such as "moral" power, the power of public opinion, will power? What are the relationships among all of these—how do they conflict and how do they reinforce one another? In this investigation of alternative arms policies, the primary focus must be on military power, but the various schools look differently not only at military power itself but also at its relationship to other forms of power.

Power, however, is not the same in all areas of the world, and indeed, the analysis of *allies and neutral countries* has some overlap with several other of the analytical headings. What kinds of power are most appropriate for use in the different portions of the globe? How important are these different areas to us, and how does our policy in one area (e.g., NATO) affect our policy in other areas (e.g., colonies belonging to our NATO allies)? The competing analyses of the relationship of the United States to NATO and that of NATO to the rest of the world form an important portion of arms policy disputes; in addition, within the area of the Atlantic Alliance, the specific picture of Germany is for historical reasons particularly important.

Finally, it does not suffice to analyze the rest of the world; analysts also look at *ourselves*. Can the United States and the Soviet Union be treated as symmetrical opponents, or are they so different that the same rules cannot be applied to them? Whether or not this is true of the rules of world law and morality, what about the rules of logic? Independent of value judgments concerning what *should* motivate American arms policy, what in fact *does* motivate our decision makers? The analysis of what we are relates back to the previous value discussion concerning threats to freedom from the right. Does the military power *of* the United States imply military power *in* the United States to an extent which might endanger democracy?

Because marginalists optimize, they must analyze the world

in all of these complex categories in order to arrive at recommendations which do some rough justice to all of their relevant values. As suggested above, not all of these analyses are explicit—some matters are just assumed—but even implicit analysis comes under the definition of analysis. Further, the discussion of the analyses which characterize the three marginal schools of arms policy runs into one additional problem not encountered in describing values. In the determination of values, every man is, in a real sense, his own philosopher. In the United States, the values relevant to arms policy are not accepted by the individual makers of recommendations as received doctrine, but are matters of personal belief. The values of elected decision makers are compounds of personal belief and the beliefs of their constituents.

This system of arriving individually at one's beliefs on all matters, which is the usual method for personal choice of values in a free society, however, is not the ordinary mode of choice for policy analyses, where receipt of doctrine from experts is much more common and acceptable. In the process of analysis there is usually a division of labor. Most of those who write about arms policy are specialists who prefer to put down on paper that which they know best, and assume the rest on the basis of learned analyses they trust or find compelling. This is true of all the marginal schools, but particularly of the middle marginal group because it is much the largest of the three—large enough to allow a division of labor and "economies of scale" beyond those available to either the anti-war or the anti-Communist marginal schools. The division is not always completely successful—discrepancies sometimes exist between the partial analyses made by the specialists in one category (e.g., Sovietologists), and the partial analyses in the same category assumed by specialists on another topic (e.g., military analysts' assumptions about the Soviet Union)—but by and large, specialization increases the level of sophistication brought to policy analysis by all three schools.

This specialization of analysis, however, compounds an-

other difficulty which affects the identification of the values
and recommendations of the three marginal groupings as
well as their analyses—where to draw the lines dividing the
schools. The lines are *defined* on the basis of recommendations, but even here they are both idealized and arbitrary.
The specialized analyses of different individuals cannot even
be arbitrarily classified into schools on the basis of their
content. These analyses are intended to be objective pictures
of the world and cannot be called anti-war, anti-Communist,
or intermediate. Rather, analyses can be classified according
to the way in which each specific one forms a portion of the
world picture of individuals who make classifiable recommendations. Such individuals ordinarily carry with them
complete pictures of the world, including analyses which
come under each of the five headings. The recommendations
and the people who make them are real and whole, but because of the specialization problem, few individuals record
their complete pictures of all aspects of the world—and if
they did so, it would characterize themselves but probably
not their schools of thought. The analyses discussed below
as being characteristic of the schools themselves, then, are
synthesized from the writings of many persons. Although
what are described are ranges of analytical views rather than
single viewpoints for each school, marginalists are eclectic
enough that even the ranges might not catch all individuals
whose recommendations fall within the schools. The problem, however, is not a serious one for two reasons. First,
almost all of the writers quoted to illustrate the analyses
synthesized into the world pictures of the three schools do
in fact make recommendations which fall into these schools.
And second, in those few cases where this is not true or where
there is some doubt, it is because a particular point or entire
category of analysis is shared by more than one school (as is
the case in more than one instance). Because of these considerations it is not possible to do justice to every individual
with a viewpoint on arms policy; fortunately, in order to
describe the bases of policy disputes, it is also not necessary.

✣   ✣   ✣   ✣   ✣

CHAPTER 7

MARGINALIST ANALYSES: THE ANTI-WAR MARGINALISTS

ANALYSIS OF WAR

The major motif in the arms-policy analysis of the marginal anti-war school is that of thermonuclear war between the United States and the Soviet Union. This is the theme; all else is counterpoint. Such a concentration upon thermonuclear war is to be expected, given the anti-war value system which emphasizes the avoidance of such a war; indeed, because of the terrors involved in any such war, much of the middle marginal school, too, concentrates its analysis on nuclear holocaust.

A distinguishing characteristic of the marginal anti-war school, however, is that *it pays much more attention than any of the other marginal groups to the kind of thermonuclear wars which it believes cannot be avoided by human rationality acting through deterrence.* The more extreme members of the anti-war marginal school, those near the border with systemism, although they are willing to envisage deterrence of war as a temporary expedient, worry about undeterrable wars of two types. The first of these is war to which they believe deterrence is essentially irrelevant because the war stems from human irrationality or mechanical unreliability; the second, nuclear war which may actually be started by the attempt to deter nonnuclear attack.

The category of wars stemming from causes beyond human

rationality is particularly important to the anti-war group—
its members concentrate largely on the imperfection of both
machine and man. Etzioni writes that ". . . like any super-
complex mechanism, in this apparatus of automats and ex-
plosives, human commanders and computers, electronic
beams and buck privates, something—something basic—is
quite likely to go wrong. The very fact that the parts are in-
terdependent means that when one goes, the whole system
might be undermined. The larger, the cleverer, the more
complicated the military machine, the more likely it is to
break down. It is simply impossible to have any assurance
that such a system will function reliably."[1] Etzioni then goes
on to catalog what he feels to be the major ways in which a
nuclear war might start. Under the heading of "War by Mistake," he lists four subcategories: "War by Mechanical Failure or Human Miscalculation"; "Unauthorized Action" ("a
group of Communist pilots incensed at increasing 'softness' in
the Kremlin or a group of SAC pilots who are also members
of an aggressive dissident group may deliberately unleash a
war."); "War by False Alarm," on a radar screen or something similar; and "War by Brinkmanship," which, he writes,
"is in my opinion most likely to be the immediate cause of
World-War-III-by-miscalculation." In addition, he lists war
started by an "Nth Country," (considered particularly likely
by many anti-war marginalists) and thermonuclear war stemming from escalation.[2] Etzioni concludes: "Deterrence strategies assume that people make rational responses; but men
with their backs to the wall are not in a 'normal' psychological state. If there are buttons to be pushed, such men may
very well push them."[3]

Related to the fear of such "inadvertent" war is the fear
of the use of deterrence to prevent nonnuclear aggression.
The chance that such aggression may occur in spite of the

[1] Amitai Etzioni, *The Hard Way to Peace: A New Strategy* (New York:
Collier, 1962), p. 44.
[2] *Ibid.*, pp. 45–60.
[3] *Ibid.*, p. 58.

attempts to deter it can lead to the possibility that we will start a war by executing the deterrent threat. Walter Millis criticizes the ambiguous use of the word "deterrence"; "When a President says that the great weapons 'are not to be used,' he is talking about the absolute prevention of any nuclear war whatever. But when he says (as President Eisenhower has said) that the United States will 'not fight a ground war' for Berlin, he is talking about the discouragement of a nuclear war, yet at the same time calling the weapons to his aid in a situation which might well require their employment."[4] Although President Kennedy has weakened the threat of immediate and automatic use of nuclear weapons for the defense of Berlin, he has not fully cancelled it, and only an unconditional pledge never to use such weapons first would be likely to satisfy Millis and the others who consider this to be one of the most likely ways in which a nuclear war might start.

Though many of the anti-war marginalists thus worry most about war between the United States and the Soviet Union starting from one of the twin possibilities of undeterrable accident or undeterred United States response to aggression, the more moderate members of the school place a good deal of stress as well on using "stable" deterrence to avoid those wars which *can* be deterred. According to Wiesner: "The importance of a stable deterrent system used as a component of an arms-limitation arrangement is that it provides a means of reducing the danger from clandestine nuclear weapons and long-range delivery vehicles . . . While this situation is not as desirable as would be the actual elimination of all such weapons, it must certainly be preferred to the present unlimited arms race and actual elimination probably cannot be achieved."[5]

In any case, the anti-war marginalists' concern with ther-

[4] Walter Millis, "A Liberal Military-Defense Policy," in *The Liberal Papers,* ed. James Roosevelt (Garden City: Doubleday, 1962), p. 101. Copyright © 1962 by James Roosevelt.

[5] Jerome B. Wiesner, "Comprehensive Arms Limitation Systems," in *Arms Control, Disarmament, and National Security,* ed. Donald G. Brennan (New York: Braziller, 1961), p. 218.

monuclear war, however it might start, extends well beyond
the immediate future. A major analytical point is that, even
if deterrence can prevent war in the short run, a deterrence-
based arms race must bring it about in the long. Harrison
Brown and James Real write: "For fifteen years we have been
in the largest and most frantic arms race that the world has
ever known. During this period the Soviet Union and the
United States have recognized that war between them is a
possibility. Under the circumstances each nation has attempted to put itself in the position of winning the war
should it come. Actions have brought reactions, which in turn
have brought new actions. Military expenditures in both nations have increased to staggering size. With the mobilization
of science and technology, capabilities for destruction have
increased explosively."[6]

And for the future, they conclude: "The arms race, already
almost incomprehensible in its capacity for mass annihilation,
will be elaborated with new elements—chemical, biological,
psychological—until the arsenals are packed with devices to
destroy all the peoples of the world many times over. Yet in
the long run the grisly 'race' can produce no winner. In any
future war the consolation prizes can only be surrender, stalemate, or death."[7]

Thus, the arms race with its action-reaction reciprocation
can lead ultimately to the use of thermonuclear weapons
either through overfamiliarity and consequent contempt or
through technological breakthrough which causes one side to
believe that it can win finally and absolutely. This provides a
political-military explanation of the anti-war marginalists'
fears for the long run, but in addition, there is a more purely
mechanical and statistical basis for such worry. The best-
known version is that of Sir Charles P. Snow who wrote in
1960:

We know with the certainty of statistical truth that if enough
of these weapons are made—by enough different states—some of

[6] Harrison Brown and James Real, *Community of Fear* (Santa Barbara:
Center for the Study of Democratic Institutions, 1960), pp. 10–11.
[7] *Ibid.*, p. 40.

them are going to blow up. Through accident, or folly, or madness—but the motives don't matter. What does matter is the nature of the statistical fact . . . [This] is not a risk but a certainty. It is this. There is no agreement on tests. The nuclear arms race between the U. S. A. and the U. S. S. R. not only continues but accelerates. Other countries join in. Within at the most six years, China and several other states have a stock of nuclear bombs. Within the most, ten years, some of these bombs are going off.[8]

This is the cumulation of Etzioni's fears. If all of his multifarious wars by mistake imply say a five per cent chance of nuclear war in each year, then the mathematical probability of such a war in a ten-year period is about 40 per cent. If each year's chance is higher than the last, perhaps due to the joining of the race by new countries, the cumulative number is even higher. By choosing annual probabilities high enough, it is possible to show that the ten-year probability is indeed a virtual certainty (although, Sir Charles notwithstanding, never an absolute certainty, not in any finite period of time). And the members of the marginal anti-war school are afraid that the real probabilities are in fact high enough.[9]

[8] Sir Charles P. Snow, "The Moral Unneutrality of Science," address to the American Association for the Advancement of Science, New York City, December 27, 1960, published in *The New York Times*, December 28, 1960, p. 14.

[9] In order to avoid double counting of the type which might lead to the nonsense result that a five per cent per annum chance of war for twenty-one years means an over-all total probability of 105 per cent, the probability of war in a given period is computed as the probability of "not not" having it. If the probability of having a war in a particular year is five per cent, the probability of not having one is 95 per cent. The probability of not having one in ten years, then, is $.95^{10} =$ about .60, and the probability of not not having it is .40 or 40 per cent. If the annual probability increases from year to year, multiplying the probabilities of not having a war is computationally a bit more difficult than raising a decimal to the tenth power, but the principle is the same. In any case, the probability of war in any period, no matter how long, cannot be 100 per cent unless the probability of not having it is zero. And the product of a string of annual probabilities of not having a war cannot be zero unless the probability of no-war in a *particular* year is also zero and there is thus a 100 per cent probability of war in *that* year. Sir Charles does not contend that the probability of war in a particular year in this decade will rise to an absolute certainty.

These probabilities are at the very center of the analytical world picture of the marginal anti-war school. The anti-war marginalists' value-reinforced analysis leads them to the belief that, *given no changes in policy, thermonuclear war of an undeterrable type is a very high probability in some future time period—perhaps ten years, perhaps more or less.*

But this fear of nuclear conflict in our time does not complete the school's picture of war. Not only is such war likely if the future stretches before us without change, but all efforts to meliorate it are likely to be fruitless. Waskow criticizes the theory that melioration of thermonuclear war can be achieved because, he says, it is based on "the belief that intensely rational control over the fighting of a thermonuclear war will be possible even after it has been begun." He feels, contrariwise, that "the careful, second-by-second control that would be absolutely necessary . . . would be impossible, and the . . . war would degenerate into a completely disordered thermonuclear disaster."[10] And even those anti-war marginalists who believe that civil defense might help save lives in the event of such a war, doubt that such defenses could do much in terms of preventing such a war from being a national holocaust in which the United States as a viable entity would disappear. In answer to Kahn's succinct question "Would the survivors envy the dead?" they answer "yes."

The concentration of the marginal anti-war school on thermonuclear war has left them with little to say about other less violent wars between the United States and the Soviet Union. They are interested in such conflicts mainly as they might escalate to the thermonuclear level, rather than for themselves. Etzioni writes:

. . . escalation can take us not only from cold war to hot, from limited war to world war, and from conventional conflict to nuclear attack—it may also lead us that one step further to nuclear cataclysm.

10 Arthur I. Waskow, *The Limits of Defense* (Garden City: Doubleday, 1962), pp. 26–27.

Moreover, under certain circumstances last escalation might be very tempting, for it *does* after all grant the loser a last chance for survival, if not for victory . . . Pulling the biggest trigger gives him one slim, final opportunity to save the day, pull his scattered army together and perhaps even be the sole survivor of a nuclear war.[11]

In the specific case of Europe, they feel that any war would rapidly grow to the thermonuclear level, and their typical recommendations are based more on substituting other political methods for war in Europe than on any attempt to subdue the level of violence in any war which might occur. Similarly, with respect to the underdeveloped world, the fundamental ideas of the marginal anti-war school are based on a belief that other methods must be substituted for military ones—that the Russians have chosen nonmilitary methods of competition in the underdeveloped areas, and by trying to combat them militarily, not only might we get into a war, but with or without war, we are likely to lose.

ANALYSIS OF THE OPPONENT

No marginalist analysis of war can be completely independent of the analysis of what the Russians are about. In some cases, such as that of a war starting via an escalation process, the likelihood of war depends not only upon what we do, but also on what the Soviets are trying to do and how they are trying to do it. In other cases which, like "accidental" war, stem from proximate causes not directly associated with the political conflict between the United States and the U.S.S.R., the risks of Soviet expansion must be estimated in order to put them into the optimizing mechanism for matching against the risks of a war not intended by either side.

The marginal anti-war school's picture of Soviet objectives, like their picture of war, can best be described in terms of a range. Those anti-war marginalists who are closest to systemic anti-war views (and who put the greatest stress on un-

11 Etzioni, pp. 57–58.

deterrable wars) are most inclined to believe that *current Soviet policy is becoming conservative, defensive, and consolidationist throughout; that the Russians, since they are growing toward an affluent society, are gradually becoming less and less willing to risk wars which might upset the internal and external status quo.* This view is distinguished from that of the systemists by the use of the verb, "becoming." The Russians are not yet there and it may take a while; our policy must encourage their moving in this direction; but we cannot let our guard down until we are much more sure. But those anti-war marginalists on the other end of the range, who are closest to middle marginalism (and who also worry about deterrable wars), are more likely to emphasize that *the Soviets are still primarily opportunistic—still willing to take by force or the threat of force what they can get on the cheap.* The border with middle marginalism is blurred, but can be defined according to the answer to the question, "How cheap?"

One corollary of the general belief that the Russians are not now strongly expansionistic has been developed into a major analytical base for policy by some anti-war marginalists. The proposition is that most of the remaining world tensions are caused not by real clashes of interest between Soviet expansionism and our defense of the status quo, but are illusory remnants of past conflict. As Etzioni puts it, "the objective situation calls for settlement, but psychological factors on both sides block it."[12] It is this sort of belief upon which Osgood's "Unilateral Initiatives" proposals are based. If Soviet tendencies toward military risk-taking are waning, then it may be possible to get them to reciprocate American steps taken in the interest of reducing the "psychological" tensions between the two countries. Osgood believes that:

. . . the Russians would accept an unambiguous opportunity to reduce world tensions for reasons of good sense *even* if not for reasons of good will . . . Recent travellers to Russia . . . have been impressed by the "mirror image" of our own attitudes that they

12 *Ibid.*, p. 95.

find among both the people and the leaders there . . . They blame their warlike behavior on us, just as we blame ours on them . . . According to the Twelfth Report of the Commission to Study the Organization of the Peace, Chairman Khrushchev has definitely scrapped the Marxist-Leninist notion of the inevitability of war with the capitalist nations and is sensitive to the need to meet growing consumer demands, to the popular opposition to war, and to the uncertainty of what might happen in the satellite states in the case of hostilities.[13]

Such beliefs about the Soviet Union are sustainable given that the Russians are growing conservative; they become less sustainable as one moves toward the middle-marginal end of the anti-war scale and believes that the Russians might find low-risk opportunities to take partisan advantage of tension-reducing initiatives, rather than accepting them in good faith and reciprocating. At any rate, the tendency of at least part of the marginal anti-war school is to believe that the Soviets would respond to our explicit good will; for the rest of the school, the belief can be better expressed by saying that they *might* respond.

The possibility of Russian responsiveness, however, is a dynamic concept which must start from an analysis of where the Soviet Union stands now, where it wants to go, and how it wants to get there. Osgood's general belief that the Russians are moving away from a warlike state is backed up by considerable further anti-war marginalist argument. To begin with, there is rather general belief within the school that the major Soviet challenge to the West lies in those areas of the world where the military threat is least relevant. After interviewing Khrushchev in 1958, Walter Lippmann expressed a belief espoused by most anti-war marginalists: "I have come home convinced that the most pressing issue is the Russian and Chinese challenge for the leadership of Asia and of Africa. If we are to meet it with reasonable success, we must, I am sure, abandon the notion that the Russian and Chinese

---

[13] Charles E. Osgood, "Reciprocal Initiatives," *The Liberal Papers*, pp. 207–210. Copyright © 1962 by James Roosevelt.

revolutions can be reversed or that the spread of Communism in the surrounding countries can be contained by giving armaments to the local military commanders and by establishing our own bases."[14] To which he added, after a second interview in 1961: "The Soviet government has great confidence in its own military forces. But it regards them not as an instrument of world conquest, but as the guardian against American interference with the predestined world revolution."[15]

And even in West Europe, although the military danger there may be greater than elsewhere—great enough so that no marginalist would propose any *unilateral* disarming or withdrawal which might open the Western areas to possible Soviet military attack—even here the military danger is less than many believe. George Kennan writes:

> We must get over this obsession that the Russians are yearning to attack and occupy Western Europe, and that this is the principal danger. The Soviet threat, as I have had occasion to say before, is a combined military and political threat, with the accent on the political. If the armed forces of the United States and Britain were not present on the Continent, the problem of defense for the continental nations would be primarily one of the internal health and discipline of the respective national societies, and of the manner in which they were organized to prevent the conquest and subjugation of their national life by unscrupulous and foreign-inspired minorities in their midst.[16]

Yet most anti-war marginalists would nonetheless agree that the Russians do still have military interests in Europe outside of Soviet borders. These interests, however, they see as primarily defensive and consolidationist, with the Soviet Union consolidating its East European and East German positions and protecting itself against West Germany. The anti-war

[14] Walter Lippmann, *The Communist World and Ours* (Boston: Little Brown, 1959), p. 41.
[15] Walter Lippmann, *The Coming Tests with Russia* (Boston: Little Brown, 1961), p. 29.
[16] George F. Kennan, *Russia, the Atom, and the West* (New York: Harper, 1958), pp. 62–63.

marginalists, whether they believe this Soviet fear of West Germany to be well founded or not, generally agree that it is a real fear. Lippmann reported after the second interview:

> It was clear to me at the end of a long talk that in Mr. Khrushchev's mind the future of Germany is the key question . . . He said . . . there must be a German solution before "Hitler's generals with their twelve NATO divisions" get atomic weapons from France and the United States. Before this happens there must be a peace treaty defining the frontiers of Poland and stabilizing the existence of the East German State. Otherwise, West Germany will drag NATO into a war for the unification of Germany and the restoration of the old eastern frontier.
>
> His feeling of urgency, then, springs from two causes: his need to consolidate the Communist East German state . . . and second, his need to do this before West Germany is rearmed.[17]

This picture of Soviet fear of Germany and desire to consolidate and stabilize the satellite areas of Europe, however, is coupled with the hope of many anti-war marginalists that over the very long run it may be possible to induce the Russians to loosen their control in East Europe. The analysis is quite different from that of members of the anti-Communist schools who hope for ultimate "liberation" of the area. Rather than forcing the Russians back, the anti-war marginalists feel that it may be possible in the long run to convince them to back off, to disengage militarily without abandoning the area either to a rampant Germany or, for that matter, to Western democracy. However desirable democracy in Eastern Europe might be, the analysis of the anti-war marginalists does not predict it under any circumstances in the foreseeable future. The best expression of all this is again that of Kennan:

> Let us not forget that thoughtful people in Eastern Europe, both of Communist and of non-Communist persuasion, would have an interest in assuring the success of any scheme that held real prospects for changing, if only slowly and gradually, the abnormal situation that has prevailed there in recent years. The problem is to provide these people with an alternative some-

17 Lippmann, *The Coming Tests with Russia*, pp. 23–24.

where between the extremes of a continued slavish and hopeless subordination to Soviet power and a sharp, defiant break with the "socialist camp" . . . The West can afford to be relatively relaxed about the name by which the social and economic institutions of the East European peoples are described. What is immediately important is that development of national life there should not be impeded by abnormal military strictures . . . and that some progress should become possible in the creation of the prerequisites of a true European community.[18]

Thus, the anti-war marginalists' picture of the Soviet Union: a nation which is growing more conservative and less willing to take military risks; is perhaps responsive to tension-reducing initiatives; is more interested in political action in Asia and Africa than in military action in Europe; even in Europe, is defensive and consolidationist rather than trying to enlarge its sphere of influence; and finally, may ultimately be willing to withdraw at least its military influence from Eastern Europe.

To this picture of the Soviet Union as an entity, it is necessary to add one last touch. The U.S.S.R. may not be the political monolith implied by the above description; it may instead be ridden by political factions. Rather than Khrushchev being in absolute command, he may be the leader of a majority "moderate" group, which, because it is constantly being challenged by a much more bellicose and anti-American radical faction, deserves our subtle encouragement. World-wide, this theory is most closely associated with the name of Marshall Tito. According to a similar American interpretation by Louis Halle, however:

Premier Khrushchev's leadership is more strongly challenged, and his authority less firmly established than we had thought . . .

What is the issue between Mr. Khrushchev and his domestic opponents—the so-called Stalinists?

All of the evidence suggests that the main issue is whether the progress and promise of the Soviet Union, in its domestic

18 George F. Kennan, "Disengagement Revisited," *Foreign Affairs*, 37:190–191 (January 1959).

development, shall be safeguarded by a policy of relative moderation abroad, or shall be exposed to the risks inherent in a militant foreign policy based on an acceptance of war as an eventuality . . .

If Mr. Khrushchev's words and actions since last spring are superficially inconsistent with this view, that inconsistency may represent simply a classic gambit of domestic politics—that of disarming one's opponents by stealing as much of their program as may be necessary for the purpose . . .

I am aware of how delicate and tricky are the circumstances that have to be dealt with here. It means political tight-rope walking, for the actions that leadership on one side feel compelled to take in order to build a backfire against its own extremist opposition have the effect of strengthening the extremist opposition on the other side.[19]

And what may be true about politics within the Soviet Union may also apply to Russo-Chinese relationships, where it may be in our interest to encourage the Soviet Union's relatively peace-loving side of the quarrel.

Much less can be said about the marginal anti-war school's (or for that matter, any other school's) analysis of China than about Russia, mainly because Communist China has replaced the Soviet Union as the world's chief enigma. But the anti-war marginalists should probably be credited with recognizing at least as early as any of the others that China and the Soviet Union had separable and even conflicting interests. What to make of this conflict is another question—few anti-war marginalists would follow some of the systemists in making a cult of Communist China as a representative of the rising masses of the underdeveloped world (certainly not after the Chinese invasion of India); but the value-orientation of the school toward the poorer nations of the world makes it difficult to hope that China will be suppressed by the Soviet Union. Perhaps the one point on which the anti-war marginalists can unite is that China must be dealt with (not neces-

[19] Louis J. Halle, "On War in Gestation—and the Possibilities of its Abortion," *The New Republic*, November 20, 1961, pp. 10–12.

sarily recognized, but dealt with). China is too big to be ignored, particularly when it comes to the cause dearest to the hearts of most anti-war marginalists—disarmament. Adlai Stevenson in 1960 put the dilemma of the anti-war marginalist who is disturbed by Chinese bellicosity but realizes that China is nonetheless the key to many problems: "Yet it is clear that no general control of disarmament has any value unless it includes China, and it is difficult to see how China can accept international control when it is not, formally, a member of international society. Moreover, as a member of the United Nations, Communist China, with a quarter of the world's population, would be more accountable to world opinion than as an outcast."[20] The anti-war marginalists do not necessarily or particularly believe that China can be readily kept in check, but they see China as a huge fact. And since we do not want to fight her, we must try to housebreak her by peaceful methods.

ANALYSIS OF POWER

Stevenson's reference to the possibility of curbing China by making her "accountable to world opinion," however, leads to consideration of anti-war marginalist analyses in the third category—those having to do with the different modes of power which can be used to achieve national objectives. Although anti-war marginalists put little weight on power-as-a-value, this does not imply an *automatic* rejection of military power-as-a-tool for achieving the national values they do favor. Nonetheless, much more than the other schools, the anti-war marginalists tend to prefer the carrot to the stick— rather than driving the world in our direction, using the power of public opinion, moral power, political-economic power to lead it. Chester Bowles credits Lenin with seeing "that military and industrial power had their strict limita-

[20] Adlai E. Stevenson, "Putting First Things First," *Foreign Affairs*, 38:203 (January 1960).

tions and that the decisive advantage would be held by those who understood the political, economic, and ideological forces which increasingly would shape the minds of men," and Bowles then asks: "How can America and her Atlantic Community associates meet this broader challenge? How can we regain the initiative? Above all, how can we achieve the urgently needed balance between military security and positive political and economic action for peace?"[21]

This stress on the battle for "the minds of men" can lead on specific issues to the need for a balancing against one another of the demands of military strength and the demands of world opinion, which, according to the analysis of the antiwar marginalists, is repelled by these military demands. In opposing United States resumption of atmospheric nuclear testing in 1962, the Federation of American Scientists admitted that resumption might have military utility, but argued that the negative effects of resumption on Soviet and American, as well as "world" opinion, would outweigh this utility:

The social and political repercussions are quite as important as, and perhaps even more important than, the technical and military factors.

. . . If we refrain from testing, . . . such an act of self-restraint on our part may help to convince the Soviet leaders that the United States is in earnest about slowing the arms race and sincere in its dedication to disarmament.

We scientists are also concerned about the effect resumption of testing may have on our own public attitudes. For resumption of tests now cannot help but foster the impression that our security can in the long run be maintained solely by military strength . . .

A decision to resume atmospheric testing would turn world public opinion against us. But an announcement to refrain from testing would make a very favorable impression on the non-

21 Chester Bowles, *Ideas, People, and Peace* (New York: Harper, 1958), p. 6.

nuclear powers, and would strengthen international efforts to obtain a more stable world.[22]

In addition to arguing that moral, political, and economic power factors should be balanced against military, the anti-war marginalists also question more directly the utility of military power. The biggest weapons have no political utility in the world power struggle—they exist only to foreclose the possibility of their use by the other side: "The sole purpose of the nucleonic mass-destruction arsenals is to prevent their use by anyone under any conditions. They do not, as President Eisenhower has said, exist to be used but to make certain that they are not used by anyone . . ."[23] according to Millis. And even the smaller weapons may have a political disutility if their use is to reinforce governments so unpopular that in the long run our support will turn the people of the nations against us. Because of this, because the real power in such areas is political and economic rather than basically military, Bowles argues, for example, that "In many countries our efforts should put less emphasis on the maintenance of outsize and out-of-date military machines and more emphasis on people—on efforts to raise the level of literacy, to provide equitable distribution of land, to foster community development projects, to stimulate the growth of free institutions such as labor unions, to establish adequate public health programs, and to train public administrators in modern techniques."[24]

But the anti-war marginalists' view of power in such parts of the world can probably be best put into its political context by the use of a specific example, that of Cuba. Writing of the failure of the April, 1961, Bay of Pigs landing by Cuban exiles, Theodore Draper presented a thoroughgoing anti-war marginal interpretation. As Draper himself pointed out, however, the invasion was "one of those rare politico-

[22] "Scientists Appraise Atomic Tests," *The Bulletin of the Atomic Scientists,* 18.4:33 (April 1962).
[23] Millis, p. 109.
[24] Chester Bowles, *Agenda 1961,* The Rosenfield Lectures at Grinnell College, Grinnell, Iowa, April 1960, p. 35.

military events—a perfect failure. So many things went wrong that it was relatively easy to fix the blame on anyone or anything connected with it."[25] Thus most of the anti-war *systemists* claim that the invasion failed because it deserved to fail—that the United States was attempting to interfere unjustly with a people's social revolution, and that in this case at least, right made might; many *middle* marginalists argue that the fiasco was to be blamed on military factors such as the failure to provide air cover from American carriers; and *anti-Communist* marginalists blame both military factors and American failure to understand Castro as part of the worldwide Communist movement. But Draper's own interpretation, which would probably be subscribed to by most anti-war marginalists and a number of middle marginalists, is that the most fundamental of the many reasons for the perfect failure was because ". . . the Eisenhower administration was, at best, cautious and indecisive; at worst it played into Castro's hands. Such an administration was attracted, in time, to a military "solution" of the Cuban problem—tightly controlled from above, with a minimum commitment to any program that might disturb the sensibilities of the Cubans or the Americans who had benefited most from the *status quo ante.*"[26] Thus, the invasion failed because it was purely military and took no account whatever of the strong social forces involved in both the Castro movements and the various anti-Castro groups. Draper's solution would have been to encourage an internal guerrilla overthrow of Castro by those anti-Castroites who had been anti-Batista and most of whom had backed the Castro revolution until it turned toward Communism.

And on the basis of this analysis of the failure of one American action vis-à-vis Cuba, it should not have been very difficult to predict the anti-war marginalists' position in the controversy over a more successful action—the forced removal of Soviet missiles from Cuba. Although most anti-war

25 Theodore Draper, "Cuba and U.S. Policy," a supplement to *The New Leader,* June 5, 1961, p. 6.
26 *Ibid.,* p. 12.

marginalists backed President Kennedy's action in quarantining Cuba in order to force the removal of the missiles, they looked at it (as did the administration) as a direct issue between the United States and the Soviet Union, an issue which could hardly be interpreted as anything but one of military power. The reservations which some anti-war marginalists held concerning the forcefulness of this use of our power had less to do with their analysis of the uses of power in underdeveloped areas than with their analysis of and fear of war. But on the matter of the use of our power against Castro, as compared to its use against Soviet missiles, the attitude the anti-war marginalists took could have been deduced directly from analysis of the Draper type. They were clear that American military power should be limited to the issue of the missiles; that lacking an invasion of Cuba, which they would have favored only under the direst of circumstances (if at all), the question of the government of Cuba remained a political rather than a military one. And this belief, though certainly not confined to anti-war marginalists, remains typical of the anti-war marginalists' interpretation of power in such areas of the world, as being basically nonmilitary, even so close to our own shores.

ANALYSIS OF ALLIES AND NEUTRALS

Few anti-war marginalists, however, would argue that military power is not relevant in one area—Western Europe. Most would follow Kennan in the belief that although the military portion of the Communist threat to Europe has been overplayed, the threat does exist. The whole issue of geography—the questions of where the struggle with Communism is centered—thus becomes very important. If the challenge for Asia and Africa is much more important than the challenge in Europe, then arms policies should put less stress on our basic NATO alliance. And most anti-war marginalists do believe that American policy is too Europe-oriented. Thus James Warburg writes that "there is no evidence that the

Soviet Union has ever intended to attack Western Europe. There is ample evidence that Soviet intention has been to outflank Western Europe in Asia, the middle East, and Africa."[27] Although, as has been pointed out, not even those anti-war marginalists nearest to systemism would absolutely dismiss the possibility of a Soviet military threat in Europe, the analysis which argues for more attention to the rest of the world does make a difference. There is some feeling, allied to the belief in the power of public opinion, that "tough" American military policies in Europe antagonize the neutral nations such as India, and thus act against our interests in vital areas of the world. More specific, however, is the feeling that too close an alliance with the colonial and former colonial nations of NATO hurts the West's long-run interests in the former colonies. One expert expression of this is Rupert Emerson's:

. . . the imperial powers which carved up Africa among them remain the principal allies of the United States. NATO embracing these powers, is the cornerstone of the coalition which the United States has shaped to meet the Communist challenge, and Britain and France are our closest friends.

. . . in 1960, when the General Assembly debated the declaration on colonial independence, the Soviet bloc went all out for immediate freedom for colonies while the United States backed and filled, and ultimately abstained in the company not only of its NATO allies but also of Spain, Portugal [sic], South Africa, and the Dominican Republic. Here, if the reports which circulate are correct, was a splendid example of the fact and the folly of yielding to the pleas of an ally.[28]

More extreme versions of the same feeling about our alliance with the former colonial powers carry with them an implication that Europe (with the possible exception of the left wing of the British Labor Party) is old and conservative, and, how-

27 James Warburg, "A Re-examination of American Foreign Policy," in *The Liberal Papers*, p. 54. Copyright © 1962 by James Roosevelt.

28 Rupert Emerson, "American Policy in Africa," *Foreign Affairs*, 40:305–308 (January 1962).

ever prosperous it may be now, will ultimately be over-whelmed by the large majority of the world's population which is not white and not rich. Another, *realpolitik,* version suggests that we need worry little about upsetting our Euro-pean allies because they have nowhere else to go anyhow.

The anti-war marginal feeling about Europe, however, is related not only to colonialism, but also to a specific fear of a resurgence of German militarism and Nazism. While not approaching the fear of some anti-war systemists that the rearming of West Germany will lead to a Fourth Reich, the anti-war marginalists feel that a major criterion for American policy in Europe is the effect on Germany—both on the stability of internal German democracy and on the ability of Germany to engage independently in European power poli-tics.

The anti-war marginalists' feeling about Germany has several aspects. There is some concern over the long-run viability of German democracy. According to the view of Gerald Freund, moderate enough so that it would be shared by many middle marginalists:

A sound foundation for democracy has been provided . . . The prestige and immense authority of an antimilitarist Chan-cellor has shown all Germans that an efficient government can operate under democratic institutions. Adenauer, moreover, al-most singlehandedly restored the moral worth of Germany in the society of free nations.

. . . [but] the democratic institutions and practices in the Fed-eral Republic are not steeled against a political or an economic crisis—the Republic has experienced neither since its founding—and there has been as yet no change in the party in power, the acid test of democracy. It takes more time than the Germans have had since 1945 to build sound democratic traditions. They must overcome important shortcomings in their political practices before the Federal Republic can be described as a mature democracy.[29]

29 Gerald Freund, *Germany Between Two Worlds* (New York: Harcourt, Brace, 1961), pp. 47–48.

Warburg, who joins Freund in the marginalist policy recommendation that we should be willing to negotiate with the Russians about German reunification based on military neutralization, feels more strongly about the dangers of a rearmed Western Germany and looks less benignly on Adenauer:

In 1959 our government has agreed to give Germany everything except nuclear warheads and has permitted our war industries to go into partnership with Krupp, Kloeckner, Heinckel, and Messerschmidt in re-creating German capacity to build almost every kind of war equipment.

If we are serious and sincere in wishing to halt the arms race and to reach a European settlement, the least we can do is to call a halt in rearming Germany while we negotiate.

Unfortunately it is true that the approach we advocate would run counter to the wishes of West German Chancellor Adenauer, whose belief in the intransigent policy of refusing to negotiate except from a "situation of strength" remains as unshaken as that of its author, former Secretary of State Acheson.[30]

Probably the most prudent statement of all, expressing a middle-marginal view also held by many in the anti-war school, however, comes from Michael Howard, a Briton who feels that *he's* not worried but our policies must take account of those who are:

The nations of Western Europe which have accepted, not without qualms, the Federal German Republic as an equal and necessary ally in an international organization might look with different eyes on a Germany enlarged, separate, and perhaps strengthened by a train of East-European satellites. Could international control prevent rearmament today any more effectively than it did after the First World War? And if it could, would not Germany be all the more formidable as an economic competitor? Such emotions may be parochial, anachronistic, and unworthy, but they exist and as a factor in the problem they cannot be ignored.[31]

30 Warburg, p. 70.
31 Michael Howard, *Disengagement in Europe* (London: Penguin, 1958), p. 50.

These three views on Germany are by no means all the same. But they have one thread in common, a fear which, although it is held by other marginalists outside of the anti-war school, is by far the strongest within this group. This is that recent German history is by no means completely obsolete—that what we do in Europe must be conditioned by the fact that Germany is a different and special case and cannot be regarded simply as another member of NATO. This view makes the anti-war marginalists rely less than the other marginal groupings on NATO as such; it helps to reinforce the view that our world policies are too oriented toward the alliance and toward Europe.

ANALYSIS OF OURSELVES

Those who are most worried about a resurgence of German militarism are also inclined to worry about the effects of arms policy on possible reaction and militarism in the United States. There are two aspects to this worry: concern with *who* will gain domestic political power from a policy of heavy armament, and concern with *what* such a policy will do to the psychology of the American people as a whole.

Some of those who are bothered with the effect of the political power of the military are inclined to argue or imply that the reason we are where we are today is because the military already have and have had far too much power. Such dark hints, however, are much more common among the anti-war systemists than among the marginalists. More typical of the marginalists is some concern with the past but much more worry about the future. President Eisenhower's farewell speech did not argue that the military had had too much power through 1960—he hardly could have stated that the generals had forced *him* to do anything against his will. His worry was rather for the future: "In the councils of Government, we must guard against the acquisition of unwarranted influence, whether sought or unsought, by the military-industrial complex. The potential for the disastrous rise of misplaced power exists and will persist."[32] Eisenhower is no anti-war marginalist, and he was more concerned with vigilance than with changing the policy which caused the need for the vigilance. Waskow puts the worry into terms more directed at a change of policy: ". . . none of the deterrents so far examined would permit even the representatives of the people in Congress to make the crucial decisions upon which would depend war and peace. In fact, the power of directing the whole society would more and more come to be centered in a small clique of defense experts if under these theories we gave our whole future to the permanent establishment of an atomic force. The ancient democratic fears of a standing army are multiplied geometrically by the fantastic speed and destructiveness of thermonuclear arms."[33]

And so far as the psychological effect of arms upon the American people is concerned, Osgood is willing to argue not only that this effect will be bad: "It would seem, then, that to pursue the policy of mutual deterrence *successfully* will require us to give up as rapidly as possible a system of beliefs and practices which ill fits us for the race. As I have defined the nature of the real conflict with communism, this would mean losing what we are really fighting for in the course of fighting for it.

. . . mutual deterrence fosters the very conditions, both in the United States *and* in Russia, which support a totalitarian way of life. In the most basic sense, then, this is a weapon turned against ourselves."[34] but also that the psychology of the arms race has already begun to feed upon itself and become self-perpetuating. Commenting on Sidney Hook's belief that Communism brings to the top "power-mad fanatics," Osgood says: "Now I certainly do not claim any exclusive possession of the truth, and it could be that Hook is more nearly right in this than I am. But I can show how such bogy-man con-

---

[32] Dwight D. Eisenhower, address from the White House, January 17, 1961, published in *The New York Times*, January 18, 1961, p. 22.
[33] Waskow, p. 74.
[34] Osgood, pp. 167–168.

ceptions of the enemy develop naturally out of the dynamics of human thinking—when little minds seek simple consistencies in a complex world, or big minds like Hook's operate under intense emotion, as I suspect was the case."[35] Thus Osgood adds to his picture of the Soviet Union willing to respond to our tension-reducing initiatives, a picture of the United States whose fear of the Soviet Union may well be based on self-reinforcing "bogy-man" reasoning. And from this reduction of the ordinary picture of two vastly different world opponents to similarity and near-symmetry stem most of the anti-war recommendations for preventing open combat between these near-equal opponents.

[35] *Ibid.*, p. 189.

✤ ✤ ✤ ✤ ✤

C H A P T E R 8

MARGINALIST ANALYSES: THE ANTI-COMMUNISTS

ANALYSIS OF THE OPPONENT

Just as the world picture of the anti-war marginalists is centered around the thermonuclear war they consider the greatest danger to world and national well-being, the thinking of the marginal anti-Communist school starts with an analysis of "the opponent." The opponent is not a nation or nations—it is world Communism as such. The anti-Communist school's picture of the opponent is detailed enough to distinguish among the Soviet, the Chinese, and the East European members of the Communist camp, but they feel nonetheless that as a general rule, American policy should treat with Communism as a single movement, with the different components differing only in tactical detail. Robert Strausz-Hupé, in the spring of 1962, during one of the recurrent crises in Sino-Soviet relations, still felt that the common interests of the bloc governed their relationships with the West. He wrote, in a few paragraphs which provide a succinct description of the Communist world as seen by the marginal anti-Communist school:

Conceivably, in some distant future, the rulers of the Soviet Union, frustrated by "capitalist" resistance, might jettison Communist ideology and seek to consolidate the Greater Soviet Union as a status quo power. Given enough time, anything can happen. There is, however, something bizarre and eery in the notion which seems to have gained ground in certain academic quarters, that Moscow, perturbed by the tensions within the Communist bloc and fearful of the proliferation of bigger and more obstreperous Yugoslavias, would like to halt the world revolution—and keep the United States and Western Europe in business as a counterweight to Red China. Soviet power has thrived on the increasing momentum of the world communist movement. The Soviet rulers could not—even if they wanted to— call off the permanent world revolution. It is only the international gains of communism and the promise of a communist world that give meaning to the deprivations of the Soviet people and divert attention from the social, the human failure of communism.

For the time being, the interests of all communists—Soviet, Chinese, or Cuban—still coincide on one objective, namely to wrest world supremacy from the heretofore dominant Western powers. It is ludicrous to assume that Moscow prefers to conciliate the Western states under capitalism in order to stem the tide of "national" or "polycentric" communism—that the more successful communism becomes as a political doctrine, the more unhappy feels the Kremlin.

. . . [Further] there seems to be no major issue on which communist leadership could find itself in a serious conflict with Soviet military leadership.

In sum, the ruling groups within the Soviet Union and the leaders of other communist states are still united on one overarching objective, namely to expand communism. They are—and it would be surprising if they were not—disagreed on specific strategies and tactics, on the where and the how much. Even here, the tenor of their *public* controversies might be deceptive: the Chinese communists, despite their insistence on an aggressive strategy, have been more pacific in their Far Eastern bailiwick than has Khrushchev, notwithstanding his digressions on "peaceful coexistence," in his dealings in Western Europe.[1]

Short-run tactical changes thus do not change the basic picture. Now, just as in 1959, when Robert Strausz-Hupé, William Kintner, James Dougherty, and Alvin Cottrell wrote *Protracted Conflict,* "For the Communist there is only one

[1] Robert Strausz-Hupé, "The Sino-Soviet Tangle and U.S. Policy," *Orbis,* 6:32–34 (Spring 1962).

war, namely the war to the finish."[2] Just as in 1961, when Strausz-Hupé, Kintner, and Stefan Possony wrote *A Forward Strategy for America,* the single basic objective of Communism is "world domination by the communist elite and destruction of that freedom of man that ennobles our civilization."[3]

Given this anti-Communist picture of a Sino-Soviet camp which, while not monolithic, is basically united on the objective of substituting their way of life for ours throughout the world, the questions which the *anti-war* marginalists ask must be rephrased to have any meaning for the anti-Communists. Rather than "is the major Communist challenge to the West in Europe or in the underdeveloped world?" the marginal anti-Communists ask "what do the Communists now believe is the best tactical order of procedure for our ultimate complete defeat?" Rather than "will the Russians risk war?" the marginal anti-Communists ask "under what conditions and for what specific objective will they take what risk of what kind of war?"

But the surprising point is that, having rephrased the questions—having substituted the basic anti-Communist belief that the Communists are implacably out to get us, for the basic anti-war belief that the Soviet Communists are becoming defenders of a stable *status quo*—*the answers given by the anti-Communist marginalists to a number of detailed questions of Communist tactics and risks are not very different from those given by the anti-war marginalists.*

On the question of Communist geographical priorities, for example, although the anti-Communists would disagree with the anti-war analysis that the Communist challenge to the West is in the underdeveloped world (for the anti-Commu-

---

[2] Robert Strausz-Hupé, William R. Kintner, James E. Dougherty, and Alvin J. Cottrell, *Protracted Conflict* (New York: Harper, 1959), p. 109.

[3] Robert Strausz-Hupé, William R. Kintner, and Stefan T. Possony, *A Forward Strategy for America* (New York: Harper, 1961), p. 406. Copyright © 1961 by Robert Strausz-Hupé, William R. Kintner, and Stefan T. Possony.

nists, the challenge is everywhere); and although the anti-Communists are more definite than the anti-war school that the Communists' penultimate goal (prior to defeat of the United States) is control of Western Europe; the two schools nonetheless join in denying that the Communists give their West European objectives the clear *current* priority frequently assumed. In 1959, for instance, *Protracted Conflict* described "Afro-Asia" as "the battleground chosen by the Communists."[4] In 1961, *A Forward Strategy,* on the basis of shifting evidence, inverted the argument: "To guess at the communist schedule of priorities is a hazardous game. Yet it is likely that the principal, if not the first, objective of the communist strategic plan is the neutralization of Germany followed by the break-up of the various European agencies of integration; the next target might well be the neutralization of Japan and reduction of the American base system off the coast of China." But the operative sentence in this latter statement is the next one: "Depending on developments, this sequence can, of course, be reversed."[5] Thus Western Europe may have a current (1961) priority, but these priorities are easily reversible and in fact did reverse between 1959 and 1961. This is far from a belief that the Communist strategy is constantly and primarily "European."

On another, related, question, the anti-Communists are even closer to the anti-war marginalists. This concerns the importance to the Communists of their hold on the East European satellite area. George Kennan has been quoted as representing the anti-war marginalist analysis that there is some hope in the long run of getting the Russians to at least loosen and liberalize their hold on the satellites. The anti-Communist picture of protracted and implacable conflict does not, of course, place any credence in such voluntary relaxation of tyranny, but a major aim of their policy is to

---

[4] *Protracted Conflict,* p. 104.
[5] *A Forward Strategy for America,* p. 399. Copyright © 1961 by Robert Strausz-Hupé, William R. Kintner, and Stefan T. Possony.

gain a similar goal with completely different methods. Rather than the liberalization of existing regimes, the anti-Communist school favors a strategy which:

> . . . seeks to detach Eastern Europe from the communist bloc and to create a united Europe possessing geographical depth and all the other prerequisites of an independent power center . . .
> Soviet diplomacy persistently seeks to wrest from the Western powers the admission that the present arrangement in Eastern and Central Europe is permanent. In Eastern Europe, the Soviet rulers have sought to cow the peoples into a resigned acceptance of communist domination. An active American and Western policy toward Eastern Europe would require that we (a) refrain from any action that could be construed by the people of Eastern Europe as a ratification of their present fate, and (b) demonstrate, Soviet contentions to the contrary, that the balance of power remains favorable to the West.
>
> . . .
>
> It might be argued that liberation movements within the communist bloc, triggered by the assurance of American military help, might drive the communists to preventive war . . . But [communist doctrine] also makes provision for tactical retreats.[6]

This is at the center of the school's strategy and, as a strategy, it is obviously almost the exact reverse of that of the anti-war marginalists. But the interesting point is that the analytical view that the Soviet domination of Eastern Europe may not be unalterable is not dissimilar from that of some anti-war marginalists. And this view is in opposition to a strategy which would resign itself to Russian domination of these areas in perpetuity.

Thus on two points in their analysis of the opponent's interests in particular areas, the two more extreme marginal schools are rather close to one another. And on another, vital, analytical question, which completes the anti-Communists' analysis of the opponent, there is even greater agreement between the anti-Communist and the anti-war

6 *Ibid.,* pp. 29–31.

marginalists—but perhaps even less agreement concerning what to do about it. This concerns the risks the Communists are willing to take to advance their power. Much of the anti-war analysis is predicated on the idea that the Soviets will not take great risks for purposes of expansion. *The anti-Communists agree with this basic analysis.* The difference between the two groups is that the anti-war marginalists then finish off the analysis with statements such as "And the Communists would therefore like to lower their risks by a joint demilitarization of the world. Thus we can exploit their dislike of risk-taking in order to reach a *détente.*" The anti-Communist marginalists complete the analysis by saying "and the Communists therefore look for low-risk methods of expansion. Thus we can exploit their dislike of risk-taking by making an expansive course too risky for them." Strausz-Hupé's picture of the Communists' relatively riskless use of military power in 1962 is that:

Now, more than ever, weighty technical considerations are likely to dissuade the Soviet military from wanting to fight a war in Europe for the sake of expanding the Soviet realm, not to speak of fighting a nuclear war for the purpose of expanding communism in Europe. Soviet conflict strategies assign to military power an essentially *political* role. They aim at the defeat of the West by means short of war and, preferably, by the use of military force as a blackmail counter. From a military point of view, this is a sound strategy—and a relatively safe one in the light of unpredictable nuclear hazards.[7]

Thus the Soviets do not want to fight in Europe. This does not mean, of course, that the time is ripe for *détente.* Rather, they are continuing their use of military power as a political weapon, and their proximate goal in Europe is still the one quoted above from *A Forward Strategy:* "the neutralization of Germany followed by the breakup of the various European agencies of integration."

This over-all Communist strategy of always advancing with minimum provocation to the West is applicable not only in

[7] Strausz-Hupé, *Orbis,* pp. 33–34.

Europe and not only in 1961 and 1962, however, but is *the* basic Communist protracted conflict strategy for the world, succinctly described by Kintner a few years earlier:

How can the greatest freedom of maneuver be maintained so that power and space may be gradually amassed without the risk of being plunged into a full-scale atomic war?

Protracted conflict is the obvious answer. A strategy of limited actions, of indirect threats, it is also one in which no single move constitutes adequate provocation for the unleashing of the West's engines of nuclear destruction. And for its success it relies most heavily on our fears that any introduction of such weapons would surely produce a global chain reaction. Because Western strategy has been mainly predicated on the concept that war, if it comes, will be total in character, involving maximum violence, we are still ill-equipped to meet the diffuse and dangerous challenges offered by that form of conflict at which the men in Moscow and Peiping are most proficient.[8]

Such an analysis of the Communist desire to minimize their risks is not unlike the anti-war marginalists' picture of the Soviet Union as a nation unwilling to risk reversing its own past successes, domestic and foreign. And the picture differs from the popular one of Russia as a nation which considers nuclear weapons as the basic currency of conflict. But the anti-Communists' implication is not at all the same as the one drawn by the anti-war group—that we can therefore strive to minimize our *joint* risk of holocaust and work out our differences, if not peacefully, at least at very low levels of violence. Rather the anti-Communist conclusion is that "the communists must be convinced that politico-military adventures beyond major thresholds court the danger of the U.S. resorting to general nuclear war. Such an American aggregate capability must be real—so real that the communists cannot labor under any misapprehension about it." In any case, because the Communists apparently wish to avoid nuclear war for now, this does not necessarily imply that they

[8] William Kintner, "The Orchestration of Crisis," in *American Strategy for the Nuclear Age*, eds. Walter F. Hahn and John C. Neff (Garden City: Doubleday, 1960), p. 107. Reprinted from *Esquire*, May 1959.

will for all time. If we ever allow them to gain the power to hurt us without being severely hurt in return, Communist doctrine may change rapidly: "That in the near future the communists may prefer to apply these limited techniques of conquest—techniques short of a direct military assault on the continental United States—should not obscure the totality of the communist threat . . . The communists might be tempted, within the next few years, to achieve and exploit missile superiority and to inflict upon the United States the military or psychological *coup de grâce.*"[9] And finally, whatever may be the Soviet fears of war, they do not impel or imply a serious quest for disarmament or even for real measures of arms control acceptable to both sides. As put by British Sovietologist Harry Willetts: "The Soviet leaders, to judge by their behavior to date, are unlikely to accept as in their national interest any major measures of disarmament or arms control that do not give them substantial strategic or political advantages. They may well be interested in reducing the dangers of war and the burden of armaments. But they apparently do not regard either of these tasks as so urgent that it cannot be combined with and made dependent on achievement of broader political objectives."[10] Soviet positions on arms negotiations are merely another portion of the protracted conflict.

Thus the fundamental anti-Communist picture of the Communist world—a united, implacable, expanding enemy, bent on substituting its political and social system for all others on the surface of the globe—differs completely from the fundamental picture drawn by the anti-war marginalists —that of a divided and hesitant competitor, with the Russian segment gradually turning inward and searching for *détente* in order to consolidate the positions it already has. But on many important matters of detail, there exist peculiar simi-

[9] *A Forward Strategy for America*, pp. 115, 400. Copyright © 1961 by Robert Strausz-Hupé, William R. Kintner, and Stefan T. Possony.
[10] Harry T. Willetts, "Disarmament and Soviet Foreign Policy," in The American Assembly, *Arms Control: Issues for the Public*, p. 172. Copyright © 1961. By permission of Prentice-Hall, Inc., publisher.

larities: both schools find the underdeveloped world a vital area of conflict (or competition); both schools conceive of the Soviet Union as flexible enough to tolerate an eventual relaxation of the hold on Eastern Europe; both see the Communists as being very much afraid of nuclear warfare in today's world.

The detailed similarities of these views—views which are rather different from those of many middle marginalists—do not unite the anti-war and anti-Communist marginalists on policy. If the underdeveloped world is important, this implies, to the anti-war group, competition for the minds of men; to the anti-Communists, Western self-assertion. If the Soviet Union might relax its hold on the satellites, this implies to the anti-war school, Gomulka; to the anti-Communists, Nagy. And, as pointed out, if the Soviets have a distaste for nuclear warfare, this means to the anti-war school, *détente;* to the anti-Communists, deterrence of aggression. These wide differences in the interpretation of similar analyses are fundamentally based, of course, on fundamentally different pictures of what the Communist bloc is. But in addition to this, the anti-Communist and the anti-war marginalists differ deeply in the beliefs which come under the other headings of arms-policy analysis, and these companion beliefs react back upon the analysis of the opponent, turning analytical similarity into interpretative difference.

ANALYSIS OF POWER

Although the picture of *war* joins the picture of *the opponent* as one of the two major categories of analysis determining arms-policy recommendations, war, for the marginal anti-Communist school, is mainly a Clausewitzian means of utilizing power against the Communists in the various parts of the world. Because of this, it is most convenient here to link the anti-Communist analyses of the opponent and of war through the other two key analyses of *power* and of *allies and neutrals.*

And power-as-a-tool—how the Communists try to make

the world run in their direction, and how we can make it go in ours—is as much as anything the specific matter which causes similar analyses of the anti-Communist and anti-war marginalists to produce different end results. The basic difference in the two schools' interpretations of the uses of power is the difference between conviction and coercion. The anti-war marginalists want to convince the rest of the world of the need to move voluntarily in our direction; while they do not reject military power, they use it reluctantly and mainly to preclude its use by the other side. The anti-Communists just do not see much good coming out of the carrot. They feel that the rest of the non-Communist world should realize that its long-run interests lie in staying with us to avoid Communism; that short-run inducements, material or moral, should not be needed and will not be successful (although we should try through propaganda to convince other peoples of their true interest in the matter). But in any case, we must face up to the use of the stick as necessary:

The requirements of foreign policy are to assert authority, to enhance prestige, to stand firm, to face down threats, to take risks, to stand by one's allies, to punish one's enemies, and, whenever pursuing these tasks calls for the use of force, to use force. The single-mindedness and intransigence of the communist bid for world power leave us no other choice but to think soberly about force and to accept the ever-present contingency that force will be used against us and that we will have to counter it in kind. Our essentially "other-directed" foreign policy has not only failed to alter the international equation in our favor, but has also managed to deceive our own people about the grim, the true nature of the struggle.

Compassion and generosity are not alternatives for resolution in taking the risks and bearing the sacrifices with which the use of power is fraught. If men of good will, when they confront the challenge of the aggressor, shirk the use of power, they court not only their own defeat, but also the defeat of those humane causes which they seek to further.[11]

11 *A Forward Strategy for America*, pp. 10–11. Copyright © 1961 by Robert Strausz-Hupé, William R. Kintner, and Stefan T. Possony.

It is this analysis that leads the anti-Communist marginalists' interest in Afro-Asia to be expressed as a need for greater self-assertion by the West; their tool for loosening the Communist hold on the satellites to be Hungarian-style revolutions; the implication to them of the Soviet fear of risk-taking to be that we should create risks. Force, toughness, coercive power, are the instruments which move the hard real world of men.

Again, an excellent demonstration of the application of this theory of power is given by the example of Cuba. If the anti-war marginalists blamed the Bay of Pigs fiasco mainly on the militarization of an unpopular movement, the editors of *Orbis* disagreed:

> One of the more facile rationalizations of the Cuban debacle to make the Washington rounds this past spring was that the "invasion" failed essentially for the same reason that outside intervention had proved vain against the French and Russian revolutions—namely, gross underestimation of the degree of popular support enjoyed by the incumbent radical regime.
>
> Actually, it would be more accurate to attribute the failure of the expedition to deficiencies of intelligence and planning and to a lack of political sureness on the part of a new Administration which had scarcely had time to get its bearings. The responsible agencies seemed not to appreciate the extent to which the Soviets had buttressed Castro with the most modern arms prior to the crisis, nor the position they were in to supply him with on-the-spot tactical guidance when the challenge was hurled down on the beach . . . Not popular support for Castro frustrated those who awaited an island revolt, but the repressive power of totalitarian terrorism . . .
>
> Finally, and most tragically of all, the climax of the brave venture was a military fiasco.[12]

Thus the invasion failed because both sophisticated knowledge of how to combat world-wide Communism and military power are needed for such affairs. In 1961, the knowledge was not possessed by the young administration, and the power was

12 "Reflections on the Quarter," *Orbis*, 5:132–133 (Summer 1961).

not used. And, predictably, the marginal anti-Communists applauded the use by President Kennedy of American military power in the 1962 affair of the Soviet missiles in Cuba, but were disappointed that lack of a sophisticated anti-Communism caused the administration to stop short of using this power plus political weapons for the purpose of finally overthrowing Castro.

Throughout, the anti-Communist marginalists have put much of the blame for the failure to get rid of Castro on the homage paid to the anti-war marginalists' false god of "world opinion." Thus, the editors of *Orbis*, in a statement written apropos of the Bay of Pigs fiasco which could as easily have been applied to the failure to overthrow Castro in the missile affair, stated that:

Within recent years, the American approach to international relations has reflected an overweening desire to curry favor with nations abroad. The diplomatists, to be sure, cannot ignore the factor of national popularity, but they should never look upon it as the *unum necessarium*. Too often the United States has tailored its substantive positions to the anticipated response of an abstraction known as "world opinion," especially as registered in the votes of the UN General Assembly. At best, however, the erection of a foreign policy upon the rapidly shifting sands of international political attitudes is a risky venture. It can bring serious losses with scant chance of durable gains, as the reaction to our exemplary conduct in the Suez affair demonstrated.

At worst, the compulsive quest to be liked rather than respected by those neutralist tribunes who allegedly sit in judgment upon the world will slowly erode not only America's security posture but her cherished ideals as well.[13]

This analysis of the lack of power of public opinion, however, although it illustrates the point that the carrot is not a proper instrument of public power, does not imply that intangibles such as "moral leadership" in the world are negligible in creating such power. Moral leadership is necessary, but it is not the type of moral leadership designed by the anti-war

[13] *Ibid.*, p. 135.

school—*convincing the nations of the world that we are with them*. Rather, the moral leadership of the anti-Communists is leadership *in convincing the world that it should be with us*—that we are right, and that it should come along:

> Only by a clear understanding and a forceful presentation of our goals, of communist objectives, and of the irreconcilable conflict between the two ideologies, can American leaders blunt the Soviet psychological offensive, set the record straight, and restore unity of purpose to the West . . .

> In the vital theater of the uncommitted and new nations, the United States must help create a realistic image of the future, free from the chimeras of utopian states . . .

> In Eastern Europe, the communist puppet governments are politically and militarily dependent on Soviet support . . . The desire for national independence, most dramatically asserted by the Hungarians, is thus a basic factor of East European politics. This, too, is a potent psychological weapon, if we but have the skill and determination to use it against the Soviet Empire.[14]

And, aside from such moral or psychological leadership of the rest of the world, the power of the United States is dependent upon a similar intangible at home: the will power of the American people. Without American determination to use them, all the military and other instruments of power are as naught. Senator Margaret Chase Smith (Republican, Maine), in a widely reported major speech criticizing the Kennedy administration for allegedly substituting "conventional" for tactical nuclear weapons in the defense of Europe, argued strongly that:

> We are, as the President has said, engaged in a contest of will and purpose as well as force and violence . . .

> The greatness of this country was not won by people who were afraid of risks. It was won for us by men and women with little physical power at their command who nevertheless were willing to submit to risks. Could it not be lost for us by people with

14 *A Forward Strategy for America*, pp. 265–275. Copyright © 1961 by Robert Strausz-Hupé, William R. Kintner, and Stefan T. Possony.

great physical power at their command but nevertheless willing to risk submitting? I believe it could.

. . . Is it conceivable that Khrushchev could assess that the will of the American people has collapsed?

. . . we have the nuclear capability—and he knows and fears it. But we have practically told him that we do not have the will to use that one power with which we can stop him.[15]

Thus, American power throughout the world is essentially coercive: possession of the means of using force and the will to use it as necessary. Moral leadership is a necessary supplement, and indeed becomes a means of turning both Western and subversive Eastern force against the Communist system. But power, in all parts of the world, is a function of military strength, resolution, and confidence that we are in the right.

ANALYSIS OF ALLIES AND NEUTRALS

The marginal anti-Communists' picture of power as being coercive means that the importance they place on the under-developed areas of the world does not carry the implication of peaceful competition which attached to the similar geographical emphasis of the anti-war marginalists. Such an implication would in any case be difficult to make compatible with the basic picture of the deadly world struggle with Communism. Rather, the anti-Communist marginalists, though favoring economic aid, psychological warfare, and the like, still feel that the military component of the struggle is important in the underdeveloped world, particularly Asia:

Were the strength of the West to decline in relation to that of the Soviets and Chinese, the nonaligned states of Asia would face the alternative of submitting to increasing communist pressure or casting their lot with the West. In fact, Asian neutralism is buttressed by Western military strength. It follows that, even in the face of neutralist complaints, the United States should

15 Senator Margaret Chase Smith, United States Congress, 87th Congress, First Session, *Congressional Record*, pp. 19385–19387 (1961).

demonstrate its determination to protect the Asian rimlands against communist aggression; maintain or increase its military capabilities in or near the region and strengthen SEATO. While we should be respectful of neutrals' desires and attitudes, the United States should not feel compelled to modify its defense arrangements to placate neutralist opinion. Indeed, it is more than likely that most of the neutral and noncommitted states of Asia are not entirely displeased with an American posture of strength.[16]

Thus there is no respite from the tough power struggle, even in the underdeveloped world. Asia and Africa, even though they receive a good deal of attention in the analysis of the anti-Communist marginalists, have no special *mystique* for this group, as they do for the anti-war group. It was suggested above that in their analysis of the geographical aspects of Communist strategy, the anti-Communists are not far from the anti-war school, giving considerable emphasis to the conflict in Asia and Africa. But this is not because the anti-Communists *downgrade* the relative importance of Europe; control of Europe they believe to be still the ultimate if perhaps not the immediate goal of Communists. Rather, the anti-Communists *upgrade* the relative importance of the struggle with Communism, wherever in the world it appears. They find the underdeveloped world almost as important as do the anti-war marginalists; but *they also find the struggle in Europe at least as important as does the most enthusiastic middle-marginal partisan of NATO.* Relatively they must give less weight to either of the two areas than do the advocates of strategies centered on these areas, but the relative relationship becomes important only in terms of conflicts between the areas. In absolute terms, the anti-Communists pay as much attention to the struggle in *any* area as do most pleaders for such an area.

But so far as relative geography is concerned, the authors of *Protracted Conflict,* after describing "Afro-Asia" as the "battleground chosen by the Communists" (in 1959), as quoted above, went on to warn: "If the United States, mistaking the place where the issue was met for the place over which it arose, should abandon the primacy of Europe to the expediency of Asiatic strategy, it would play the game of Soviet strategy."[17] And the anti-Communist marginalists make clear that in case of conflict between Western European and non-Communist Asian or African powers, they would choose Europe. In contrast with Professor Emerson's criticism of the Eisenhower administration for having sided with our colony-holding allies in UN votes (quoted on page 122), the editors of *Orbis* criticize the Kennedy administration's UN votes which sided with the Afro-Asian bloc:

In recent months the United States has voted in the General Assembly for resolutions censuring NATO allies. For example, the U.S. neither assisted constructively in the development of politically stable independent states—avowedly one of our national objectives—nor did it strengthen the Western Alliance—another crucial element in our foreign policy—when our United Nations delegation voted for Afro-Asian resolutions censuring Portugal, but not Angolan terrorists, while demanding "immediate independence of all African peoples" regardless of their capabilities for self-government.[18]

Thus, in spite of their very intense awareness of the struggle with Communism in Asia and Africa, as well as Europe, they are clear which comes first. As put explicitly in *A Forward Strategy:*

The Atlantic Alliance is the core of the West's federative powers and its mightiest bulwark against communist expansion. The basis for community among the Atlantic peoples is present in their common strategic interests, their economic and social interdependence, and their shared cultural heritage. This does not mean that the West, no matter how strong its common bonds, can thrive in isolation, nor that the United States can cold-shoulder its friends in Asia, Africa, and Latin America and renounce making new friends. To the contrary, the United States does and must pursue policies which will ease the transition of

17 *Protracted Conflict*, p. 105.
18 "Reflections on the Quarter," *Orbis*, 6:10–11 (Spring 1962).

former colonial areas to independence and responsible statehood. But national sovereignty would avail the emancipated peoples little if the communists were to prevail over the West . . .[19]

The previous discussion of the *anti-war* marginalists' analysis of third nations in general and of NATO in particular, was not complete, however, without specific mention of their attitude toward Germany. And the unusual point about the anti-Communist marginalists is that, unlike their anti-war brethren, and unlike, indeed, many middle marginalists who are in no way anti-German, they do not have a differentiating picture of Germany. West Germany is one of our NATO allies, and should be treated strictly as such. *A Forward Strategy* has no references to any German problem with antecedents before 1945, to any question of German nationalism, German *rapprochement* with the Soviet Union, or anything of the kind. American NATO policy is criticized for singling out Britain as a special ally, but this is in the context of difficulties between France and Britain, rather than having anything to do with Germany.[20] This anti-Communist treatment (or lack of treatment) of Germany is all the more striking because, unlike some middle marginalists who take no special notice of Germany because they are concerned purely with military-strategic matters, the over-all analysis of the anti-Communist marginalist school is political to the core.

But the only struggle is with Communism, and, except for Western Europe, the various regions of the world are arenas rather than independent participants. Within this context of a world-wide power struggle with an implacable foe, it finally becomes possible to examine the anti-Communist marginalists' picture of war.

ANALYSIS OF WAR

It was suggested above that in considering the ways thermonuclear war might start, the *anti-war* marginalists placed greatest emphasis on two types of undeterrable wars: those

---

[19] *A Forward Strategy for America*, pp. 50–51. Copyright © 1961 by Robert Strausz-Hupé, William R. Kintner, and Stefan T. Possony.
[20] *Ibid.*, p. 227.

to which deterrence is, in their view, irrelevant because they stem from irrationality, and those for which deterrence is relevant but likely to be unsuccessful. The anti-war school treats these as a pair, the existence of which places severe limits on the uses of deterrence.

The anti-Communists separate these two types of war, and treat them quite differently from one another. Nuclear wars stemming from irrationality they dismiss in an interesting manner:

Wars, including general nuclear war, are fought to achieve objectives that lie beyond war. We must presume that the strategic dialogue between the U.S. and the U.S.S.R. is governed by rationality. If it were not, strategy would be a child's tale told by an idiot. Hence we have little choice but to preface our strategic planning with an act of faith. The U.S. and the U.S.S.R. leaders will seek to preserve the value of their respective societies and will strive to limit war to conditions under which both sides can not only survive, but also attain those objectives that lie beyond war.[21]

And throughout the anti-Communist marginalist literature, it is very difficult to discover any discussion of what happens if rationality fails.

But *undeterred* wars, as compared to those which may be *undeterrable* because they are irrational, provide another instance in which the analysis of the anti-Communists is quite close to that of the anti-war marginalists, but the ultimate implications are completely opposite. The anti-Communists would agree with the anti-war marginalists that a chief—the chief—risk of a nuclear war lies in the chance that a nation might, in spite of its opponent's deterrent threats, go ahead and start one. *The difference is that the anti-Communists are for this risk*—the key to the anti-Communist analysis is that war, even nuclear war between the United States and the Soviet Union, is an instrument of policy:

If we should elect to abstain from nuclear warfare under all circumstances, the most rational course would appear to be not to fight at all, but surrender on the most advantageous terms.

21 *Ibid.,* p. 99.

But if we choose to stand, our agenda will include at least the following items:

1. Security of the North American base and the survival of its peoples.
2. Maintenance of Free World positions in the regions along the periphery of the Sino-Soviet bloc.
3. Control of the seaways, the airways, and outer space.

These are our minimum objectives. We must seek to obtain them, even at the risk of general nuclear war. Such a war *is* "thinkable."[22]

Indeed, it is the anti-Communists and those middle marginalists who are allied with them on this issue about whom the anti-war marginalists are thinking when they worry about undeterred wars.

And it follows as a matter of course that on the third type of thermonuclear exchange, that which is deterrable in principle, and, given proper strategy, is in fact deterred, the anti-Communists are interested in one direction of deterrence only. They want us to deter Soviet attack on the United States and they devote a good deal of discussion to how to go about it, but they are not interested in the "stable mutual deterrence" of anti-war marginalists such as Wiesner, who wants *us* to be deterred as well.

Similarly, the anti-Communists interpret the arms race differently from the anti-war marginalists who find in the race the cumulation of all their fears that if the bomb does not go off today it will be sure to go off tomorrow. The arms race exhilarates the anti-Communists:

The U.S. is caught inescapably in an "arms race" with the Soviet Union, whether it wishes to recognize this deadly competition or not. Contrary to general belief, such a race need not work against world stability and peace. It could serve as the most effective means to bring the communist rulers to reasonable terms. *For the Free World can far better afford such a competition than the communist bloc.* The economic resources of the Free World are so much greater than those of the communist

22 *Ibid.*, pp. 109–110.

bloc that, combined with a masterful exploitation of technology, a strategy based on overwhelming military means is well within our reach.[23]

Thus the arms race, like war, is an instrument to be exploited for political purposes, rather than a horror to be prayed against. Part of the difference between the anti-Communist and the anti-war interpretations of war stem from vastly different analyses of what nuclear war will look like. The *anti-war* marginalists, just as they minimize the importance of human rationality, doubt the chances of human control, once war with nuclear weapons has begun. They believe that the antagonists in such a war will strike out blindly in successful attempts to destroy one another. But the anti-Communists believe that the effects of even thermonuclear war between the United States and the Soviet Union can be made tolerable. Civil defense is, to them, not merely the mitigation of disaster which it represents to many people, but it is an aid to making thermonuclear war "thinkable." Civil defense plus control over nuclear war to keep it military can lead to really striking results in the minds of some of the more extreme anti-Communist marginalists. According to Robert C. Richardson, III:

Thus, we see that, once the full implications of atomic age warfare are understood and strategy is tailored to these implications, the destruction of property and of non-combatants will probably be less than in past wars of attrition . . .

Clearly there would be no purpose in destroying non-military targets where this in no way would affect the capability of the military forces to carry out their mission . . .

The sooner we accept the fact that atomic munitions are here to stay and will in due course become a normal element of military force just as gunpowder did in its day, the safer the world will be.[24]

23 *Ibid.*, pp. 101–102.
24 Robert C. Richardson, III, "Atomic Bombs and War Damage," *Orbis*, 4:51–52 (Spring 1960).

Thus thermonuclear war as well as the other lesser varieties are all legitimate and possible instruments of the protracted conflict. Indeed, although the conflict comes in all sizes, the very existence of thermonuclear weapons will dominate even lesser wars.

The conflict between the Free World and the communists embraces the full range of force and persuasion from peaceful competition and negotiation at one end to nuclear wars of annihilation on the other . . .

American strategy does and must assign primacy to the contingency of thermonuclear exchange in a general war, the most frightful aspect of a future conflict. Yet war has many faces. To shy away from one is to withdraw into the illusion that war comes in pieces. War is an organic whole. If we must fight a war, its course will be governed by the contingency of thermonuclear exchange, no matter whether nuclear weapons will be used or not. If we do not go to war, nuclear power-in-being will weigh heavily in the scales of peace.

Hence the capability for waging general nuclear war is the keystone of American defense.[25]

And even small wars may use small nuclear weapons, a fact which disturbs the anti-Communists not in the least. They look benignly at American use of tactical nuclear weapons in Europe, favor strongly American equipping of an independent NATO nuclear force,[26] and contemplate the use of nuclear deterrence in Asia.[27] All of these positions are taken by some middle marginalists too; the middle marginalists take them agonizingly, the anti-Communists willingly. For most marginal anti-Communists, Richardson's picture of atomic munitions replacing gunpowder may be slightly extreme, but only slightly.

The predominance of nuclear warfare, from the tactical to the general, however, does not mean a complete anti-Com-

25 *A Forward Strategy for America*, pp. 98–99. Copyright © 1961 by **Robert Strausz-Hupé, William R. Kintner, and Stefan T. Possony.**
26 *Ibid.*, pp. 141–142.
27 *Ibid.*, p. 153.

munist preoccupation with the most violent levels of combat. They also have a particular interest in the least violent unconventional nonbattlefield war:

Guerrilla or revolutionary war has become the principal communist military technique for the reduction, by installments so to speak, of Western influence in the underdeveloped regions of the world. Ideally, the operation consists of two phases: the establishment of a national government and then, after liberation has been won, the subversion of the national government by a communist or communist-controlled faction.

The United States and its allies, if they propose to check this particular communist gambit, have little choice but to maintain forces equipped for scotching civil or regional "liberation warfare movements." This is especially true of Southeast Asia, the Middle East, Africa and Latin America.[28]

The most nearly unique contribution of the marginal anti-Communists to current analysis of warfare, however, is their argument that guerrilla and other forms of unconventional warfare are not merely Communist weapons we must defend against, but must be used offensively by us against the Communists. Slavko Bjelajac states that "the lessons of the past and the opportunities of the future can be summarized in the following propositions: Unconventional warfare is a vital segment of the total spectrum of conflict in the mid-twentieth century. We must take up this weapon if only to parry the thrusts of our opponent. Beyond that, however, unconventional warfare can play a decisive role in winning the Cold War, in deterring Soviet aggression, or, should deterrence fail, in bringing a hot war to a victory which would not be steeped in the ruins of nuclear devastation."[29] He proposes subversive organization by the West of underground cadres and partisan groups within the Communist countries, forces which would not only keep the Communists on edge by their passive existence during the Cold War, but would make it difficult for the

28 *Ibid.*, p. 156.
29 Slavko N. Bjelajac, "Unconventional Warfare in the Nuclear Era," *Orbis*, 4:327 (Fall 1960).

enemy to start any hot war, would fight on our side in a conventional war, and would help us to win the world even after a thermonuclear exchange.

Where this concentration on the most and least violent sorts of warfare leaves nonnuclear "conventional" warfare is an interesting question. At best it must be somewhat squeezed between the cases in which the use of tactical nuclear weapons is appropriate and those where counterguerrilla techniques rather than standard infantry tactics are called for. Perhaps the most accurate statement about the conventional war doctrine of the anti-Communist marginalists is that it is evolving toward a more important position in their strategy. Early in 1959, Strausz-Hupé downgraded the importance of such nonnuclear capabilities:

The idea that conventional forces can persuade the Communists to desist from starting small wars for fear of landing in unprofitable stalemates or of "tripping off" a nuclear holocaust is based on the assumption that they will and can confine their operations to "conventional" weapons. Now, in fact, nuclear weapons are already an integral part of the Communists' war machine, and it is highly unlikely that they could fight a "limited" war of, say, the dimensions of the Korean war without the use of tactical nuclear weapons even if they wanted to. It is true that they maintain large standing forces that are not equipped with nuclear warheads. But the principal mission of such forces is to keep down rebellious peoples in the satellite countries and at home rather than to fight foreign wars . . .

Thus far, Communist strategies have been far more limited than those of "limited war." Without firing a shot of old-fashioned gunpowder, they have penetrated deeply into what is called euphemistically the Free World. There is no reason that the West should not be able to counter and turn back their advances, but to do so it must not waste its resources on "limited wars" that will not be fought and on "conventional" forces that cannot be used except to their own detriment.[30]

[30] Robert Strausz-Hupé, "Nuclear Blackmail and Limited War," *The Yale Review*, 48:177–181 (Winter 1959).

But in 1960, Cottrell and Walter Hahn seemed rather explicitly to disagree with Strausz-Hupé. The disagreement was embodied in a paper adapted from a part of a multiauthor report to the Senate Foreign Relations Committee,[31] which was dated October 15, 1959, only eight or nine months after the Strausz-Hupé piece. According to Cottrell and Hahn:

So long as the weaknesses of allied conventional forces in central Europe compel the Western powers to contemplate the ultimate choice between a nuclear holocaust and limited defeat, for just as long are the Soviets able to drive their psychological advantage home.

Therefore, an effective conventional capability—on a scale at least twice the force levels available to NATO today—is imperative if NATO is to be prepared to (1) wage limited nonatomic conflict and (2) cope with the new Soviet crisis strategy in Europe.[32]

And although in 1959 this might well have been a difference of opinion between Strausz-Hupé on the one side and Cottrell and Hahn on the other, by 1961, the situation had evolved to the point where *A Forward Strategy* with Strausz-Hupé the chief author, accepted the Cottrell-Hahn thesis: "Despite the change wrought in the balance of power by the growing Soviet nuclear missile arsenal, the United States and its allies need, for political and psychological reasons, the ability to respond to any given communist aggression at a high level of violence, *without* automatic resort to nuclear weapons."[33] The evolution has taken place, partly in response to an intellectual evolution in strategic thinking, partly in response to political developments in Europe, partly, perhaps, in response to the fact that by 1961 it began to appear more possible that the United States would be willing to

31 Committee on Foreign Relations, United States Senate, *United States Foreign Policy—Western Europe*, Report #3 (Washington: U.S. Government Printing Office, 1960).
32 Alvin J. Cottrell and Walter F. Hahn, "Needed: A New NATO Shield," in *American Strategy for the Nuclear Age*, p. 281.
33 *A Forward Strategy for America*, p. 138. Copyright © 1961 by Robert Strausz-Hupé, William R. Kintner, and Stefan T. Possony.

spend more money on conventional forces. (*A Forward Strategy*, although published in 1961, has an authors' preface dated November, 1960, the time of the Presidential election. By then it was becoming obvious that both Kennedy and Nixon were concerned with the state of our conventional forces.) But even after the evolution, the greater marginal anti-Communist willingness to use tactical nuclear weapons and the greater interest in unconventional warfare, appears to leave conventional forces in something of a residual position. It is worthy of note that Cottrell and Hahn, and, to an even greater extent, the authors of *A Forward Strategy*, appear at least as interested in the political and psychological effects of conventional forces as in their more purely *military* capabilities.

At any rate, the war philosophy which distinguishes the anti-Communists from the other marginal groups is that they consider war, of all varieties and levels of violence, as the Clausewitzian "continuation of politics by other means." This distinctive analysis of war as pictured by the anti-Communists can be summarized by the contrasts between their views and those held by most other marginalists concerning the highest and lowest levels of violence:

1. Most marginalists consider the use or the threat of war legitimate and necessary, at least in the short run, in order to prevent thermonuclear war by deterrence. Some marginalists of the middle school reluctantly consider the use or the threat of thermonuclear war necessary to deter or combat lesser aggression. *The anti-Communist marginalists consider all forms of nuclear war, if used with circumspection, as useful weapons in winning the protracted conflict.*

2. Most marginalists consider guerrilla and unconventional war to be threats to the West which we must find some way to combat. *The anti-Communists, like Bjelajac, consider unconventional war to be a powerful offensive weapon which the West can use to help win the protracted conflict.* War may not be desirable, but it is an inevitable and necessary human activity.

ANALYSIS OF OURSELVES

It is useful, for purposes of symmetry, to include this category of analysis here, even though the findings in relation to the anti-Communist marginalists are entirely negative. They are not worried about militarism (although they do not particularly advocate it for its own sake). As is obvious from all the foregoing, they do not treat the United States and the Soviet Union in any way as symmetrical opponents in the cold war. This is true not only of the Osgood anti-war marginalist sort of symmetry, in which each side misunderstands the other; it is also true of the "gaming" symmetry of some strategists. Because the anti-Communists are basically *political* analysts, the fact of the real political asymmetry is the important one to them. And finally, unlike those of some of their *systemic* anti-Communist cohorts, the writings of the anti-Communist marginalists exhibit no concern with any possible internal Communist threat.

✤ ✤ ✤ ✤ ✤

C H A P T E R   9

MARGINALIST ANALYSES:
THE MIDDLE MARGINALISTS

The middle marginal school has been defined, somewhat circularly, as containing all of those marginalists whose arms-policy recommendations fall between those of the marginal anti-war and anti-Communist schools. To some extent, this recommendation-based definition applies also to the *analyses* of the middle marginalists. On some analytical issues, the typical middle positions fall within a range extending from the most moderate anti-war marginalists on one end to the most moderate anti-Communists on the other. If some anti-war marginalists consider the Soviet Union to be mildly opportunistic, for example, and some anti-Communists think of the Soviets as being carefully malign, most middle-marginal analyses can be thought of as falling on a continuum between these positions. But this idea of middle-marginal analysis as being merely "between" the other two cannot be applied very easily to very many analytical topics—for two reasons.

First, on many issues it is impossible even to define a meaningful continuum between two polar analytical positions. Thus, if, as has been suggested, *both* the anti-war and the anti-Communist marginalists tend to think similarly that the Communists will shy away from nuclear risks, many middle marginalists believe that they still may be nuclearly inclined, a position which in no sense is between two "poles."

The second reason for not describing most middle-marginal

analyses as portions of an intermediate range may be even
more important. This is that most middlemen are highly
eclectic, accepting analyses from where they will, without
taking over-all positions which can be consistently defined as
being a fixed distance from either of the two borders of
middle marginalism. Rather, the differences within the middle-marginal school over specific issues of arms policy tend to
take place each in its own dimension, with an individual's
position in a particular matter not necessarily very closely
correlated with his other positions. One example of this has
already been discussed under the heading of value systems—
the "balanced-value" and the "analytical" middle marginalists tend to base their recommendations on quite different
sets of values, but the differences bear little relationship to
differences of opinion over analyses and recommendations.
Similarly, it would be difficult to deduce a person's stand on
one particular analytical issue from his stand on another.
Indeed, many middle marginalists agree with some of the
analyses which characterize one or the other of the anti-war or
anti-Communist marginal schools. Some, for example, appear
to be anti-Communist in one area of the world and anti-war
in another. It would be difficult for a person to accept *all* of
the analyses and the values of another school and still make
middle-marginal recommendations, but to take one example
of an analytical belief shared by the middle and another
school, many middlemen agree with the belief of the anti-
Communists that world Communism is immutably expansionist. But these middle marginalists nonetheless come up
with different recommendations because they are more ap-
palled by war than are Strausz-Hupé and his marginal anti-
Communist cohorts.

Because of all this, the discussion of middle-marginal analyses makes no attempt to place particular beliefs on a nonexistent continuum which can be represented as a straight
line connecting the anti-war and the anti-Communist marginalists. Rather, what is attempted is a *pointillist* picture of an

eclectic and heterogeneous school—a picture of the school which tries, by describing some "typical" analyses, to give an impression of both its differences from the others and its internal disagreements.

ANALYSIS OF WAR

In one very important way, the over-all world picture of the middle-marginal makers of arms recommendations, rather than being "between" the other two schools, is quite close to that of the anti-war marginalists. Most middle-marginal study, like that of the anti-war group, is generally oriented around war as such, instead of being centered on the Communist menace, as is the work of the marginal anti-Communist school. This is not due to middle-marginal *analytical* belief that war is objectively more "important" than Communism, but rather to values which lean toward the anti-war side. Middle-marginalist analyses of war and of Communism resemble those of the anti-Communists more than they do those of the anti-war school, but the middle, like the anti-war group, puts its picture of war at the center of the considerations relevant to arms policy. The basis for this can be found largely in what has been called the "analytical" strain of middle-marginal values which, rather than being balanced between dislike of war and of Communism, comes to middle recommendations from anti-war values. There are few adherents to a "pure" analytical strain of middle marginalism, who really just don't care about Communism as such. Implicit in much of the writing, however, is the idea that recommendations for policies which are obviously anti-Communist (e.g., an arms build-up against Chinese Communists) can and should be explicitly derived from a less simple chain of logic based on their contribution to the prevention of war. It is difficult to discover how far this tendency toward anti-war argumentation is based on value systems which are weighted toward the anti-war side, and how far on a feeling that an anti-war case for these recommendations is a politically strong case because it is a logically dominant one—making the policies appear preferable from both the anti-war and the anti-Communist points of view. It is also not very important to make this discrimination among the motives for a particular type of argumentation; what is important is that, whatever its motivation, the anti-war "bias" in middle-marginal thought leads to the centering of analysis on war rather than on Communism. This does not imply *less* analysis of Communism than of war, although a content analysis would probably show proportionally less; it merely means that even the analysis of Communism is to a great extent an analysis of how to avoid war with Communists.

And, for similar reasons, the middle-marginal analysis of war, like the anti-war marginalists' analysis, has centered on the picture of general thermonuclear war between the United States and the Soviet Union. Big war is the big danger. There is plenty of interest in and analysis of limited war—considerably more than is provided by either anti-war or anti-Communist marginalists, both of which schools, as has been seen, tend to downgrade limited war for different reasons. But much of the middle-marginal limited-war analysis is concerned specifically with the connections between limited and general war. Although considerable thought is still given to "classical" analysis of how to fight a limited war, an increasing emphasis is being put on the problems of the escalation process which can lead from "small" war to the general war which occupies the center of the stage. Thomas Schelling makes explicit the belief that this should be so: "Discussion of troop requirements and weaponry for NATO is much concerned with *battlefield* consequences of different troop strengths and nuclear doctrines . . . The idea that European armament should be designed for resisting Soviet invasion, and is to be judged by its ability to contain an attack is based on the notion that limited war is a tactical operation. It is not. What that notion overlooks is that a main consequence of limited war, and a main purpose for engaging in it, is *to raise the risk of general war.* Limited war does this whether it intends to or not."[1] Schelling does not use this as an argument for any particular limited-war doctrine. His implication is rather that all sides in the discussion should concentrate on the key analytical question of expansion to general war—both its danger and its use as a threat for political objectives. And much middle-marginal military analysis does concentrate on general war. This colors the middle-marginal analysis of limited war, and it has also tended until recently to lead to an analytical slighting of unconventional war. Middle-marginal writing on guerrilla and similar war does exist, and, since the Cuban invasion fiasco and the continuous Southeast Asian situation have made obvious the necessity for more thought on these problems, it exists in increasing quantity. But until lately, compared to the anti-Communist school, the interest of the middle marginalists in this warfare bordering on the political has been relatively small.

The middle marginalists thus tend to orient their analyses around the same phenomena as the anti-war school: their picture of the world is centered on war; their analysis of war is oriented around general thermonuclear war. Once this is established, however, one must note that the two schools diverge. To begin with, if the anti-war marginalists worry most about thermonuclear wars which they consider undeterrable, the middle marginalists' picture of war centers on deterrence and deterrable wars. These two categories—wars which the anti-war group feels are undeterrable and wars which the middle marginalists believe to be deterrable—are not mutually exclusive; not only do they overlap, but sometimes the debate makes them appear to be almost exactly the same. But the approach of the two groups to such wars is markedly different.

Perhaps most basic is the different approach to rationality. The anti-war school tends to deprecate deterrent strategies whose deterrence they feel depends on the rationality of the

[1] Thomas C. Schelling, "Nuclear Strategy in Europe," *World Politics*, 14:421 (April 1962).

decision makers. This anti-war belief is based on the dual fear of the failure of nonrational humans and nonhuman machines. The middle marginalists, while they, too, worry about the failure of deterrence, worry less. They make several arguments on these points. The first is that human rationality is not an on-off proposition—that rational strategies are possible even with irrational individuals. Schelling points out that rationality can be used *by* the irrational: ". . . even among the emotionally unbalanced, among the certified 'irrationals,' there is often observed an intuitive appreciation of the principles of strategy, or at least of particular applications of them. I am told that inmates of mental hospitals often seem to cultivate, deliberately or instinctively, value systems that make them less susceptible to disciplinary threats and more capable of exercising coercion themselves."[2] And Herman Kahn argues that, similarly, rational strategies can be used *against* the irrational:

Moreover, we want to deter even the mad. It is sometimes stated that even an adequate . . . Deterrent would not deter an irrational enemy. This might be true if irrationality were an all-or-nothing proposition. Actually, irrationality is a matter of degree and if the irrationality is sufficiently bizarre, the irrational decision maker's subordinates are likely to step in. As a result, we should want a safety factor in . . . Deterrence systems so large as to impress even the irrational and irresponsible with the degree of their irrationality and therefore the need for caution.[3]

But even beyond the argument that "irrational" people or organizations retain elements of rationality, it is possible to use rational systems even in a context of absolute irrationality. Kahn also points out that:

Many people feel that it is useless to apply rationality and calculation in any area dominated by irrational decision makers.

[2] Thomas C. Schelling, *The Strategy of Conflict* (Cambridge, Mass.: Harvard University Press, 1960), p. 17.

[3] Herman Kahn, *Thinking About the Unthinkable*, pp. 111–112. Copyright © 1962 by Herman Kahn. This quotation and all subsequent quotations from this book are reprinted by permission of Horizon Press and George Weidenfeld and Nicholson, Limited.

This is almost comparable to feeling that it would be impossible to design a safety system for an insane asylum by rational methods since, after all, the inmates are irrational. Of course, no governor or superintendent would consider firing the trained engineer, and turning the design over to one of the lunatics. The engineer is expected to take the irrationality of the inmates into account by a rational approach. Rational discussions of war and peace can explicitly include the possibility of irrational behavior.[4]

Thus, without denying that people can be irrational, the middle marginalists believe that this irrationality need not lead to war, that systems can be designed to prevent war by taking account of the irrationality.

The arguments by Schelling and Kahn apply specifically to human irrationality, mainly on the part of national decision makers. This sort of irrationality might be defined as action which is likely to be detrimental to the decision maker according to his own values. But what of the class of irrational or nonrational wars which result from either insanity on the part of an individual who is not a top-level decision maker but has some control over a nuclear weapon, or from sheer mechanical failure? These are the wars that Etzioni lists under the headings of "War by Mechanical Failure or Human Miscalculation," "Unauthorized Action," and "War by False Alarm." Kahn lumps these together under "Inadvertent War," and *he agrees with Etzioni that this is the most likely way in which general war can start:* "I believe that the current probability of inadvertent war is low. It is at the top of the list for two reasons: first, because I believe that the other ways in which a war might occur today are even less probable; and, second, because I believe that inadvertent war might well become a much more dangerous possibility in the not too distant future . . ."[5]

Not all middle marginalists would agree that this sort of war is the *most* probable; none, however, would dismiss it

4 *Ibid.*, p. 30.
5 *Ibid.*, p. 40.

out of hand. But even here the fact that the immediate causes of such war are beyond rationality does not preclude the use of rationality first, to reduce the chances that such nonrational occurrences will take place and second, to reduce the chances that if they do take place they will lead to war. The former is the more familiar idea, agreed to by all schools of thought—that, all other things being equal, it is useful and possible to design weapons so that they are less likely to go off accidentally, and to design weapon-triggers so that it is less easy for a madman to set them off. Nuclear weapons designed so that it requires a near-impossible sequence of events to set them off accidentally; nuclear delivery systems designed so that no single lunatic can send them on their way, are examples of reducing the chances of irrational war by rational design. But beyond these, the middle marginalists feel that it is possible to arrange things so that rationality can prevent a central thermonuclear war *even after a nonrational or irrational incident which shows danger of setting it off.* According to Schelling and Morton Halperin:

The problem . . . is not solely one of preventing the "accidents"; it is equally, or more, one of forestalling the kinds of *decisions* which might lead to war as a result of accident, false alarm, or mischief . . .

Cooperative or unilateral measures to improve the ability of each side's strategic forces to survive an attack . . . might slow down the tempo of decisions. Slowing down decisions on the brink of war not only means that either side, if it wishes to, can take more time to clear up whether or not the war has already started; it also means that each can impute less impetuous action to the other, and reduce thereby the need for its own quick reaction.

Measures to reduce the incidence of false alarm could be helpful . . . Agreements to limit the kinds of activities and deployments that might create misunderstandings or false alarms could also be helpful . . .[6]

6 Thomas C. Schelling and Morton H. Halperin, *Strategy and Arms Control* (New York: Twentieth Century Fund, 1961), pp. 15–16.

This idea that it's not the accident, it's the reaction, is extended by Fred Iklé to another case of war stemming from causes "beyond rationality"—war started by an "Nth country," beyond the control and therefore beyond the rationality of major-power decisions. This is another possibility that concerns many anti-war marginalists. Iklé minimizes the importance of this problem, and summarizes his arguments by saying that they ". . . do not deny that the diffusion of nuclear capabilities might make local nuclear disasters more likely, either in an 'Nth country' conflict or as a result of irresponsible action. What they question is the notion that such local disasters would necessarily increase the risk of global war. The more critical factors that determine that risk are the reaction time, the decision-making processes, and the vulnerability of the major powers, all of which are more or less independent of 'Nth countries.' "[7] Not all middle marginalists would agree with Iklé's implied optimism, but most would subscribe to his idea that even "Nth country" wars are susceptible of some control, and to his further arguments that in any case there is not much that can be done to keep nuclear weapons out of the hands of nations not now possessing them. There is policy disagreement among middle marginalists about what sacrifices we should make (e.g., of our good relations with our allies) in order to limit the nuclear club, but there is little belief on any side that such limitation is going to be easy no matter what we do.

Thus, although the middle marginalists tend to agree with the anti-war school that the possibility of war starting from accident or other proximate cause beyond the rationality of the major powers remains an important one even after all that can be done is done, the middlemen believe that it is within the scope of human rationality to do many things

[7] Fred Charles Iklé, "Nth Countries and Disarmament," *Bulletin of the Atomic Scientists,* 14:392 (December 1960). Iklé adds in a footnote that "To the extent there is a dependence, [of major powers on 'Nth countries'] it might well work in the other direction; the presence of 'Nth countries' might stimulate the major powers to institute more cautious reaction and decision processes."

which will reduce this possibility. By design of systems which are stable against irrationality; even by the use of rational deterrence against partially irrational individuals, "accidental" war can be made less likely. And there is no agreement between the schools about the relative importance of the reduction in this likelihood as against the importance of the possibilities that remain after rationality has done all that it can—this is a major analytical issue dividing them.

If the middle marginalists agree with the anti-war school that wars stemming from immediate causes beyond rationality cannot be dismissed out of hand, however, the middle also puts great weight on two other general ways in which a thermonuclear war might begin. One of these, a war starting from political causes, is the kind of war which the anti-war school thinks is deterrable but may not be deterred, and the anti-Communists tend to concentrate on as being the major type of thermonuclear war. The third type of war-start is discussed mainly by middle marginalists, although the other two marginal schools take some cognizance of it. This is the war stemming from war itself—primarily the "preemptive" attack designed to disarm an enemy who it is believed is trying to disarm you first. In a sense these preemptive wars are also political: they start with the idea of a political enemy (we are not very likely to get into such a war with Great Britain), but the theory is that from a small kernel of political war-danger, a much greater danger of self-generating war can grow.

Political thermonuclear wars can be of two general types, based on either a relatively cool decision to go to war for particular political objectives, or a more cursory step taken to raise the level of violence in a smaller war. The first, the cool decision, would probably manifest itself in a surprise attack upon an enemy; once the decision has been taken it is best to get maximum effect from the strike by careful planning and coordination, although if the attacking side thinks the defenders have gotten wind of its plans, cool surprise can rapidly turn into hot preemption. Most middle-marginal analysts consider a cool political attack by the Soviet Union relatively unlikely. As of 1962, they agree with Kahn's statement: "I believe that the probability of war by calculation is low because I think that this is the place where deterrence is most likely to work and—perhaps optimistically—that we are going to be competent about deterrence. If we weaken our deterrent prematurely, however, the possibility of war by calculation may move to the top of the list."[8] But there are some exceptions to this. One is based on time and the pre-1962 belief that we were heading toward the short end of a "missile gap." In 1959, most middle marginalists adopted (with lags up to two years) Albert Wohlstetter's belief that ". . . strategic deterrence, while feasible, will be extremely difficult to achieve, and at critical junctures in the 1960's, we may not have the power to deter attack. Whether we have it or not will depend on some difficult strategic choices as to the future composition of the deterrent forces as well as hard choices on its basing, operations, and defense."[9] This does not imply a difference of basic analysis by Kahn and Wohlstetter. Kahn, too, was worried in 1959, and both analyses stress that deterrence is not automatic but depends on "competence." But it does indicate that the near-universal (among middle marginalists) belief that deterrence of calculated Soviet attack has been achieved as of 1962, is not necessarily a stable one.

The probability of a cool, political, thermonuclear war, however, is not merely one of Soviet attack; we might attack too, and the 1962 belief that we can readily deter Soviet attack implies an asymmetry which may allow us to attack them first. On whether we have the capability for such a cool attack, there is no agreement among middle marginalists. Objective analysis of the *probability* of such a war started by us is inextricably connected with subjective value judgment about the *desirability* of risking war for political purposes,

[8] Kahn, *Thinking About the Unthinkable,* p. 56. Copyright © 1962 by Herman Kahn.

[9] Albert Wohlstetter, "The Delicate Balance of Terror," *Foreign Affairs,* 37:217 (January 1959).

and on these issues there is a range running from the near-anti-war to the near-anti-Communist middle marginalists. James King, Jr., a middle marginalist whose values put him near the anti-war border, believes that there will be an inevitable shrinkage of our ability to strike first. His picture of the future is one in which the dominant strategic fact is a

. . . convincing stalemate of long-range nuclear strike forces that appears likely to be the initial consequence of the substitution of missiles for air power . . .
Even though the Russians may not be convinced at first, . . . in time we may hope to convince them that it is not our intention to rehabilitate the first-strike advantage, nor to impose stability, but that we are seeking another basis for our security.[10]

But Kahn's analysis envisages situations where it will be desirable for the United States to maintain a credibly high probability that we will take a cool decision to strike the Russians without their hitting us first:

Suppose . . . that there is a device which restrains the President of the United States from acting for about twenty-four hours . . . which forces him to stop and think and make his decision in cold blood . . .

Let me give an example of a crisis that the Soviets could precipitate that would, by forcing both the Europeans and the Americans to face the possibility of a war seriously, give the effect of a 24-hour waiting period. Assume that both the United States and the Soviet Union could reliably annihilate each other in a retaliatory blow so that there was no special advantage in one side hitting the other first. Assume also that the Europeans had bought their own independent nuclear deterrents . . . The European deterrent . . . can only inflict about as much damage on the Soviet Union as the Soviets suffered in World War II. Therefore, the Soviets can threaten the Europeans with a disarming attack if they go first, and with an annihilating retaliation if the Europeans go first . . .

10 James E. King, Jr., "Arms Control and United States Security," in The American Assembly, *Arms Control: Issues for the Public*, p. 110. Copyright © 1961. By permission of Prentice-Hall, Inc., publisher.

The Soviets might couple their disarming ultimatum with another one that would make specific their immediate goals. They could announce that from then on, Europe, Asia, and Africa would be considered as being in the Soviet sphere of interest . . .

While the above will strike most people as being closer to paranoia than to analysis, it is still worth while to observe that the basic assumption of a firm belief on both sides of a reliable balance of terror is not unreasonable. Given this belief, it is most unlikely that even a Soviet ultimatum as provoking as the above would result in an attack by the United States.[11]

And Kahn favors steps to correct the situation where reliable mutual annihilation would make us fear to strike first in cold blood; he envisages the possibility of political wars started by a cool and deliberate United States decision.

This sort of scenario in which the United States would strike first, coolly and "out of the blue," however, is bizarre enough that Kahn's reference to paranoia seems well-taken, and, indeed, in his later writing, he has kept much more closely to United States-strikes-first situations without cooling-off periods, in which actual Soviet attack on Europe rather than mere threat or blackmail is the immediate trigger. The sort of situation which worries most middle-marginalists more than Kahn's extreme one is described by Richard Fryklund: "It is our stated policy now, and was our unstated policy under Eisenhower and Truman, to defend Europe if possible with nonnuclear weapons or small nuclear weapons on the scene. But if these weapons are not adequate, it is and has been our public policy to use SAC and Polaris rather than abandon Europe."[12] This statement carries an implication that war in Europe is already under way when the decision to strike at Russia is taken. So now we are no longer talking about a cool and deliberate decision. Rather, such a decision to strike the Soviet Union without our having been struck first provides a link between the two types of political wars—the deliberate one and the one based on a raised level of violence in a war which already exists.

[11] Herman Kahn, *On Thermonuclear War* (Princeton: Princeton University Press, 1960), pp. 29–32.
[12] Richard Fryklund, *100 Million Lives* (New York: Macmillan, 1962), p. 64.

Escalation from general Soviet attack on Europe to thermonuclear war between the United States and the Soviet Union is the easiest of the relatively "hot-headed" political wars to conceive of. Most middle marginalists agree that in the event of a Soviet attack on Europe, central thermonuclear war becomes a strong possibility. The possibility can be decreased by proper actions before the attack, but nobody contends that war in Europe and central war between the United States and the Soviet Union can be so insulated from one another that all-out escalation is made impossible. Nor is there agreement that it should be made close to impossible; Kahn and Fryklund, for example, favor the maintenance of some possibility precisely because such a threat that a thermonuclear war will stem from a Soviet attack tends to deter the initial attack.

Indeed, this principle of the danger of war deterring its own initiation can be generalized to events other than a full-scale attack in Europe. Middle marginalists reject the anti-war analysis that a small war will inevitably lead to a big one via an irresistible temptation for the losing side to try to gain its political goals by increasing the level of violence. Rather, the very chance that limited war will expand to unlimited deters putative attackers from starting such wars; it also deters the expansion of the wars if they do start. According to Henry Kissinger:

In a limited war between major powers both sides, by definition, have the technical ability to expand the war. It is easy, therefore, to "prove" the unreasonableness of any restraints. As long as either side has uncommitted resources at its disposal, any limitation can be made to appear arbitrary or ridiculous. However paradoxical it may seem, the danger of escalation is one of the chief reasons why a strategy of limited war contributes to deterrence and also why, if deterrence fails, there is a chance of keeping a conflict limited. A strategy of limited war adds to deterrence for the very reason usually invoked against it. The danger that limited war may expand after all works both ways. An aggressor may not credit our threat of massive retaliation because it would force us to *initiate* a course of action which will inevitably involve enormous devastation. He may calculate, however, that once engaged in a war on any scale neither he nor we would know how to limit it, whatever the intentions of the two sides.[13]

This paradox is the very foundation of the middle-marginal analysis of war and deterrence; it extends across the board to many more cases than escalation. War, particularly thermonuclear war, is a terrible thing; the Soviets know, as we do, that it is a terrible thing; this terror helps to prevent war. The paradox is related to the value conflict between the prevention and melioration of war, but it is also part and parcel of the analysis of prevention itself. The basis of middle-marginal deterrence analysis lies in the belief that *the chance of war deters war, and an attempt to reduce this chance too low can actually encourage war.* Dropping too low the probability that if certain initiating events occur thermonuclear war will result can make the events themselves more likely— enough more likely that the over-all probability of thermonuclear war (the product of the probability of initiation and the probability of escalation) is greater than otherwise. Conversely, raising too high the probability that *if* the first events occur, thermonuclear war will result, although it will discourage the events, can leave a substantial enough residual probability of their occurring that it too will raise the overall probability of such a war. This is the dilemma. For the middle marginalists, the "truth" of how best to prevent ultimate holocaust lies neither in no deterrence nor in all-out deterrence, but somewhere in between. There is a need for careful calculation, even mathematical computation. Because middle marginalists disagree with one another about the factors entering this calculation; because they disagree with one another about the weight to be given values other than the prevention of war as they enter the final decisions, they disagree on the precise policy recommendations they make. *But the middle marginalists as a group differ from the anti-war*

[13] Henry A. Kissinger, *The Necessity for Choice* (New York: Harper, 1961), p. 60. Copyright © 1960, 1961 by Henry A. Kissinger.

school in that they believe that the answer to the question of how best to stay out of war lies in the results of these calculations; they differ from the anti-Communist school in that they put the answer to the question much closer to the center of arms-policy decision.

The deterrence dilemma applies to the prevention of the growth of a small war into a big one: too high a likelihood that the small one will get big may tend to deter the small one but ensure its turning thermonuclear if it does occur; too low a likelihood may make the small one more likely and make it more possible that it will after all turn big. The truth lies somewhere between. And as a result, the middle marginalists assess the probability that a thermonuclear war will start via such a process of political escalation in much the same way as they assess the probability of an accidental war —not as being inevitable, but as a danger which can be reduced by proper and very careful rational action.

But beyond the process by which limited war escalates to the thermonuclear level for *political* reasons, because neither side wants to lose its objectives, there is another sort of connection between the small wars and the big ones. This links political war with the self-starting variety in which each side is afraid the other is about to attack and one or both therefore attempt to "preempt"—to hit before being hit—and thus gain the military advantage accruing from a first strike. Halperin distinguishes between the political and the self-starting military wars: "The process by which extraneous events lead to general war results either from changing estimates of the future without general war or from changing estimates of the likelihood of general war." The former is political, the latter preemptive. But he then goes on to argue that limited "political" war makes self-starting preemptive situations more likely: "Even at low levels local war will increase tensions. Both sides will become increasingly aware of the hostility between them, more aware of the possibility that all their disputes will be settled by force, and perhaps more prone to decide that general war has become so likely that it is time to strike. Finally, literal accidents of various kinds (explosion of nuclear weapons, for example) are much more likely during a period of local war, and such accidents are more likely to trigger general war during a period of tension."[14] The decision to preempt can thus be based in part on an attempt to anticipate the escalation of a small war. Indeed, self-generation, while it can be considered a separate and distinct way in which thermonuclear war might start, is closely related to the other ways. Once the decision maker feels that the avoidance of thermonuclear war is no longer open to him but the only available alternatives are striking first or striking second in an inevitable big war, the situation is drastically different from what it was before. The possibility of escalated political war can convince him that big war is likely and make him more prone to believe (in the case of a nonrational event) that it has indeed started, and that he had better strike while the striking is possible.

Preemptive war is thus most likely to begin in times of tension, when decision makers are half-expecting war anyhow; it can also start, however, without a previous high-tension level. If there is a reason to believe that the enemy is about to strike, and if there is substantial premium on going first, a preemptive situation is set up. The possibilities of this sort of preemptive war can be reduced, however, by proper rational action. Glenn Snyder points out that: "There may not be a first-strike advantage in an all-missile or predominantly missile environment if one makes four quite plausible assumptions: that the targets of a first strike would be the opponent's missile bases; that missile sites are well dispersed and hardened, or mobile; that a given number of missiles aimed at missile bases would cause less damage to the population and economy than a smaller number of retaliating missiles aimed at cities; and that the primary targets of

---

[14] Morton H. Halperin, *Arms Control and Inadvertent General War*, Institute for Defense Analyses, Special Studies Group, Study Memorandum no. 6, March 10, 1962, pp. 3, 6.

a retaliatory blow would be cities."[15] Thus, preemptive dangers can be decreased, although at the present time not all the conditions are fulfilled—and even if they were, preemption could not be ruled out completely, particularly in a tense situation.

In any case, although self-generating "military" starts to thermonuclear war, of which preemption is the major example, are intimately related to the other ways in which it might begin, the purely military aspects have tended to preoccupy many middle marginalists in recent years. Schelling writes, for example: "The premise underlying my point of view is that a main determinant of the likelihood of war is the nature of present military technology. We and the Russians are trapped by our military technology. Weapons developments of the last fifteen years . . . have enhanced the advantage, in the event war should come, of being the one to start it. They have inhumanly compressed the time available to make the most terrible decisions."[16] Indeed, if the anti-war school considers irrationality to contain the major danger of thermonuclear war and the anti-Communists consider such war to be a political phenomenon, it seems accurate to state that *the distinguishing characteristic of the middle-marginal analysis of war is that thermonuclear war may well be self-generating,* and that therefore measures designed for stabilization should in part aim for decreasing the likelihood of preemptive situations. The chances of self-generation make the problems of deterrence immensely more complex than the simple discussion above implies; the question of whether a terror weapon deters the enemy from striking or tempts him to strike in order to wipe it out provides one example of the intricacies. But if the calculus of deterrence becomes

---

[15] Glenn H. Snyder, *Deterrence and Defense* (Princeton: Princeton University Press, 1962), p. 106.

[16] Thomas C. Schelling, "Reciprocal Measures for Arms Stabilization," in *Arms Control, Disarmament, and National Security,* ed. Donald G. Brennan (New York: Braziller, 1961), p. 170.

more complicated, it must be pursued with even more diligence and sophistication.

It is at this point that the anti-war marginalists come back in and argue that the whole thing is so complicated that it gets beyond human rationality, that the residual risk of war which remains after rationality has done its damnedest is too large to be tolerable and that we must therefore aim at disarmament—the abolition of the weapons that might go off. To this the middle marginalists have three answers. The first, that human rationality can go a long way—that complicated reasoning is not impossible reasoning—and the second, that there are political values for which the residual risks are tolerable, have been discussed above. The third answer, however, is that, even though risks exist and some anti-war school criticisms may be well-taken, there may be nothing better available—that the anti-war school's solutions may actually increase the risks. As stated in one terse anonymous review of Arthur Waskow's book, *The Limits of Defense*,[17] which makes many of these anti-war marginal criticisms: "Mr. Waskow's petulant criticisms are often good [but] . . . One trouble with his book is that nobody actually holds the theories that Mr. Waskow despises—at least not in such a simple form. The last part of the book presents Mr. Waskow's constructive ideas. He . . . combines elements of arms control and disarmament by stages with, among other things, an international police force, a special armaments panel of the World Court, universal training in guerrilla warfare, and a large portion of wishful thinking."[18] In other words, he's not all wrong, but his 'ole don't look much better in this world-as-it-is as compared to the world-as-Waskow-wishes-it-to-be. And Schelling argues against the idea that disarmament is less complicated or dependent upon human rationality than is deterrence—or indeed, that they are alternatives rather than being different faces on the same coin:

17 Arthur I. Waskow, *The Limits of Defense* (Garden City: Doubleday, 1962).
18 *The New Yorker*, May 12, 1962, pp. 178–179.

If disarmament is to discourage the initiation of war and to remove the incentives toward preemptive and preventive war, it has to be *designed* to do that. Disarmament does not eliminate military potential; it changes it . . .

There should be no divorce between deterrence and disarmament. If disarmament is to work, it has to improve deterrence and to stabilize deterrence. Until a much greater community of interest exists in the world than is likely in this generation, war will have to be made unprofitable. It cannot be made impossible.[19]

Thus the middle marginalists argue that the complexities of deterrence are due to the complexities of the world, and that simple answers are useless. This is true of the short-run probabilities of war starting from one of the causes discussed above; it is also true of the long-run probabilities, the arms race. There is no unity within the middle-marginal group on the effects of the race. Some are optimistic, agreeing with Samuel Huntington that as increasing terror deters war, the arms race provides an alternative outlet: "As wars become more frightening and less frequent, arms races may become longer and less disastrous. The substitution of the one for the other is certainly no mean step forward in the restriction of violence."[20] Others agree with Kahn that: "It is most unlikely that the world can live with an uncontrolled arms race lasting for several decades. It is not that we could not match Soviet expenditures; it is simply that as technology advances and as weapons become more powerful and more diverse, it is most likely that there will have to be at least implicit agreements on their use, distribution, and character, if we are not to run unacceptably high risks of unauthorized or irresponsible behavior."[21] But even this statement diverges from the anti-war marginalists' fear of the arms race because Kahn

[19] Thomas C. Schelling, "The Role of Deterrence in Total Disarmament," *Foreign Affairs*, 40:396, 406 (April 1962).
[20] Samuel P. Huntington, "Arms Races: Prerequisites and Results," in *Public Policy*, eds. Carl J. Friedrich and Seymour E. Harris (Cambridge, Mass.: Harvard Graduate School of Public Administration, 1958), p. 83.
[21] Kahn, *On Thermonuclear War*, p. 574.

hints that implicit agreements, which are not too different in type from what has occurred in the past and continues to occur, may suffice. Further, most middle marginalists would apply to the arms race a previously cited statement of Kahn's, that the most important task is to "concentrate on the problem of avoiding disaster and buying time."[22] Even if the future looks dismal if the arms race continues, this is no reason to take measures now which will be so disastrous as to literally preclude our reaching this future.

The middle-marginal picture of rational human control over the way thermonuclear war might start is related to a similar picture of the course it might take once it has started. In contrast to the anti-war marginalists' belief that any war involving the homelands of the United States and the Soviet Union will necessarily become a holocaust in which each side tries to annihilate the population of the other, the middle marginalists believe that, in greater or lesser degree, human control can be exerted to prevent even thermonuclear war from being absolute Armageddon—that neither we nor the enemy need attempt to annihilate each other. This attempt to survive thermonuclear war may involve civil defense; it may also involve strategies for the use of thermonuclear weapons.

Middle marginalists have debated two major strategies for control of a thermonuclear war: "counterforce" and "limited retaliation."

Counterforce, the more familiar one, tries to keep thermonuclear war from being absolute by directing such a war against military targets in the Soviet Union and making at least some attempt to avoid population centers. The theory is, first, that by destroying enemy weapons, we weaken their ability to hurt us; and, second, that, prodded by our retention of an ultimate ability to retaliate against population later if necessary, the Russians will similarly avoid hitting our population centers. The total number of lives lost on both sides will be numbered in the millions rather than the hundreds of millions. According to Fryklund's analysis:

[22] *Ibid.*, p. 7.

This strategy also relies upon our long-range weapons to deter attacks on the United States and its major allies, but it would control the use of these weapons to give us the maximum chance of winning with the minimum amount of death and destruction. . . . Deterrence would be continued *during* the war . . . The cities of the enemy would be held in hostage to keep him from blasting ours . . . Blades of grass in the Soviet would remain unseared; the Main Streets of Painesvilles and the Center Cities would remain intact.[23]

If death and damage can be kept down, winning the war becomes a more meaningful concept than it would be in maximum holocaust, and the counterforce strategy has particular appeal to those who put great value weight on "prevailing" either for its own sake or for freedom's sake, although it is not limited to them.

Two basic doubts are expressed concerning the analysis of our capability to control war via a counterforce strategy. One is that by explicitly sparing Soviet cities even in a retaliatory second strike, it reduces our devastating deterrence of Soviet attack upon ourselves. Fryklund makes a reluctant and partial admission of this possibility:

The Kremlin, in weighing the pros and cons of an attack, might mark down one more pro if it were confident that our retaliation would spare Red cities.

The backers of the No-City strategy must agree that this might be true in this one deterrence situation—deterrence of a direct attack on this country.

A threat to wipe the Soviet Union from the map might make the Kremlin hesitate longer than a threat to fight back against Soviet weapons, sparing cities.[24]

He then goes on to argue, however, that our deterrence of many actions other than this calculated Soviet first strike is heightened by a counterforce strategy. The opponents of the strategy feel much more strongly about the decrease of deterrence of direct Soviet attack; some of them also oppose the

23 Fryklund, pp. 40–41.
24 *Ibid.*, p. 57.

counterforce strategy because it implies that *we* might strike first (an American first strike would most probably concentrate on Soviet weapons as targets, in order to decrease their ability to retaliate) and they oppose striking first. Perhaps an even more telling argument among middle marginalists, however, is that although control might be better than no control, it is just not within our capabilities to develop the kind of forces necessary for a counterforce strategy which could make the difference between a few million lives and a few hundred million. Kissinger contends that:

> Only on the assumption of an almost 100 per cent effective air defense can we even conceive of victory in a *defensive* all-out war. Such a defense is not now in prospect and if it came into being, we could not stake our entire strategy on it . . .
> The effort to develop such a counterforce capability would involve us in a *tour de force*. It would impose staggering force requirements on us, draining off all other military capabilities. The mere effort to develop such a force could not fail to lead to a spiralling arms race and perhaps provoke a pre-emptive attack . . . A counterforce strategy designed to win a victory *after* we concede the first blow is an illusion.
> It is conceivable that we could develop a retaliatory force capable of winning a war provided we struck first—though the technical difficulty of even this task in the age of mobile missile systems should not be underrated. But its utility as a threat in crisis situations is limited by the Soviet capability for a devastating pre-emptive blow.[25]

Kissinger's book, however, was written in 1960–1961, at a time when the prevailing belief was that, far from being able to develop such a superior counterforce, we were quite possibly at the wrong end of a missile gap. Since then, the belief has moved 180 degrees to a feeling that not only do we possess such a force, but that we have possessed it all along.[26] And the debate has thus become one over how long we can keep

[25] Kissinger, *The Necessity for Choice*, pp. 37–38. Copyright © 1960, 1961 by Henry A. Kissinger.

[26] See, for example, Senator Stuart Symington, "Where the Missile Gap Went," *The Reporter*, February 15, 1962, pp. 21–23.

it in the face of Soviet efforts to build a force which will be secure even against our counterforce attacks. Fryklund suggests that we can keep it for a long time, given annual expenditures of $5–$10 billion.[27] Others believe that if we still do have it, we are on the verge of losing it.

Faced with the possibility that a full counterforce strategy may be becoming less and less feasible, some middle marginalists have arrived at an alternative means for the controlled use of thermonuclear weapons for political means. This strategy, called "limited retaliation," envisages at least some possibility of bombing of populations in addition to military targets, but bombs them selectively, rather than in an all-out attempt at annihilation. According to Morton Kaplan, one of its originators:

> The process of employing limited retaliation might begin merely with threats. One might threaten reprisals, perhaps using an envoy to explain the policy and the reasons necessitating it, hoping this will be sufficient. If this does not work, one might then sink a ship or two of the aggressor at sea. If this does not work, perhaps an oil well or mine in his territory might be hit with conventional weapons. If this does not work, perhaps because the aggressor is not convinced that any of these measures represent a threat to use nuclear weapons, one nuclear weapon might be exploded in a largely uninhabited area.
>
> If this last measure does not work, the situation becomes grave. At this point . . . the limited reprisals might enter the city-busting phase. One might, at this time, pick out a small city of the aggressor and demand that he evacuate it prior to attack . . . If the aggressor does not enter into political negotiations now . . . the city must be destroyed.

Kaplan admits that "the very idea of limited nuclear retaliation seems bizarre; and it is,"[28] but he argues that it is no more bizarre than other nuclear strategies, and is more likely

27 Fryklund, p. 160.
28 Morton A. Kaplan, *The Strategy of Limited Retaliation*, Princeton University Center of International Studies, Policy Memorandum no. 19, April 9, 1959, two-paragraph quotation p. 14; brief quotation p. 2.

to succeed. Kissinger, however, has at least as many doubts about this as about counterforce:

Reliance on either limited strategic war or graduated retaliation would in fact confront us with an almost hopeless dilemma. In case of Communist aggression, an American President would be faced with the decision of initiating a type of conflict which could not protect the victim of the aggression and which might expose the United States to fearful devastation. This becomes clear if one imagines a Communist note to the United States . . . somewhat along the following lines: ". . . To show our good intentions we will overlook attacks you make in the first few hours after this communication. From then on, we will devastate the United States in precise proportion to your attack but no more."

But if many middle marginalists have qualms both about the lessening of deterrence which might proceed from the less-than-all-out-devastation implied by control and about the feasibility of a highly controlled use of thermonuclear war, this does not imply that they are against all attempts at control. All things being equal, if big weapons are to be used, it is certainly preferable to kill fewer people with them rather than as many people as possible. Thus almost all middle marginalists favor measures for civil defense. And Kissinger, even though he doubts the possibility of a Fryklund-type counterforce, writes: "The difficulty with the dispute is that our options are often vastly oversimplified. The choice is not between a complete counterforce capability or none at all nor between a strategy of pure devastation or a strategy which guarantees victory in all circumstances. Between these limiting conditions many other possibilities exist, each with its own implications for deterrence and for strategy should deterrence fail."[29] And in general, the concept of control as such, as compared to lack of control, is quite attractive to most middle marginalists (as indeed, it must be, put in these terms—opposing control is like favoring sin). Middle-mar-

[29] Kissinger, *The Necessity for Choice*, first quotation p. 67; second quotation p. 29. Copyright © 1960, 1961 by Henry A. Kissinger.

ginal estimates of the expected number of American casualties in a thermonuclear war thus range from Fryklund's very few million up to the anti-war marginalists' almost 180 million owing to the failure of control. Where the middle marginalists as a school differ from the anti-war group is in their belief that the highest estimate of casualties is not the necessary number, that control is worth trying and may even work. This difference of opinion runs parallel to that over the likelihood of war starting at all—some middle marginalists agree with the anti-war school that war stemming from causes beyond rationality is a substantial danger—but even they feel that it is well worth while to push rationality as far as possible.

The same can be said of the middle-marginal attitude toward "limited war." The middle marginalists do not think that they have solved all of the problems brought up by either the anti-war or anti-Communist schools, but they do think they have some ideas about how to approach the problems. As has been suggested, the middle-marginal analysis of wars not involving the American or Soviet homelands is increasingly concentrated on the problem that such wars may escalate and ultimately become "central." Much of the analysis has been covered under the discussion of thermonuclear war, but two questions are important enough to warrant further investigation. These are the use of "tactical" nuclear weapons in limited war, and the required size for "conventional" limited war forces. The questions are intimately related to each other; they are also related to the problem of escalation—how to prevent American fear of thermonuclear war from giving great political advantage to the Russians.

Middle marginalists are not united on their policy recommendations concerning the use of nuclear weapons in limited war. Halperin argues against:

There is now a tacit and informal agreement not to use nuclear weapons [in a local war].
There is a net advantage to the United States to transform this

tacit understanding into a formal agreement. A formal treaty would strengthen present practice by spelling out the risk for the decision-maker. It would increase confidence on both sides that nuclear war was neither imminent nor inevitable. This confidence could help to dampen the preemptive urge.[30]

Not many middle marginalists would agree that a formal treaty banning such local use of nuclear weapons would be advisable, but most would agree that the tacit agreement is worth maintaining under most circumstances. Not Edward Teller, however: "We must prepare psychologically. Since the devastation of Hiroshima, the American people have convinced themselves that any use of nuclear weapons constitutes all-out war. This erroneous notion must be corrected before we can begin to prepare for limited nuclear warfare. The American people, as well as free people throughout the world, must be educated to the fact that wars are divisible, that we can limit the scope of war, and that the use of nuclear weapons in a war limited by territory and purpose would not lead inevitably to a global nuclear disaster."[31] The intriguing thing about these two statements is that in spite of their clear policy disagreement, they betray a similarity of analysis on the key point in the analysis of tactical nuclear weapons. This analytical conclusion is described by Schelling:

The first conclusion to be drawn . . . is that there is a distinction between nuclear and nonnuclear weapons, a distinction relevant to the process of limiting war. It is a distinction that to some extent we can strengthen or weaken, clarify or blur . . . Which policy we should follow depends on whether we consider the distinction between nuclear and other weapons to be an asset we share with the USSR, a useful distinction, a tradition that helps to minimize violence—or instead a nuisance, a propaganda liability, a diplomatic obstruction, and an inhibition to our decisive action and delegation of authority. Those who believe

30 Morton H. Halperin, *A Proposal for a Ban on the Use of Nuclear Weapons*, Institute for Defense Analyses Special Studies Group, Study Memorandum no. 4, October 6, 1961, p. iv.
31 Edward Teller, with Allen Brown, *The Legacy of Hiroshima* (Garden City: Doubleday, 1962), p. 288.

that atomic weapons ought to be used at the earliest convenience, or whenever military expedience demands, should nevertheless recognize the distinction that exists so that we can take action to erode the distinction during the interim.[32]

And in fact, Teller has followed precisely the prescription of the last sentence. Analytically, he agrees that the distinction exists—he is out to erode it and to establish a new distinction between "limited nuclear" and "all-out" war. Some middle marginalists agree with him; most believe, together with the anti-war marginalists, that the distinction should be maintained. But all agree that the distinction as it now exists is the key to the question of the use of tactical nuclear weapons.

The problem of the size of conventional nonnuclear forces, both for the United States and for NATO, is, of course, related to the question of tactical nuclear warfare, since to some extent, small nuclear weapons are believed to be substitutable for manpower in ground warfare. In 1960, before the election of President Kennedy, there was an increasing agreement, at least among the nongovernmental members of the middle-marginal school, on two general propositions—that the United States needed more conventional ground forces, and that NATO needed more. But there was no agreement as to how much more, and in the face of some success in 1961 and 1962 both in increasing United States forces and in moving toward the NATO goal of 30 divisions, the middle-marginalist consensus has been breaking up over the question of how much further to go.

Recommendations concerning conventional forces in Europe depend not only upon the analysis of war, but also on analyses of Soviet intentions in Europe and of our relationships with our European allies. Nonetheless, two relevant analytical questions under the current subheading are debated by middle marginalists. One concerns the military capabilities of different-size NATO forces; the other the economic and other feasibility of obtaining these forces. On the

---

[32] Schelling, *The Strategy of Conflict*, pp. 263–264.

capabilities question, Alastair Buchan, a Briton, put forth in 1960 the classical "pause" argument for a 30-division NATO force (rather than the 22 then available): "Its real function is to contain a Soviet attack with conventional weapons on Western Europe, springing, perhaps, from the miscalculation of a local commander in a tense situation—such as that created by the East German uprising of 1953—in order to give both sides the necessary hours or days to reach a considered political decision on whether they will turn aside to the conference table or progress to total war and the partial obliteration of the Northern Hemisphere."[33] Other middle marginalists now feel that not many more than 30 first-line divisions are necessary to hold a Soviet attack for a much longer period of time. But Kissinger, although preferring 30 divisions to fewer, doubts whether the 30 solve very many problems. He argues that the purpose of increasing the number of divisions is ". . . to strengthen the shield forces and ready reserves so that they could hold, not for 30 days, but for long enough for the West's superior potential to make itself felt. The objective of the conventional forces would be to achieve a local stalemate equivalent to the stalemate in strategic forces which made the buildup necessary . . . If this option is chosen, the goal of 30 divisions will have to be substantially increased."[34] Some analysts carry the argument even further, suggesting that a conventional-force build-up to 30 divisions is harmful because, although it is insufficient to hold the Russians for a long enough period of time, it is sufficient to convince them that we are going to try to hold them conventionally rather than using nuclear weapons. And, once again, through the dilemma of deterrence, such a build-up might thus actually encourage Soviet attack. This is a rather common view among European middle marginalists.

The second limitation in increases in conventional forces is one which cuts across all strategy, but is most relevant here.

33 Alastair Buchan, *NATO in the 1960's* (New York: Praeger, 1960), p. 96.
34 Henry A. Kissinger, "The Unsolved Problems of European Defense," *Foreign Affairs*, 40:524-525 (July 1962).

It is that of cost—mainly financial, but also in terms of manpower, etc. A study of the logical basis of arms-policy disputes in the middle 1950's would have had to divide its schools of thought according to cost as well as other considerations, or would perhaps have had to create an additional "low-cost" school. Through most of the Eisenhower administration, particularly from the "New Look" of 1954 through the severe economies of Defense Secretary Wilson in the summer of 1957, cost considerations dominated strategy. The belief that the Russians were out to bankrupt us was adhered to by the President himself and by Treasury Secretary Humphrey in particular. With the shock of the Soviet sputnik, the cost limitations on strategy began to recede, and by the 1960 election, Vice President Nixon, as well as Senator Kennedy and Governor Rockefeller were all committed to increases in the defense budget. In 1963 Congress shows very little disposition to cut defense costs, in spite of former President Eisenhower's continued adherence to his belief, and the idea that the real Communist target is our domestic economy is almost the exclusive possession of a small group somewhere to the "right" of the anti-war systemists.

None of this implies, of course, that costs no longer constrain arms policy. They do, but for the most part the constraints are not so strong as to have the sort of primary effect on the choice of alternative strategic postures that they did when the "New Look" deliberately set out to get "more bang for a buck" by substituting a nuclear strategy for a conventional one. The one issue, however, on which such constraints still play a crucial rôle in such decisions is the question of the size of the nonnuclear forces needed by NATO—and the constraints are not only those of the United States, but are imposed by all of the members of the alliance. As Buchan wrote, at a time when he almost despaired of even the 30 divisions: "What is required is an intellectual appreciation of the problems and dangers of the next decade, and intellectual appreciations are notoriously hard to sell to Treasuries or Parliaments . . . Even if it were politically possible, the effects of a general increase in defense expenditure of the order of, say, 15% on internal price and wage structures might be very unfortunate."[35] There are those who feel we should try, but as a matter of analysis, the most common middle-marginal picture of conventional forces does not envisage much more than 30 NATO divisions, nor, for that matter, a United States Army of much more than 1,000,000 men.

Finally, the middle-marginal picture of "unconventional" war is underdeveloped in much the same way that the anti-Communist picture of conventional war is underdeveloped, if for different reasons. It is not that the middle-marginalists are not interested in unconventional war; almost the first military move made by President Kennedy was to give increased size and status to the Army's special-warfare troops. Nor is it that the middle has been paying no attention to this sort of warfare; the literature is proliferating.[36] But there is no distinct middle-marginal viewpoint or contribution toward guerrilla and other unconventional strife. As is suggested below in the discussion of the middle-marginal analysis of power, the attempt to synthesize the anti-war view of power-as-conquest-of-the-minds-of-men and the anti-Communist view of power-as-force, has not yet come to fruition. Further, the fact that much more than the other schools, the middle-marginalists concentrate their military analysis on Europe where, Bjelajac to the contrary notwithstanding, most of them feel warfare will remain conventional, has tended to leave few analytical resources available until recently for the study of unconventional warfare.

The middle-marginal analysis of war, then, is the most complex of the three marginal schools. Because it is primarily concerned with deterrence and deterrence is a very intricate subject, it is of necessity a detailed analysis. Compared to the

[35] Buchan, p. 33.

[36] See, for example, "Unconventional Warfare," in the May 1962 issue of *The Annals of the American Academy of Political and Social Science*, which contains some articles by marginal anti-Communists, but also a number by various middle marginalists.

analyses of the other two groups, it resembles more than anything else the anti-Communist picture of war as focused through the anti-war set of values. Middle-marginal arms-policy analysis, like that of the anti-war marginalists and unlike that of anti-Communists, focuses on war rather than the opponent; on thermonuclear war rather than the lesser varieties; on avoiding such war, rather than using it as a political instrument. The orientation is not exactly the same as that of the anti-war school; it is pushed in the anti-war direction by the "analytical" middle marginalists, but pulled away by the "balanced-value" wing. But it resembles that of anti-war marginalism more than anti-Communist. Having said this, however—given this focus and the "distortions" it causes—the detailed analysis itself is much more like that of the anti-Communists. According to both schools, humans are rational animals, able to control even irrationality. They use weapons for purposes which, although they may cumulate through self-generation processes like preemption, are initially political. In the real world as it is, war is avoided by the sophisticated possession and deployment of weapons, including nuclear weapons, rather than by their abandonment and avoidance. Such sophistication can not only avoid the worst kinds of war while maintaining our political objectives, but it can even control the conduct of war and prevent it from becoming the inevitable holocaust feared by the anti-war school. Conflict is the way of a world containing the United States and the Soviet Union.

ANALYSIS OF THE OPPONENT

If the middle-marginal analysis of war resembles a differently proportioned version of that provided by the anti-Communists, the two schools' pictures of the Soviet Union are similar in both focus and general outline but differ somewhat in detail. Both groups picture Communism as expansionistic; both argue that the Soviet Union makes use of its military power, but uses it in a subtle political manner;

both agree (as do the anti-war marginalists) that the Russians are afraid of nuclear war. Differences do exist. The middle substitutes a picture of aggressive Soviet opportunism for the anti-Communist sketch of constant hard-eyed malevolence, and this has important policy implications. Further, the policy conclusions drawn from the belief that the Soviets fear big war are quite different from those of the anti-Communists. The middle has some hope that this Russian attitude will allow ultimate stabilization on this portion of the arms race (though little hope for the general *détente* looked for by the anti-war school), whereas the anti-Communists want to use Soviet fears against them; but this is more a question of aims than analysis of what is possible—either may be possible. There are also some important divergencies on such matters as the geographical emphasis in Soviet strategy, the role of China, and the analysis of the Soviet satellites. But the general picture of the Communists using military weapons in a political way is much the same for both the middle and the anti-Communist marginalists.

The basic middle-marginal view of the Soviet Union, then, is of a nation and system which, in a careful way, is out to dominate the world. The Russians may be changing over the long run, but the evidence of short-run change is much too meager for us to drop our guard. Much basic middle-marginal expertise is summarized in a report prepared for the Senate Foreign Relations Committee by a Columbia-Harvard research group, two excerpts from which give the flavor of the analysis of Soviet motivations and limitations, as they relate to the policies required from us:

Much as we, as individuals, may dislike the Soviet system, the proper point of concern of our national policy is not with the internal organization of the Soviet Union but with Soviet behavior in the world. It is the Soviet commitment to the inevitable transformation of all other states to the Soviet system, by whatever means, that is the essential cause of ineradicable conflict. If this commitment were to change with time, the fundamental conflict would be eased, or at least it would no longer have its present unlimited character.

It is true that Soviet totalitarianism is a factor in Soviet foreign policy . . .
Whether time will have an effect upon Soviet totalitarianism is conjectural, as will be more fully discussed in Chapter 4, but in any case, it is the question of the unlimited expansionism of Soviet policy which is the point to which we must direct our concern.

But can this struggle be waged on some plane other than war? This is what Mr. Khrushchev is asking. It seems reasonable to believe that the Soviet leaders do now have a serious realization of the destructiveness of nuclear weapons, that they would genuinely prefer to achieve their objectives without total war, and are confident that they can do so. It is less certain what the response of the Soviet leaders would be if their choice were between total war and a decisive loss of important objectives. Our past experience with Soviet policy does not encourage the belief that the Soviet Union has given up for all time the use of force or the threat of force as an instrument of policy.

And the Chapter 4 analysis of the effect of time alluded to is summarized succinctly in the final paragraph of the chapter:

In short, while we must be constantly prepared to reassess the evidence of change in the Soviet situation, or to take into account the effect of forces and processes at work in Soviet politics and society which may not now be apparent to us, the weight of present evidence would seem to be against the likelihood that evolutionary changes can be expected to moderate Soviet foreign policy objectives in any short-term projection. In the foreseeable future as well, it appears more probable that a modification of Soviet foreign policy will result from persistent failure abroad than from changes in Soviet society.[37]

The impact of this is much the same as that of the anti-Communist analysis of the Soviet Union, but the differences between the two do exist and do go beyond the differences between understatement and overstatement. The middle school has some hope for the long run: although it claims no basis for optimistic prognostications, it is willing to hold the

[37] United States Senate Committee on Foreign Relations, *U.S.S.R. and Eastern Europe,* A Study by a Columbia-Harvard Research Group (Washington: U.S. Government Printing Office, 1960), pp. 16–17, 44.

future open. Further, and perhaps more important, middle marginalists have some hope for useful if not fundamental changes in Soviet policy in the short run. Marshall Shulman, the Director of Research for the project which produced the report to the Senate, writes of the Soviet attitude toward the sort of arms-control steps aimed at current stabilization rather than general and complete disarmament: "At the present time, the Soviet response to such middle-range measures of arms control and arms reduction is negative: any form of 'control' is regarded by the Soviet Union as simply a device by which we hope to gain relative advantages. But whether the Soviet leaders recognize it or not, they have a self-interest in exploring with us this middle-range of safeguards, and we must do what we can to bring them to an awareness of this fact."[38] This is still a long distance from the anti-war marginalists' belief that the Russians will soon recognize their own interest in *détente*, but it carries with it more hope than the anti-Communist attitude that the Soviets are interested in arms talks *only* to exploit them for political purposes.

This concept of Soviet expansionism, however, is a general one. More specifically germane to arms policy is the role of military power in this drive. And here, the middle-marginal Sovietologists again agree with the anti-Communists. Both believe that military power is an important, even essential, component of Russian maneuvers, but both stress that military force is important primarily for its political impact. Military strength is used more subtly, politically and psychologically, than is implied by the traditional picture of armed aggression. According to the Senate Report:

It is not that the Soviet leaders will automatically attack the moment they feel they have attained a clear military superiority in the various significant categories of military strength. Indeed, this seems improbable unless other factors intervene. What is more likely is that an imbalance of military power in favor of the

[38] Marshall D. Shulman, "Russia's Gambit on Disarmament," *The New York Times Magazine*, March 11, 1962, p. 108.

Soviet Union will have . . . serious political and diplomatic consequences. If a man who lives in Berlin, for example, comes to believe that the West does not have the will or the capability of coming to his defense, he does not need to wait for the Communist forces to move before he decides where the better part of valor lies. In a large measure, confidence is the essential though intangible binding force of the non-Communist world—confidence mainly that the United States can and will support resistance to aggression.[39]

This analysis by no means implies that the purely military aspects of deterrence are irrelevant—neither United States deterrence of direct Soviet attack on ourselves, nor deterrence of lesser Russian actions—but it does carry with it the idea that deterrence is at least as complicated on the political level as on the military. Raymond Garthoff puts even more explicitly both the relevance and the irrelevance of deterrence. He agrees with the general middle-marginal idea of a Soviet calculus of risks in which our deterrent policy plays a vital part, but believes that nuclear weapons enter this calculus in a much less precise way than is sometimes assumed:

. . . in Soviet policy-making, questions of war and peace, and of the role of military strategy, are decided essentially on the basis of calculations of relative power and of relative risk.

Mutual deterrence has resulted from the acquisition of global thermonuclear striking power by the United States, and more recently by the Soviet Union as well. Mutual deterrence has been described as a "delicate balance of terror." While this balance is indeed insecure and by no means inevitably enduring, it is not fragile. The risks and consequences of a global thermonuclear holocaust are recognized by the Soviet leaders, and they strive to avoid any "adventurist" gamble. The importance in Soviet policy of the overall balance of power, the "relation of forces in the world arena," militates against a preoccupation with purely military solutions. Soviet leaders are not poised to unleash their —and our—military power as soon as the theoretical probability of military victory crosses some calibrated balance of 50 percent or 70 percent or indeed perhaps even 90 percent. In the Com-

39 *U.S.S.R. and Eastern Europe*, p. 22.

munist view, history cannot be made hostage to the mathematical probability computations of some "communivac."

Thus total nuclear war—though not necessarily other, limited, forms of war—seems ever less likely as a rational tool for the Soviet Union to advance its position. Assuming that we maintain our strategic nuclear deterrent capability, this may then be taken as a prediction that a Soviet "Pearl Harbor" attack is not likely in the foreseeable future, although by no means can we rest *assured* by this prediction.[40]

Garthoff's interpretation of Soviet unwillingness to risk nuclear war is rather similar to those of both the anti-Communist and anti-war marginalists. The Sovietologists of all three schools agree that the Russians do not now consider nuclear weapons to be a basic currency of conflict, except perhaps in a very subtle political way, through exploitation of other nations' similar fears. The values and the other relevant analyses of the three schools lead them to disagree on whether we should exploit the Soviet attitude for purposes of deterrence, *détente,* or defeat of Communism, but the specific consensus on analysis of the Soviet attitude toward nuclear warfare exists.

This analysis, however, although it is shared by middle-marginal Sovietologists as well as those in other schools, is not in complete agreement with the picture of the Soviet Union implied by some of the middle-marginal strategic analysis of war and deterrence. Although any specific interpretation of Soviet attitudes is left largely implicit in much of the strategic analysis, the implication in a good deal of it is that the Soviet Union makes each military decision, including those involving nuclear action, by a calculus which carefully weighs the advantages and disadvantages of such action. And if this is the case, it follows that our side can leave no gaps in deterrence—we must insure that the disadvantages *always* outweigh the advantages for any action we do not want them to take. As Kahn writes, "Insofar as the international politi-

---

[40] Raymond L. Garthoff, *The Soviet Image of Future War* (Washington: Public Affairs Press, 1959), pp. 7–8.

cal situation involves opposition against a living, thinking enemy, if you leave yourself open to any particular form of attack you encourage that form."[41] And the point of Kahn's work, like that of many middle marginalists, is that this stricture specifically includes nuclear attack.

But if the Garthoff view is correct—if the Soviets would be unwilling to take even a 10 percent chance of defeat, then what may appear to us to be a gap in deterrence might still involve too much risk for them to exploit it. This does not imply to the middle-marginal Sovietologists that we can thus do away with deterrence—Garthoff is quite specific about that—but it does have two implications for the middle marginal analysis of war. The first, that all the complicated ins and outs of deterrence analysis, particularly in its bizarre forms, are lost on the Russians, who are deterred by a simple reasonably credible threat to deliver nuclear weapons, tends in the direction of the anti-war marginalists. The second implication, that it may be possible to use nuclear threats to deter nonnuclear Soviet actions, with a high probability of success and only a small chance of nuclear war actually ensuing, leans toward the anti-Communists. Neither of these implications is in opposition to a solid front of middle-marginal analysts of war; both can be readily assimilated into *some* of the middle-marginal war analyses discussed above. But the view implied by some other middle-marginal war analyses, that the Soviet Union is an aggressor on the style of Nazi Germany, contemplating the direct use of all the force at its command in order to gain its objectives, is specifically denied by middle-marginal Sovietologists. They see Russia as a master manipulator of military power for political ends, firing as few shots as possible, and this can have important implications for middle-marginal policy recommendations.

In any case, the middle-marginal Sovietologists believe that Russia is still both expansionistic and militaristic, but cautious, certainly in relation to nuclear weapons, but perhaps ultimately more generally. What is the geography of the

[41] Kahn, *On Thermonuclear War,* p. 643.

Soviet drive? Here the middle-marginal answer differs somewhat from those of both the other schools. If the anti-war
marginalists imply that the current Soviet drive, if not their
ultimate objective, is in the underdeveloped world, and the
anti-Communists feel that the particular arena chosen by the
Communists is a changeable tactical question, the middle is
quite clear that West Europe remains at the center of the
stage as objective and arena, currently and over the long run.
The belief is clearest in the statements of middle marginalists
about the part of the world in which *our* chief interests lie,
but it also appears in analysis of Soviet strategy. Herbert
Dinerstein, for example, writes of Soviet goals and tactics:

But the principal target of the Soviet offensive has been
NATO, not because the alliance is the easiest prey, but because,
next to the United States itself, it represents the most valuable
prize in the global struggle. Western Europe is of overriding
importance to the Soviet Union because of its economic and
political strength and its military potential. The surest way for
the Soviet Union to capture the economic resources of Western
Europe and to keep its military potential from being fulfilled
would be its communization, but this seems to be out of the
question in the foreseeable future. More promising is a strategy
aimed at reducing the commitments of various countries to
NATO and pushing them toward neutralism.
. . . The communization of Western Europe, even if it were
feasible, is probably not the most prudent way for Moscow to
pursue the aim of dominating Europe. On the contrary, the
communization of one West European country might well stiffen
the resistance of its neighbors; moreover with such an aggressive
policy in Western Europe the danger of nuclear war could not
be excluded.
Consequently the Soviet Union might be content to see the
emergence of a less-than-communist Europe—a Europe composed
of countries on the pattern of Finland, Austria, and Sweden.[42]

This reasoning is similar in its analysis *of* Europe, if not its
emphasis *on* Europe, to that of the anti-Communist margin-

[42] Herbert S. Dinerstein, "Soviet Goals and Military Force," *Orbis*, 5:427–
428 (Winter 1962).

alists. Because of these possible splitting effects on Western Europe, many middle-marginal Sovietologists oppose neutral-belt and disengagement solutions like those pushed by the anti-war school, although, as shown below, some in the middle school are interested over the long run in a neutral belt, primarily for its effects on *Eastern* Europe.

At any rate, the idea of the Soviet *political* drive in Europe is generally accepted among middle-marginal analysts of the Soviet Union. Shulman uses a similar argument to cast doubt on the long-run implications of the anti-war marginalist thesis that Soviet European aims are primarily consolidation-ist in nature: "A stabilization obtained by agreement on territorial interests—as for example in Berlin—can be expected to be effective only for limited periods while the Soviet Union is consolidating recent gains. Khrushchev has explicitly described for us his conception of a status quo agreement. He sees it, in effect, as a movable partition which would be successively adjusted to accommodate the inevitable process of change."[43]

The emphasis on Soviet European strategy, however, does not imply a middle-marginal belief that the Russians are not interested at all in the underdeveloped areas. Soviet strategy there, like that in Europe, is subtler than immediate outright Communization, although that is the ultimate goal. According to the Senate report:

The essential point is that the short-run policy of the Soviet Union in the Middle East, as elsewhere in Asia and Africa, is a policy of denial. The central purpose for the moment is to achieve the denial of the geographical positions, raw materials and markets of these areas to the Western industrial nations. It is not, for the present, a question of expansionism in the sense of seeking to acquire these territories, nor of the revolutionary transformation of these countries into "socialist" states. In the short-term perspective, the crippling effect upon the advanced industrial nations is a more decisive strategic factor than would be the

[43] Marshall D. Shulman, "The Real Nature of the Soviet Challenge," *The New York Times Magazine,* July 16, 1961, p. 42.

acquisition of additional underdeveloped populations by the Soviet sphere . . .

The next stage, belonging to a longer-term perspective, involves bringing to power in the underdeveloped countries indigenous forces oriented on the Soviet Union, and moving these countries toward membership in the Soviet sphere.[44]

This does not mean to the authors that the United States should oppose either nationalist revolutions or neutralist nations—merely that when these nations participate in this "policy of denial," then they have gone beyond nationalism and neutralism, although by no means all the way to Communism. The analysis, in fact, is not too different from those either of the anti-war or the anti-Communist marginalists. There is disagreement with both about the relative priorities of this Communist drive as against the one in Europe, and there is disagreement particularly with the anti-war school about whether this struggle in the underdeveloped areas is with thoughts, with guns, or with both. But the idea of the two-step revolution in Asia, Africa, and Latin America, is common to all of the marginal schools.

If the middle marginalists are close to the marginal anti-Communists on analyzing Russian tactics in Western Europe and not far from either school on Soviet policy in the underdeveloped areas, at least some middle Sovietologists seem closer to the anti-war marginalists in their analysis of the Soviet satellites in *Eastern* Europe. There is general agreement among the middle-marginalist students of the Communist bloc that, as put by Zbigniew Brzezinski: "The changes that have taken place and are continuing to take place, within the Communist world, have important policy implications for the West. In analyzing these changes, we should abandon the tendency to operate in simple and extreme terms. The bloc is not splitting and is not likely to split."[45] But beyond this, there appears to be a range of opinion. Writing with William Griffith, Brzezinski's analysis

[44] *U.S.S.R. and Eastern Europe*, pp. 14–15.
[45] Zbigniew Brzezinski, "The Challenge of Change in the Soviet Bloc," *Foreign Affairs*, 39:437 (April 1961).

appears not far from that of Kennan, although the ultimate policy recommendations are somewhat different in that Brzezinski and Griffith are not particularly interested in military disengagement:

In this situation it would seem that the United States should adopt a policy of what might be called peaceful engagement in Eastern Europe. This policy should: (1) aim at stimulating further diversity in the Communist bloc; (2) thus increasing the likelihood that the East European states can achieve a greater measure of political independence from Soviet domination; (3) thereby ultimately leading to the creation of a neutral belt of states which, like the Finnish, would enjoy genuine popular freedom of choice in internal policy while not being hostile to the Soviet Union and not belonging to Western Military alliances.[46]

This seems in opposition to Dinerstein's point that Finland is the Soviet ideal, but Dinerstein is talking about a Soviet goal for currently Western countries, where as Brzezinski and Griffith's Finnish model is for currently Eastern ones. But neither does the Brzezinski-Griffith paragraph seem to fit well with the argument in the Senate report that:

If we accept the improbability that the Russians can now be persuaded to undo their expansion into Eastern Europe by any argument or price that is open to us, and if we recognize that there does not now appear to be an overlapping of interest in some alternative arrangement for Central Europe, we may conclude that the most favorable opportunity for improving the situation will be found in concentrating our energies upon strengthening the economic and political vitality of Western Europe, in close association between the United States, Europe, and the underdeveloped nations of the non-Communist world, and in insuring the continued integrity of NATO. If unreasonable expectations of breaking the deadlock in Europe by some formula or phrase were to distract us from this course of action, Soviet tactics would have succeeded in one of its central purposes.[47]

46 Zbigniew Brzezinski and William E. Griffith, "Peaceful Engagement in Eastern Europe," *Foreign Affairs*, 39:644 (July 1961).
47 *U.S.S.R. and Eastern Europe*, p. 85.

Brzezinski participated in the writing of the Senate report too, and the differences may be partially based on changes between the December, 1959, submission of the report to the Senate and the July, 1961, publication of the Brzezinski-Griffith article, and partially based on the focus of the optimistic article on the long run and the pessimistic Senate document on the short. Nonetheless, some difference of emphasis does seem to remain. The Senate report almost excludes any explicit consideration of the effects in Eastern Europe as a criterion for American policy, and there thus does appear at least some range of middle marginal opinion on the question. What is also significant, however, is that the entire range is quite different from the anti-Communist focus on this issue, which emphasizes clandestine Western subversion of satellite regimes.

This coupling of a strong belief that the bloc is in fact no longer monolithic with an agnosticism about the implications of the split also characterizes the middle-marginal analysis of Sino-Soviet relations. Donald Zagoria describes the school of analysis in which he includes himself:

It contends that while there are serious differences of interest and outlook between Russia and China, the overriding common aims of both, their joint commitment to an international revolutionary process which they believe is historically inevitable and which they believe it is their duty to aid, their shared determination to establish Communism throughout the world, sets limits on the conflict between the two. The outermost limit, most within this group argue, is a break-up of the Sino-Soviet alliance; conflict and competition between the partners to the alliance will continue and may even lead to a radical deterioration of relations, the argument follows, but this will proceed within a self-limiting framework of basic struggle against the West.[48]

As for China itself, the middle-marginal analysts agree with Allen Whiting that while it is "a major opponent of United States policy," the Chinese regime is not as suicidally fanati-

[48] Donald S. Zagoria, *The Sino-Soviet Conflict: 1956–1961* (Princeton: Princeton University Press, 1962), p. 4.

cal as sometimes is pictured (by itself, as well as others), but "is a rational, calculating regime, pursuing ends and adopting means within a clearly defined framework embracing both Chinese and Communist components."[49] And as for the anti-war marginalists' concern that China must be included in disarmament arrangements, the middle-marginal picture of China adds to the implication of deterrence analysis that there are no easy answers in this field. As put by Doak Barnett: "At present the existing tensions and conflicts of interest in East Asia are so fundamental that one can question whether there is any immediate prospect of discovering successful approaches to the basic problem of arms control in that area. And if, as seems to be the case, even a 'first step' on the international arms control problem, such as a nuclear test ban, must be dealt with on a worldwide basis to be effective, this fact poses some far-reaching dilemmas."[50]

Thus China as a problem by itself as well as China as a member of the bloc, provides some new and difficult problems for American policy. Perhaps the best way to summarize the middle-marginalist analysis of the opponent in all of its Sino-Soviet-Eastern European complexity, is to quote one more paragraph from Brzezinski which provides a middle-marginal answer to those anti-war marginalists who feel that withal, it is incumbent upon us to encourage the "peaceful" elements in the Kremlin and the bloc:

. . . it would be hazardous to make concessions to Khrushchev on the assumption that he is to be preferred to other, possibly more militant Communist leaders. The paradox of the present situation is that concessions to Khrushchev weaken his argument with Mao by seemingly proving Mao's proposition that the West will yield if pushed hard enough. If the West had not been firm with Khrushchev in the past, it would have weakened his argu-

49 Allen S. Whiting, "Communist China," in *The Liberal Papers*, ed. James Roosevelt (Garden City: Doubleday, 1962), p. 302. Copyright © 1962 by James Roosevelt.

50 A. Doak Barnett, "The Inclusion of Communist China in an Arms Control Program," in *Arms Control, Disarmament, and National Security*, p. 302.

ments and would have provided him with no impetus for risking an open break with the more militant Communists. As long as we remain credibly committed to fighting the Soviet Union whenever the Soviet Union attacks our vital interests, we give the Soviet leaders the survival-inducement to take chances even with Communist unity. The Soviet leadership would prefer to have both Communist unity and peaceful victories. Our policy of firmness forces it to choose between the two, and, indeed, it may result in denying both objectives to it. Accordingly, it is essential that firmness, and a willingness to take even a high degree of risk, should continue to characterize Western policy.[51]

The belief that by firmness and even "a high degree of risk" we can push the Communists toward peace is the basis of the middle-marginal analysis which rejects immediate appeasement even though weighting short-run time preferences more heavily than long-run. It is thus similar to the other paradoxes of middle-marginal analysis. Applied to the analysis of war, these paradoxes produce deterrence. Applied to the analysis of the opponent, they oppose the Communist world as a whole even though rejecting the picture of the single, grim monolithic entity. The middle-marginal Sovietologists picture world Communism as a movement with a complex political structure internally and a subtle political policy externally. Arms policy is relevant in opposing them, but its use cannot be simple.

ANALYSIS OF POWER

The middle marginalists share the beliefs of both of the other marginal schools on what power in the world is. If the anti-war marginalists think of power to a great extent in the noncoercive terms of convincing other nations to agree with us, and the anti-Communists tend to think of power as being the capability (and the will to use the capability) to make others do our bidding whether they like it or not, the middle

51 Zbigniew Brzezinski, "A Policy of Peaceful Engagement," *The New Republic*, March 26, 1962, p. 14.

wants to use both the carrot and the stick. Ernest Lefever, who has been quoted as an example of middle-marginal belief that power-as-a-value must derive whatever importance it has from other higher-order values, both defines and points out the complexity of power-as-a-tool:

The power of a nation is its total capacity to achieve certain desired objectives. This capacity is determined by a variety of interrelated moral and material factors. The moral ingredients of national power include the fundamental values, beliefs, habits, and attitudes which make up the national character of a people. The concepts of justice and freedom which are cherished and practiced, the habits of democracy and fair play, and the attitudes toward the rights and welfare of peoples beyond our borders are elements of the American character which vitally affect our power and influence in the world . . .
Among the material factors which determine national power are the size and vocational diversity of the population, industrial potential, the general level of economic activity, the number of students pursing technical or scientific education in college, the size and location of the nation's territories, and, of course, the state of military preparedness.[52]

This includes some of both the anti-war and the anti-Communist concepts of what power consists of. Two ideas important to the anti-Communists are excluded from Lefever's book (although not necessarily from all middle-marginal analysis of power)—the concept of "will-power" does not appear, and of an American effort to "sell" ourselves to the world, Lefever writes: "The . . . proposals for launching a global psychological and ideological crusade have never been accepted by the State Department, the Congress, or the general public. This is a tribute to the good sense of the American people and their leaders."[53]

But outside of these ingredients, Lefever includes under power almost all the factors suggested by any of the other

[52] Ernest Lefever, *Ethics and United States Foreign Policy*, pp. 6–7. Copyright © 1957 by The World Publishing Company.
[53] *Ibid.*, p. 158.

schools. The difficulty with such a collection of elements, however, is that it is close to impossible to compound into a single guide to action—into an analysis of power-as-a-tool which will give guidelines as to how to choose when the moral and the physical components of power clash. Lefever has tried, but very few other middle marginalists have, and for that reason the analysis of power underlying most middle-marginal arms recommendations is *ad hoc,* rather than referring back to a relatively coherent body of thought as is done explicitly or implicitly by the marginal anti-war and anti-Communist schools.

And as a result of this, there is more of a tendency among middle-marginalists to base arms-policy recommendations almost entirely on military power-as-coercion than might be indicated by statements like Lefever's. Pure deterrence analysis makes its determinations solely by the calculus of national advantage and disadvantage. Although contrary to some anti-war marginal accusations, the deterrence calculus does not assume absolute enmity between the United States and the Soviet Union—it depends heavily on mutual recognition of common interests as well as conflicting ones—it does not include the noncoercive sort of power which might accrue from such things as international appreciation for our adherence to the "concepts of justice and freedom," or the "habits of democracy and fair play," mentioned by Lefever. Middle-marginal arms recommendations are seldom made on the basis of deterrence alone, but there is some tendency in this direction because the analysis is available and tangible, and to the extent power-as-coercion is emphasized for these reasons, the *ad hoc* analysis behind recommendations moves away from Lefever. Thus for many middle-marginalists, the implicit analysis of power becomes similar to that made explicit by the anti-Communists—power is force and toughness.

Indeed, some middle-marginal analysis of power goes even beyond the anti-Communists in dependence on force; the anti-Communists, after all, are the most political of the schools. Examples of this middle attitude can again be taken from their positions on United States policy toward Cuba.

The anti-war marginalists blamed the failure of the 1961 Bay of Pigs invasion on a lack of understanding of the political forces at work in Cuba and a consequent overmilitarization of the effort to overthrow Castro; the anti-Communists blamed it on a lack of understanding of the fundamental war with Communism, and only secondarily on military failure. A typical middle-marginal analysis, however, was that of Charles Murphy, who wrote:

If the United States military are without a peer in any one technique of warfare, it is in putting forces ashore across a hostile beach. For the Bay of Pigs, all the necessary means were at Kennedy's hand . . . But after the strategists at the White House and State had finished plucking it apart, it became an operation which would have disgraced even the Albanians. When Kennedy looked around for the blunderer, he found him everywhere, and nowhere . . . Only after the disaster was upon them did he and his men realize that the venture which was essentially a military one had been fatally compromised in order to satisfy political considerations.[54]

This goes beyond the anti-Communists in putting the blame entirely upon a failure to carry through militarily. Murphy's discounting of the importance of "political considerations" is an example of a strong tendency in middle-marginal analysis of power. This leaning toward the tangibility of power in its military forms is perhaps even better illustrated by the middle-marginal attitude toward Cuba before, during, and after the 1962 crisis over the Soviet missiles. Before the presentation of clear evidence that Soviet "offensive weapons" were being sited on the island, middle marginalists had no clear view about what to do about either Castro or the Soviet buildup of "defensive" weapons in Cuba; indeed, there was some tendency to sweep the problem under the rug and to feel that the most important thing was not to allow Cuba to distract us from the real problem in Berlin. This was consistent with the middle-marginal evaluation which puts the defense of Europe far above all other con-

54 Charles J. V. Murphy, "Cuba: The Record Set Straight," *Fortune*, September 1961, p. 96.

siderations. With the coming of the knowledge of the presence of the Soviet ballistic missiles in Cuba, however, there also came a feeling of intellectual relief among middle marginalists. This was a truly military question, and a rather narrowly strategic one at that. Questions of this nature had been studied, the available set of alternatives was well understood, and the proper one could be selected. And finally, with our seeming success in getting rid of the missiles, the question of Cuba and Castro returned in middle-marginal analysis to the category of an imprecise one, in which it was very difficult to find the proper mixture of military and other forms of power.

Because of the lack of a full-blown analysis of power which synthesizes both military and moral factors, and because of the consequent *ad hoc* nature of the application of power analysis to arms recommendations, the particular balance between tangible and intangible factors differs from recommendation to recommendation and from recommender to recommender. Thus, in relation to the "world opinion" which is dear to many anti-war marginalists and is decried by anti-Communists, Senator Henry Jackson (Democrat, Washington) takes a point of view which is at the same time both agnostic and negative: "The concept of world opinion has been, I fear, much abused. Whatever it is and whatever the importance that should be attached to it, I doubt that it can be measured by taking the temperature of the General Assembly or successfully cultivated primarily by currying favor in New York. To hide behind something called 'world opinion' is all too often the device of the timid, or the last resort of someone who has run out of arguments."[55] Most middle marginalists would agree with the indefinite nature of the importance of world opinion; some, however, would disagree with the negative implication of the last sentence. Similarly, when Kahn writes, in discussing the history of the 1930's, that, "by 1936 anybody who was making strategic calculations as opposed to applying (nonexistent) universal

[55] Henry M. Jackson in the symposium, "Do We Rely Too Much on the U.N.?" *The New York Times Magazine,* April 1, 1962, p. 110.

principles of justice and law ran some danger of being considered a warmonger,"[56] most middle marginalists would agree in decrying the ignoring of coercive power, but on the question of what proportion of "universal principles" *should* enter into our policy there would be less agreement. Both on the particular balance they give to their own values and on their *ad hoc* analysis of how important adherence to principle is to United States power in the world, middle marginalists would disagree.

ANALYSIS OF ALLIES AND NEUTRALS

A good deal of the difficulty middle marginalists have in assessing the weight which should be given to the noncoercive components of power lies in the fact that they doubt that the basic ideology of the United States is close enough to that of much of the world for us to lead them through our adherence to a moral code. Senator J. William Fulbright (Democrat, Arkansas) argues that:

History has demonstrated many times that concerts of nations based solely on the negative spur of common danger are unlikely to survive when the external danger ceases to be dramatically urgent. Only when a concert of nations rests on the positive foundations of shared goals and values is it likely to form a viable instrument of long-range policy . . .

A realistic "concert of free nations" might be expected to consist of an "inner community" of the North Atlantic nations and an "outer community" embracing much or all of the non-Communist world.[57]

And it is difficult to overemphasize the importance put on Europe by most middle marginalists. This manifests itself in nonmilitary matters in such things as Fulbright's concert and the strong pressure by the United States for Europe to unite economically under the Common market. It also mani-

[56] Kahn, *On Thermonuclear War*, p. 395.
[57] J. W. Fulbright, "For A Concert of Free Nations," *Foreign Affairs*, 40:15–17 (October 1961).

fests itself in military affairs. The North Atlantic Treaty Organization is, next to our own strategic capability to oppose the Soviet Union in intercontinental warfare, the essential ingredient of middle-marginal arms policy. This contrasts sharply to the anti-war marginalists whose attitude varies from suspicion of NATO to a desire to maintain it at some, but not all, costs; it contrasts less sharply to the anti-Communists, who feel that NATO is vital, but protracted conflict is everywhere, so that the relative emphasis on Europe is less.

Former Secretary of State Dean Acheson puts the middle-marginal position most strongly:

The most important objective today—indeed the *sine qua non* of Free World survival—is to hold together those sources of strength which we possess. These sources are North America and Western Europe—highly industrialized areas capable of a productive output which can be three times that of the Soviet Union and its satellites; of a military effort which can be as great if the will exists; and of effective manpower three times that of the Soviet Union. This equation excludes Chinese manpower. A billion people are not a power factor if they are merely a mass. Only when they become organized and possess the tools of power do they become formidable, and Communist China has not yet reached this level of development . . .

This . . . immediately draws the usual objections: "But you will throw in your lot with the colonial empires. Great new movements are afoot in the world. Don't you see how important it is to sustain American principles in Asia, in Africa, and in South America?"

If we would approach life from the point of view of formal moralistic rules, this caveat may be interesting. But if we approach our problem from the point of view of solving it, then these considerations are not at all important. It is not that we consider the French, or the Germans, or the British more desirable people than the Indians, the Burmese, or the Vietnamese; it is simply that, at the present time, the center of power in the non-communist world is in North America and Western Europe. Once this center is dissolved or fragmented, then the problems of the world, from our point of view, become unmanageable.[58] And this remains the dominant middle-marginal position, although some near the border with anti-war marginalism may demur at the strength with which it is stated. The position does not imply contempt for the importance of the underdeveloped areas, but merely a relative assessment, which goes with the analysis of power, which says that for the present it is not these areas upon which our security depends.

Even though the middle marginalists stress Europe relatively more than do the anti-Communists, however, on one question the positions appear to be reversed. The anti-Communists would almost always choose Europe in any struggle over an issue of colonialism; the middle marginalists are much more dubious. Many of them would endorse the Kennedy administration's United Nations votes against some of our NATO allies; most of them endorsed the Eisenhower-Dulles opposition to our allies over Suez. But this is not because of a relatively smaller appreciation of NATO on the part of the middle, but rather for three other reasons. The first is simply the less monolithic middle-marginal interpretation of power. The anti-Communist analysis leads to the position that one should always agree with those who agree with him. The middle marginalists feel that our anticolonial votes will hurt our primary interest (our relations with our allies) so much less than they will help our secondary interest (our relations with the former colonies) that they may be justified. Second, many middle marginalists, particularly of the "balanced-value" variety, have a first-order value judgment against imperialism which pushes them toward anti-colonialist United Nations votes. And third, the middle-marginal appreciation of NATO carries with it the idea that the alliance is a partnership, and on these issues we are right and our partners are wrong. As a result of all these factors, even a European middle marginalist like Buchan can take a position more complex than the simple "Vote-With-the-Alliance" prescription of the editors of *Orbis*. He writes:

[58] Dean G. Acheson, "The Premises of American Policy," *Orbis*, 3:271–272 (Fall 1959).

The problem of resolving differences of national policy on questions outside the NATO area . . . has been growing in importance and has now become acute as Europe's neighboring continent splits into scores of sovereign nations. Belgian policy in the Congo, British policy in the Rhodesias, Portugal's actions in Angola, French policy in North and West Africa increasingly affect the interests of their other allies. There is no simple answer here . . . as the nationalist revolution gathers force, so the white West comes more and more to be regarded as collectively responsible for the acts of individual countries.[59]

His plea is for more coordination within the West—and he does not mean coordination to back up colonial interest, but rather to decolonize gracefully. No middle marginalists endorse all anticolonial positions, and some do not endorse any, but in general, in spite of the middle-marginal emphasis on the importance of Europe there is much more tendency toward anticolonialism than among the anti-Communists.

Similarly, in spite of the importance to the middle marginalists of Europe, they do not ignore the special problem of Germany as the anti-Communists tend to. The middle agrees with the anti-war school that German history cannot leave us complacent, but whereas the anti-war analysis led to suspicion of Germany as an ally, the middle moves in the exact opposite direction—the belief that the way to make the Nazi past obsolete is to tie Germany to us, militarily, economically, and politically. Kissinger writes with great emphasis:

The anguish and suffering inflicted by Germany provide every cause for distrust—a fact well understood and subtly exploited by the Soviet leaders. Yet the countries of Western Europe and the United States must wrench themselves loose from their memories. If the West understands its interests, it *must* advocate German unification despite the experience of two World Wars and despite the understandable fear of a revival of German truculence . . . Any other course will in the end bring on what we should

[59] Alastair Buchan, "The Reform of NATO," *Foreign Affairs*, 40:174 (January 1962).

fear most: a militant, dissatisfied power in the center of the continent.[60]

Indeed, far from ignoring the German past, much of the middle analysis of and recommendation for European policy is aimed at this precise point—avoiding the creation once more of "a brilliant, dissatisfied power in the center of the continent."

ANALYSIS OF OURSELVES

The concern with Germany's Nazi past again serves to bring up the Analysis of Ourselves—the question asked by the anti-war marginalists as to whether the Cold War will drive us toward totalitarianism as the Soviets leave it. The question has two parts: the effect of the Cold War and the American military effort on the psychology of the American people, and the effect on the political power *in* the United States of the military and their backers.

On the question of the possible psychological effect of the military effort in making the American people militaristic, very little has been written from the middle-marginal viewpoint, almost a sure sign in itself that the idea is not considered very important. Some middle marginalists, however, have attempted to answer specific anti-war "psychological" arguments against civil defense. Jack Hirshleifer, for example, says of this anti-war position: "The idea here seems to be that having shelters will of itself destroy the democratic way of life. But the British survived their experience with shelters in World War II (thinking all the while that the German bombs were the main hazard), and democratic Sweden and Denmark both have completed extensive shelter programs for their populations with no visibly catastrophic effects." He then goes on, later in the article, to extend the idea of psychological irrelevance to the military effort in general: "Most of us support a huge armaments effort with-

[60] Kissinger, *The Necessity for Choice*, p. 139. Copyright © 1960, 1961 by Henry A. Kissinger.

out its affecting our personal lives. We go about our business daily under the comforting delusion of personal invulnerability."[61] There would probably be little middle-marginal dissent from either of these points.

The question of military power *in* the United States, however, is taken more seriously by at least some middle marginalists. On this there is a range of opinion. Nearest the generalized anti-war fear of an increasing and undemocratic military influence in American life stemming from continued dependence on military solutions to world problems are those who worry about specific aspects of this military influence. President Eisenhower has already been quoted on guarding against the economic and political influence of the "military-industrial complex." More specifically on the economic aspect, the editors of *The New Republic* argue that:

> The competition for defense contracts translates itself into political pressures. Idle communities want work, while employed communities are determined not to lose what they have. The political pressure bears strongly upon the policymakers. The possibility exists that obsolescent weapons systems will be kept alive to avoid the political consequences of shutdowns—at the expense of the introduction of improved systems. How long a period of grace was the manned aircraft granted because of the pleas of the manufacturers, and the politicians behind them?[62]

Many middle marginalists would agree that such pressures do affect adversely the development of the best weapons for achievement of American military objectives; some few would go further in the anti-war direction and worry about the impact of possible similar pressures against disarmament; almost none would worry about the economic pressure of defense on democracy as such. Similarly, on the more specifically political aspects of the military power in American life, incidents such as General Edwin Walker's political indoctrination of his troops do bother middle marginalists, but

[61] J. Hirshleifer, "The Civil Defense Debate," *The New Leader,* February 19, 1962, pp. 11–12.
[62] "Defense and the Economy," *The New Republic,* June 5, 1961, p. 7.

unlike the anti-war school there is little tendency to generalize them to the military as a whole.

At the other end of the range from those middle marginalists who are concerned with certain specifics of the "military-industrial complex," are those, many of them in the military, who argue that the whole question is a false one. According to Herman Wolk, writing in *Air Force* magazine:

To the historian, America was once again becoming witness to a devil theory. It is a continuing and fascinating American political paradox that both the Right and the Left of the United States political spectrum hold tenaciously to their own devil theory; to the Right evil incarnate has become the State Department and those traitorous Americans who "lost" China and so many other entities to Communism. To the Left, the military-scientific combination, the Atomic Energy Commission, the Strategic Air Command, and, of course, the Pentagon, are responsible for so much of our present predicament . . .

And yet to my knowledge, not one specific example has ever been advanced proving that the military are in fact controlling United States national policy. It is indeed difficult to avoid the conclusion that many respected Americans are venting their disillusion and frustration with the cold war and nuclear weapons problems on the man in the uniform.[63]

The range of middle-marginal opinion, then, goes from specific worry about phases of military power to general lack of worry about any part of it. The more worried end of the range is close on this issue to the more moderate of the anti-war marginalists; the unworried end is similar in view to the anti-Communists. Perhaps if there is a single consensus among middle marginalists on this question it is that whether or not military influence is a problem, it is certainly not *the* problem, nor even one of the main problems of United States arms policy. The problems to be solved are the very complicated ones of how to deal with thermonuclear weapons and how to deal with subtle enemies, and next to these, the "military-industrial complex" counts hardly at all.

[63] Herman S. Wolk, "Deterrence Under Fire," *Air Force*, March 1962, p. 33.

✦ ✦ ✦ ✦ ✦

C H A P T E R   1 0

MARGINALIST RECOMMENDATIONS

Table 1 summarizes the complex differences (and the similarities) in the values and analyses which enter into the arms-policy recommendations of the three marginal schools of thought. Just as the description in a single volume of the points at issue in hundreds of books and articles on arms policy must of necessity be a simplification, the summary in a single table of the last six chapters is a simplification compounded. This is particularly true of Table 1 because the tabulation by schools ignores the fact that the marginalists, notably the middle marginalists, are eclectic. The values and analyses listed columnarly for each school are those which are characteristic of the school as a whole. But individual members may stray on specific ideas from those with whom they generally agree, and this cannot be shown in the table.

In spite of its simplification, however, Table 1 does bring out some important points. One is the large number of value and analytical considerations which must enter into a single arms-policy recommendation made by a marginalist. For systemists, the matter may be easier; if there exists one absolute factor (e.g., peace) which is to all others as infinity is to zero, then only that single factor need be considered in order to use a maximizing mechanism of choice. But if use is made of the optimizing process of combining values and probabilities, then the entire list of factors becomes relevant. It is possible to hold most things constant within a previously determined general framework of policy (and in practice, this is what is done most of the time), but this implies not that some things are irrelevant, but rather that some things have been previously decided.

But *all* of the value and analytical factors in Table 1 are relevant to *any* arms policy recommendation, and Table 1 exhausts the list of relevant factors in a gross, although of course not in a detailed way. Fortunately, the discussion below of recommendations need not be this exhaustive. Even though all of the values and analyses listed are relevant to each recommendation, it does not follow from this that all recommendations must be described in order to understand how any is formed. What is attempted here is a summary of some of the important recommendations of the marginal schools. Most of the important ones are included, at least by example; what is omitted does not change or bias the picture, as would an omission of relevant values or analyses.

Another point illustrated by the table is the wide range of the differences of marginalist opinion on both values and analyses. The range is not the greatest possible—it excludes values and analyses so extreme that they would completely ignore either of the twin threats of thermonuclear war or Communist military expansionism—but this is all that is excluded. The major value judgment of Osgood, Etzioni, and Waskow is that the value of peace far outweighs the risk of Communist expansion; their chief analyses are that unintended war by accident or miscalculation is rapidly approaching, and that our conflicts of interest with the Soviet Union are mainly illusory and psychological. The major value judgment of Strausz-Hupé, Kintner, and Possony is that the value of the extension and preservation of freedom far outweighs the risk of war; their chief analyses are that ways can be designed by which war can be used for political purposes and that the Communists are implacably out to dominate the world. The distance between these two ends of the marginal continuum is great. Between them come all of those individuals whose unconditional recommendations for arms

TABLE 1. Summary of values and analyses by marginal schools

| | Anti-war | Middle | | Anti-Communist |
		"Balanced-value"	"Analytical"	
Values:				
Primary	Prevention of war	Prevention of war Melioration of war Defense of freedom against Communism	Prevention of war Melioration of war	Defense of freedom against Communism Forcing Communist retreat
Other	Defense of freedom against right-wing threats Defense of freedom against Communism	Defense of freedom against right-wing threats		Melioration of war Prevention of war Power-as-a-value
Time	Stress on the long run	Short run is more important than long	Short run is all-important	Some stress on long run
Analyses:				
War	War will be thermonuclear	War tends to become thermonuclear		War is a spectrum
	Weapons can only be used to prevent war if anything	Weapons are primarily to deter war but we may have to strike (first or second)		Weapons are political instruments
	War starts by irrationality, accident, miscalculation	Rationality can exert substantial control over irrationality; accidental war requires both an accident and a wrong response; the "Paradox of Deterrence"; war can be self-generating		War starts primarily for political reasons

TABLE 1. (Continued)

	Anti-war	Middle	Anti-Communist
War (cont.)	"Limited wars" escalate	Escalation can be controlled through proper attention to tactical nuclear weapons, conventional forces, etc.	Nuclear weapons dominate war and conventional forces are important mainly for "psychology"
	Arms races cause wars	The arms race can perhaps be controlled	The arms race can be exploited
	Once war starts control and melioration are impossible	Control and melioration of war may be possible particularly in those cases where we strike first	Control is possible and is necessary for the political exploitation of war
		Analysis of guerrilla warfare (in underdeveloped areas) at an early stage	Unconventional war can be exploited in Soviet satellite areas as well as being defended against in underdeveloped areas
Opponent	USSR is becoming consolidationist in order to conserve its successes; clashes of interest are psychological	USSR is still carefully aggressive in the short run but perhaps it may change in the long; clashes of interest are real	USSR is implacably aggressive and out to bury us, with no sign of change
	USSR is moving away from military means to achieve its objectives	USSR uses military means for political ends, but is willing to take little nuclear risk (perhaps less nuclear risk than implied by middle-marginal analysis of war) .	USSR is carrying on a "protracted conflict" with all means, although it now shies away from high nuclear risk

TABLE 1. (*Continued*)

	Anti-war	Middle	Anti-Communist
Opponent (*cont.*)	The Soviet drive is mainly in the under-developed areas and their aim in Europe is to consol-date current holdings	Europe is to the Soviets both the ultimate prize and the pri-mary battleground; the under-developed areas are important but secondary	Europe is the prize and the current back-ground but the struggle is everywhere and where to fight is a tacti-cal question
	It is possible to get the Communists to relax their grip on Eastern Europe	Eastern Europe will probably remain Communist but we might encourage a more lib-eral Communism; others think there is little we can do	It is possible to push the Com-munists out of Eastern Europe
	Communism is dividing and we must en-courage the peaceful ele-ments by co-operation	Communism is no longer mono-lithic; and we can encourage the peaceful tendency by re-fusing to give in to force; the internal politics of the bloc is exceedingly complex	Communism is not monolithic but we must still treat it as a unified whole
	China exists and must be dealt with particularly for purposes of disarma-ment	China is a strong and not too irrational enemy; it is moving away from the Soviet Union but we must remain agnostic about how or whether to ex-ploit this	China and the Soviet Union still act to-gether
Power-as-a-tool	The carrot; moral lead-ership	The carrot and the stick; a mix-ture of the analyses of the other two schools without an analytical synthesis; *ad hoc* power analysis	The stick; force, coercion, and will power

TABLE 1. *(Continued)*

	Anti-war	Middle	Anti-Communist
Power-as-a-tool *(cont.)*	The "minds of men"; convince them we are with them; the importance of "world opinion" Understand world political forces	Implicit emphasis on tangible military power, more or less tempered by intuitive inclusion of less tangible factors; agnosticism on "world opinion."	Convince them to be with us; military power is important, but we must understand its political uses; the unimportance of "world opinion." Understand Communism
Allies and neutrals	Our long-run interests lie in the underdeveloped world	Our major interests lie and will continue to lie in Europe; this is true both on grounds of common goals and grounds of power	Our major interests lie in Europe but the struggle is everywhere
	More or less grudging acceptance of NATO	Next to strategic deterrence NATO is at the center of our military policy	NATO is the key to our policy
	We must stress anticolonialism	We must reconcile the NATO nations to anticolonialism	We must agree with our friends even if it means voting for colonialism
	Fear of German revival	We must tie Germany to us by bonds of common interest	Germany is another member of NATO
Ourselves	We are in danger of being dominated by militaristic psychology	There is little danger of the American people becoming militaristic	The relation of the political forces within the US to arms policy is so tenuous as to require no analysis
	We are in danger of being dominated by the political power of the military	There may be some questions of the weight of military power in some particular economic or political areas but these provide a minor problem of arms policy	

policy are for change which is no greater than marginal; between them *and at some distance from either end* come most of those who actually make arms policy or who make recommendations from positions close to those who make the policy. The terrain covered by the values and analyses of all of the marginal groups is a vast and differentiated one; because of this it is not surprising that most of the recommendations they make are vastly different ones. What may be surprising is that in spite of this wide differentiation, a consensus exists on certain fundamental, if general, recommendations.

CONSENSUS

A marginalist consensus exists on two arms-policy recommendations. The first is that at least in the short run the United States must remain armed in sufficient strength to deter or prevent the Communists from taking certain actions which they might take in the absence of such arms; the second that such modern arms are so dangerous that we should maintain a continued effort to control them (defining control to include any limitations on numbers, types, deployment, *or* utilization of arms) in order to make war less likely or less terrible if it comes.

The first marginalist consensus depends on a tautology stemming from our definition of marginalism. Current United States policy is to maintain armaments and forces in sufficient strength to deter a number of Communist actions, ranging downward from attack on ourselves. Any recommendation that we *not* remain so armed would be a recommendation for *systemic* change, and nobody making this recommendation could be a marginalist within the meaning here. Thus to state that there exists a marginalist consensus on remaining armed is true by the definition used here. What is interesting then, is not the existence of the definitional consensus, but the fact that this consensus on recommendations is spread over individuals valuing and analyzing the world as differently as do the members of the three marginal schools.

More specifically, it is hardly surprising that the protracted conflict analysts of the marginal anti-Communist school or the deterrers of the middle favor continued armaments and deterrence; but it may be surprising that individuals holding the views of even the more extreme members of the marginal anti-war school do so. In some cases it is a grudging agreement—some individuals drag themselves into the position only with kicking and screaming—but nonetheless, those who see war as being caused by accidental use of weapons and see conflict with the Soviet Union as being mainly psychological in cause, still want to maintain the weapons until the psychological atmosphere is changed. And, as marginalists, they feel that we must carry out this change of psychology gradually, with each marginal step being conditioned upon the success of the previous one.

There is little question about those moderate anti-war marginalists near the boundary with middle marginalism. Wiesner writes that "while a system of mutual deterrence is less attractive in many ways than properly safeguarded total disarmament, it may be somewhat easier to achieve and could be regarded as a transient phase on the way toward the goal of total disarmament."[1] And in fact, Wiesner has few apparent reservations about basing short-run stability on a system of highly protected thermonuclear weapons targeted on Soviet cities for maximum deterrence. The more extreme anti-war marginalists, however, are more dubious about the success of deterrence, but nonetheless, they too come along. Some also favor city-busting deterrence as a stopgap until the change of psychology. Thus Waskow, who believes that "the balanced [i.e., city-busting] deterrent seems incapable of permanently protecting either the life or the liberty of the

[1] Jerome B. Wiesner, "Comprehensive Arms-Limitation Systems," in *Arms Control, Disarmament, and National Security*, ed. Donald G. Brennan (New York: Braziller, 1961), p. 215.

United States,"[2] nonetheless argues that pending the adoption (and presumed success) of his prime recommendations:

> The President and Congress should . . . deliberately choose and bring into effect the balanced deterrent. The weapons systems necessary to do this should . . . be substituted for the weapons systems of counterforce deterrence. Having moved . . . to the balanced deterrent, the President and Congress should then use the balanced deterrent as an avenue toward arms control for ourselves, regardless of Communist acceptance of arms control. Without reducing expenditure or abandoning any security whatsoever, this kind of arms control could greatly enhance the stability of the world and the safety of the United States.[3]

Waskow pinpoints the purpose of the balanced deterrent as "deliberately increasing the terror of . . . war to the nth power, thus making it as nearly unfightable as possible."[4] But some anti-war marginalists oppose such a use of terror. Charles Osgood, the originator of the "Unilateral Initiatives'" concept endorsed by many anti-war marginalists, proposes, in his first published recommendation for such a specific initiative:

> *Unilaterally Initiated and Reciprocated Nuclear Displacement:* Here both sides have achieved geographical displacement of nuclear missile and production sites away from civilian population centers. The moral and military situation is therefore clear and equivalent for both. For either we or they to launch a full-scale *strategic* attack against the civilian population centers of the opponent is clearly immoral; furthermore it is suicidal, because of the certain and heavy retaliation against the initiator's civilian centers. Therefore strategic attack by either side makes no military sense whatsoever.
> What about a fullscale *tactical* attack by one side against the other? This is the only sensible alternative for a responsible military—responsible, that is, to its own civilians. But even a

2 Arthur I. Waskow, *The Limits of Defense* (Garden City: Doubleday, 1962), p. 44.
3 *Ibid.,* p. 102.
4 *Ibid.,* p. 31.

preemptive tactical strike is rendered quite unlikely by the nature of mutual nuclear displacement. Why? Because only if one side could be certain of destroying a major portion of the opponent's retaliatory capacity, or could be certain of defending against such retaliation, would it be likely to make the gamble. It would appear, then, that reciprocal nuclear displacement provides maximum stability in a world where such weapons exist.[5]

Osgood hopes that this reciprocated step will be the first of a chain which will ultimately abolish nuclear weapons, but pending this, he too is looking for a variety of stable deterrence. He differs from Waskow in that he wants terror only in the retaliatory strike, with any possible first strike being a counterforce one avoiding population, but both have in common that in the short run, they depend upon weaponry.

The other recommendation upon which marginalist consensus exists, the desirability of an effort at some variety of arms control, is at least in part also a tautological one. The arms controls or the efforts at obtaining such controls which are contained in current American policy can be divided into three categories. One, the safety device designed to minimize the probability that literal accident or insanity will trigger a war-starting incident (e.g., nuclear weapons designed so that only a fantastic chain of coincidences can set them off accidentally) is agreed on by all schools including the systemic ones and thus cannot be considered at issue in the arms debate (and should perhaps be excluded from the definition of arms control). Such safety devices increase stability and decrease the likelihood of war with very little weakening of national capability to wage war. The second category, the unilateral measure designed for stability even at the cost of giving up some military option or capability (e.g., declining to maintain a high level of "airborne alert"— weapon-laden bombers kept aloft to protect them against surprise attack) is a fundamental portion of national policy and opposition on principle to any and all such weakening

---

[5] Charles E. Osgood, "Rational Defense: Nuclear Displacement," *Bulletin of the Atomic Scientists*, 18.6:23 (June 1962).

of military capabilities would be systemic. Not all marginalists agree on all the measures which might fall into this category, but it is implied by the definition of marginalism that there must be consensus on the need for some unilateral stabilizing measures of this type.

Arms controls of this second type may be considered as a portion of a general implicit agreement between ourselves and the Soviet Union not to do everything within national capabilities. If we refrain from airborne alert operations (for the most part), the Soviets refrain from shooting down our reconnaisance aircraft which remain outside of their borders (for the most part). Such controls need not match one another very neatly—the essence is that each side recognize the general need for self-restraint and therefore limit itself in ways more stringent than merely not attacking the other. The third category of controls, however, contain those which, although they need not be embodied in formal signed treaties, are dependent upon somewhat more explicit and specific agreement between the two opponents. This category includes signed agreements, of course, but it also includes negotiated but unsigned agreements, such as the one by which both sides stopped testing nuclear weapons for a number of years; it includes, in addition, agreements not based on any formal negotiating process. An example here, is the tacit agreement by which neither power *gave* its allies nuclear weapons (although both provided more or less technical help in developing their allies' weapons). The boundary between this third and the second category is necessarily blurred, but the difference is that the tacit agreements in the third group are agreements over a particular issue, rather than even less formal agreements for general self-restraint.

The effort to obtain explicit and implicit arms controls in the third category is also part of our current policy. Given the current small success in obtaining such agreed controls (even the implicit ones), it is debatable whether a recommendation to stop trying for agreement would fall under our definition of systemism; it would make very little difference to our arms policy if we did stop. But what is interesting, in any case, is that even with their wide divergencies, all of the marginal schools place enough importance on the effort to arrive at *some* sort of agreed controls to help avoid the worst kinds of modern war; none recommends an attitude of pure conflict with the Soviets (as do systemic anti-Communists). Some marginalists are skeptical about the short-run chances for success but all seem to have at least some residual long-run hope.

Again, it is not surprising that the marginal *anti-war* school which builds its entire policy on agreed disarmament should recommend continued effort at agreement and co-operation. (Osgood's unilateral initiation and reciprocation sequence is, of course, another way of trying to obtain agreement.) Nor is it surprising that the *middle* school wants to make deterrence more stable through mutual international recognition (perhaps implicit) of common interests as well as conflicting ones. But even the marginal anti-Communists, in spite of their emphasis on the conflicting and incompatible interests of the two international opponents, feel that some effort at agreement is necessary. In part they feel that our continuing to make attempts to agree with the Russians should be made part of our protracted conflict strategy as they have made it part of theirs. According to Harry Willetts, who was cited above as arguing that the Russians are simply not interested now in anything but their own political advantage:

. . . we risk serious disillusionment if we concentrate on devising measures which the Soviet Union might reasonably consider economically advantageous and unobjectionable from the point of view of its national security, and expect the Soviet Union to accept them in return for equal sacrifices on our part . . .

There is no reason for the United States and its allies to be excessively depressed by this prospect. There will be disappointments if the West fails to play the Soviet Union at its own game, to make its proposals on disarmament and arms control a part of a positive political strategy of its own. But once this is accepted, the West may hope to demonstrate that the Soviet Union has misjudged the outcome of the contest.[6]

Even this, in its last sentence, implies that once our political strategy has demonstrated that the Soviets have nothing more to gain by the propaganda game, they may become serious about delineating areas of mutual interest in preventing the worst forms of conflict.

But beyond using arms control as part of our international strategy, the anti-Communist marginalists feel that some good can come out of the mutual recognition of common interests implicit in the third category of arms controls. Strausz-Hupé, Kintner, and Possony, after rejecting anything coming under the heading of comprehensive schemes, whether for arms reduction or for control over the uses of armaments, nonetheless feel that:

For the United States, there is promise in an approach which might be called "security by consent." This concept is based on the assumption that the major powers have a common interest in the promotion of their own security and in the avoidance of general nuclear war. By definition, a system of security founded on mutual consent requires genuine communication on the mutual strategic interests of the contracting parties. It cannot be created in the atmosphere of propaganda and "ploymanship" which have characterized disarmament negotiations until now. ... The Soviets, not so surprisingly, are reluctant to move from a ground which has been decidedly favorable to themselves to a quieter game of genuine "give and take." But unless they do this, we should break off arms negotiations and disengage our military security from the caprices of grandstand diplomacy.

If Soviet and Western strategists were to enter into a frank, continuing dialogue at regular intervals, carried out privately and informally (without embodying the results in formal treaties) they might be able to arrive at a consensus on the objectives and methods of a security-through-consent arrangement ... By accepting the possibility of war as an aspect of the human con-

6 Harry T. Willetts, "Disarmament and Soviet Foreign Policy," in The American Assembly, *Arms Control: Issues for the Public*, pp. 172–173. Copyright © 1961. By permission of Prentice-Hall, Inc., publishers.

dition and by providing for our normal security needs, we may have the best chance of deterring war and breaking through the vicious circle of fear, insecurity and arms races.[7]

This recognition of the utility of trying to get the Soviets to explore with us the common interests contained within an over-all context of conflict is, in fact, closer to the view of the middle-marginal deterrers (many of whom also agree to the assessment that the current type of arms talks is futile) than to the systemic anti-Communist view that there can be no talk on common interests in a time of conflict.

Thus on two basic matters, the short-run need for the maintenance of military strength and the long-run need for recognizing and exploiting the mutual interests of the United States and the Soviet Union in not using that strength to its most horrifying technical limits, there is a marginal consensus. The consensus is over general recommendations, always easier to agree on than specific recommendations for acting now, and there are probably few if any direct actions upon which the extremes of the marginalists could agree. Nonetheless, because the existence of the marginalist consensus is sometimes obscured both by political and intellectual rhetoric and by the reluctance of some to admit the necessity for what they dislike, and because even the two items of consensus are attacked from the outside by systemists of one school or the other, the very existence of the areas of agreement becomes important.

DISAGREEMENT

There is, however, much more disagreement among marginalists than agreement. Particularly in their primary recommendations—those actions they wish to push as compared to those the necessity for which they will grudgingly admit

7 Robert Strausz-Hupé, William R. Kintner, and Stefan T. Possony, *A Forward Strategy for America* (New York: Harper, 1961), pp. 310–311. Copyright © 1961 by Robert Strausz-Hupé, William R. Kintner, and Stefan T. Possony.

—the three schools are quite different from one another. The recommendations described here are divided into three major categories: Strategic military policy and arms control; American arms policy in Europe; and American arms policy in the rest of the world. The inclusion of arms control with strategic policy is not entirely arbitrary; the other two categories have important control aspects and these are discussed, but what is most commonly called arms control (including disarmament) is primarily concerned with those controls which will prevent or limit strategic thermonuclear war between the United States and the Soviet Union. Not every recommendation of every school is discussed. What is drawn once more is a somewhat impressionistic sketch of how the three marginal schools believe arms should be used and limited in today's world, and how these recommendations are derived from the values and analyses to which the schools adhere. Some of the recommendations have already been mentioned or are obvious from the discussion of values and analyses; others may be less obvious.

Strategic Military Policy and Arms Control

From the combination of their values and analyses, comes the strategic belief which unites the *anti-war marginalists,* that *the* problem of nuclear weapons is to avoid their unnecessary use—and any use is an unnecessary one. This avoidance has two parts: in the short run while the weapons exist, we must stabilize them so that they will not be used; in the long run, *starting now,* we must reduce them in number and finally abolish them so that they cannot be used. The anti-war marginalists, since they fit the marginal definition, do not propose that this abolition take place quickly or unconditionally, but they are confident that their first steps will be successful in starting us on the road, and they are explicit that these steps must be successful in order to go on to the succeeding ones.

Beyond the agreement to the two principles of stabilization now and disarmament coming, however, the consensus among the anti-war marginalists begins to break down somewhat. On stabilization, the disagreement between Waskow and Osgood indicates that there is no fundamental unifying belief on how to go about it. Most would probably agree with Waskow and Wiesner that the best way to stabilize is to try for a mutual balance of population-killing terror—that any attempt to "rationalize" war by either designing American strategies of controlled war or encouraging Soviet ones, makes war more thinkable and more likely—but the moral and political implications of such terror may in the future put more anti-war marginalists into the Osgood camp on this issue. An example of the effect of the difference comes in the discussion of civil defense. One implication of the attempt to maximize the balance of terror is the marginal recommendation that the United States forswear all civil defenses. Most anti-war marginalists would agree to this, but Osgood's agreement is tentative and sounds almost *pro forma*. In the same article in which he proposes his reciprocated program for protecting civilians by removing military targets from cities, he writes: "I do not wish to imply, by making the distinction between target and nontarget areas, that I favor a fallout shelter program, even in nontarget areas. On the contrary, I believe that the only real defense against nuclear attack is to prevent it from happening. But I also believe that our citizens have a right to make their own decisions on this crucial matter."[8] If the second sentence sounds like an affirmation of faith, the third seems to be a surrender to heresy.

In any case, however, most of the anti-war marginalists still look to the balance of terror in the short run, but they are more interested in starting toward the disarmed long run, when the balance of terror will no longer be needed. Wiesner provides a connection between the two: ". . . a mutually agreed-upon stable deterrent system could provide the basis for comprehensive disarmament because it provided a means of reconciling the Soviet reluctance to permit inspection and the Western fear of clandestine weapons. The size of the deterrent force can be chosen large enough to provide ade-

[8] Osgood, p. 21.

quate security with minimal inspection and subsequently reduced as the inspection effort grows and experience establishes confidence in it."[9] Wiesner's idea is to arrive at a comprehensive disarmament scheme starting with stable mutual deterrence and phasing down through mutually negotiated stages of preparation, implementation, and consolidation.[10]

The anti-war marginalists all agree that ultimate general disarmament cannot be reached except through multilateral negotiations of the classical type, and the more orthodox also feel that the best way to begin is to continue trying to negotiate with the Russians around the conference table. Their prime recommendation then, rather than being for any specific action on the part of the United States, is that we should negotiate seriously and plan well for these negotiations. Within this context, they make negotiating proposals, but these are not unconditional recommendations to the United States government within the definition used here, since the only action they call for, lacking Soviet agreement, is to keep proposing. Given agreement, however, many sets of proposals (currently in the status of conditional recommendations) exist. One detailed set, for example, proposed by Louis Sohn and David Frisch, calls for a first stage of disarmament divided into three substages. During the first substage, an international disarmament control organization would be set up. The substantive measures to be taken during the three substages include such matters as: phasing down the number of long-range strategic delivery systems, the stockpiles of fissionable materials, and the size of conventional armed forces; limitation of production of military material including nuclear weapons and delivery systems; and prohibition of tests of both nuclear weapons and delivery systems. All of these steps are to be accompanied by inspection and control, and a good deal of study has been made of these questions.[11]

9 Wiesner, p. 219.
10 *Ibid.*, pp. 219–221.
11 Louis B. Sohn and David H. Frisch, "Arms Reduction in the Sixties," in

The continuing failure of negotiations, however, has led some anti-war marginalists to look to other techniques for obtaining agreement. Osgood, although he agrees to the ultimate need for negotiation, is not optimistic about the prospects under present psychological conditions. He believes that the conflicts of interest which now exist, although perceived by both sides as being strong, are nonetheless illusory, and that these illusions must be gotten rid of before anything substantial can be accomplished: "We have behind us a long and dismal history of unsuccessful negotiation. It is easy to blame it all on the Communists, but the [psychological] mechanisms we have been discussing operate on both sides . . . The crucial point is that *mutual agreements on arms control require commitments prior to action,* and in the present climate of fear and distrust it is hard to see how bilateral commitments of any significance could be reached."[12] He therefore favors a program of unilateral acts designed to break the "climate of fear and distrust" by showing the Soviets that we are looking for peaceful accommodation. He describes the unilateral acts as ones which must be: "perceived by an opponent as reducing his external threat"; "accompanied by explicit invitations to reciprocation"; "executed regardless of prior commitment of the opponent to reciprocate"; "planned in sequences and continued over considerable periods regardless of reciprocation"; and "announced in advance of execution and widely publicized . . . as part of a consistent policy." Osgood's analysis of the Soviet Union as already being so consolidationist that it wants nothing more than peace leads to his belief that it would welcome this opportunity to consolidate by reciprocating such actions. Being a marginalist, however, he hedges against possible Soviet exploitation of our friendly gestures for parti-

---

Arms Reduction, Programs and Issues, ed. David H. Frisch (New York: Twentieth Century Fund, 1961), pp. 24–34.

12 Charles E. Osgood, "Reciprocal Initiatives," in *The Liberal Papers,* ed. James Roosevelt (Garden City: Doubleday, 1962), p. 179. Copyright © 1962 by James Roosevelt.

san gain, by also specifying that in order to maintain our national security, unilateral acts must "be graduated in risk potential"; "be diverse in nature and unpredictable (by an opponent)"; "never endanger our 'heartland' or reduce our fundamental capacity for retaliatory second strike"; and "be accompanied by explicit firmness in all areas."[13]

Aside from the proposal which has been discussed to separate target areas from civilian population, Osgood has not specified a series of unilateral measures. Some of those subscribing to his general program have, however. Waskow lists such items as: enlarging of the Arms Control and Disarmament Agency into a National Peace Agency; economic planning for disarmament; allowing free travel of Soviet citizens within the United States (since done in part); unilateral cessation of nuclear testing; enlarging world trade; allowing Russian observers into the posts of the Distant Early Warning line so that the radars will warn them against our attacks as well as warning us against theirs; and withdrawing the United States Seventh Fleet to a position where it could still protect Taiwan from the Chinese Communists but would no longer appear to the Communists to be threatening the mainland.[14] Etzioni wants to start with a public announcement of a new conciliatory American policy and then to undertake such small steps as allowing free travel of Soviet diplomats and admitting Outer Mongolia to the UN (which had not been done at the time he wrote). He then goes on to larger steps, no more than one or two of which he feels can be taken at a time until the Russians reciprocate. Examples here are military disengagement (but not in Germany, where he feels it would be politically impossible for the Soviets to reciprocate), and cuts in conventional armaments.[15]

Etzioni's belief that conventional armaments should be

13 *Ibid.*, pp. 195–201.
14 Waskow, pp. 101–108.
15 Amitai Etzioni, *The Hard Way to Peace: A New Strategy* (New York: Collier, 1962), pp. 95–102.

reduced first brings up another interesting disagreement among anti-war marginalists. Waskow seems on Etzioni's side; he feels that "each great power should keep its own 'favorite weapon' during much of the process of disarmament as a safeguard."[16] Certainly each side would then choose to keep some variety of nuclear weaponry. But Wiesner favors parallel reductions of all sorts of arms,[17] as do Sohn and Frisch, and most of the anti-war school would probably agree with this.

At any rate, the strategic recommendations of the anti-war marginalists are built on the twin bases of stability now and multilateral disarmament later (but starting now, either through negotiation or reciprocated unilateral initiative). The primary strategic recommendations of the *anti-Communist marginal school* are, of course, completely different. Their major strategic proposals are designed first for the use of force as a political instrument, and second, as a corollary of this, for the control of force so that it can be so used with a minimum of risk and destruction. Communism is a deadly enemy, and there is no certain way to avoid the possibility of war except by surrendering, and maybe not even that will work.

Strausz-Hupé, Kintner, and Possony describe the doctrine and forces necessary for the "win strike second" posture they recommend:

We make our bid to win after we have absorbed the Soviet Union's first strike. Thus we must strike back with counterforce; hold communist bloc cities in hostage; mobilize what is left of our nation; free our allies and the satellites; and seize and occupy the Soviet Union and Red China.

This is the American ideal strategy. It is sound morally—and it may be sound militarily as we approach the late sixties and a higher degree of invulnerability in strategic retaliatory force. What is our concept of the war we would have to fight if this strategy were executed? What is required to carry it out in num-

16 Waskow, p. 113.
17 Wiesner, pp. 219–221.

bers of ICBM's of all kinds, high-speed supersonic aircraft, defense organization, command of the sea and deployed forces for the defense of forward areas? As of now, [late 1960] we do not have the means adequate for this concept, but can we ever have them? As the missile age comes along, we need active defense not only against aircraft, but also against ballistic missiles.

[The strategy includes] a military requirement for civil defense, particularly fallout shelters. It is well nigh impossible to see how this country can stand up to Soviet nuclear blackmail unless the people of the United States are protected. What is rather contemptuously called "civil defense" is an indispensable element in military strategy.[18]

It is important to note that this strategy espoused by the "toughest" marginal school *explicitly* disavows an American first nuclear strike against the Soviet Union, except perhaps in the case of preemption.[19] The anti-Communist marginalists are still unwilling to accept a Communist victory at *any* level, but their strategy calls for the ability to win a general thermonuclear war *by striking second*. They explicitly want to add to our no-first-strike strategic forces, the capability to win a war fought at any lower level of violence, in order to avoid the choice between losing and escalating. According to Richard Foster:

We cannot afford gaps anywhere in the spectrum of conflict with the Communist bloc—nor is there any need for this to happen. With a resolution at least equal to Khrushchev's, the two advantages on our side—economic supremacy and national values—represent the basis for meeting the Communist challenge without resorting to strategies of extermination.

No low cost strategies are available to us.[20]

Under this condition of "no gaps in the spectrum," our ability to strike second and win a thermonuclear war will

[18] *A Forward Strategy for America*, pp. 119–120. Copyright © 1961 by Robert Strausz-Hupé, William Kintner, and Stefan T. Possony.

[19] *Ibid.*, p. 119.

[20] Richard B. Foster, "Values, Power, and Strategy," *Stanford Research Institute Journal*, 3:194 (Fourth Quarter, 1959).

be a nonextermination strategy to prevent the Communists from raising the level of violence when we are winning at a lower level. Lacking United States forces which could win at any lower level, however—given the possibility, in other words, that *we* might want to escalate—the anti-Communist marginalists seem a little more intersted in a first-strike strategy. Strausz-Hupé, Kintner, and Possony write of such a first-strike posture: "This is the strategy of a 'hard' country, one that has the intestinal fortitude to move right to the brink of nuclear war and to leap in order to make good its nuclear threat. Given such a will, that country could chance reduction of its limited-war forces below the requirements of the [limited-war]strategy."[21] "Intestinal fortitude" is ordinarily considered a favorable attribute; the anti-war school might call it "insane brinkmanship." In any case, the anti-Communist marginalists do not feel that the United States is such a "hard" country, and they favor strong limited war (but not necessarily nonnuclear) forces. It seems likely from this, but is by no means certain, that lacking limited-war forces capable of winning in all situations, the anti-Communist marginalists would prefer first-strike strategic forces to limited losses.

The preferred strategy, however, is "win strike second." This does not imply that there is no risk of thermonuclear war. The risk remains high because the Communists may misjudge our capabilities or our will and because of all the preemptive dangers which stem from maintenance of ready forces. The supporting portion of the anti-Communist marginalists' strategy therefore involves the effort to meliorate warfare in order that it may be "thinkable" and we can use it as a political weapon, even at low levels of intestinal fortitude. This is where the recommendation to delineate jointly with the Soviet areas of mutual interest becomes applicable, but this is obviously not a major portion of the effort at meliorative control. One portion which *is* major is the effort

21 *A Forward Strategy for America*, p. 118. Copyright © 1961 by Robert Strausz-Hupé, William Kintner, and Stefan T. Possony.

to achieve a capability of winning at any level. The anti-Communists' preference is to escalate rather than lose; precluding the possibility of losing precludes the need for escalation and therefore becomes a form of melioration aimed at keeping war from becoming thermonuclear.

But even thermonuclear war can be meliorated to a point where the risks which are a necessary portion of a forward strategy (even one based on a "win strike second" force) become tolerable. Civil defense has been mentioned as "an indispensable element in military strategy"; it is indispensable because by meliorating war it makes it usable. Air defense is another such device: "Secondly [to invulnerable second-strike offensive forces] we need an active defense system with two key components. The first, defense against aircraft, must be highly invulnerable to neutralization by ballistic missile attack. If we fail to develop such a system, high-speed enemy bombers with multiple bombs will be able to penetrate the air space over our territory at will. The second component is active defense against enemy missiles."[22] Finally, the counterforce strategy endorsed in *A Forward Strategy* changes general war between the United States and the Soviet Union from one of "extermination" to one in which military weapons are targets and cities are hostages. As treated by the anti-Communist marginalists, counterforce is a strategy which, combined with civil defense and the other meliorative ingredients, makes thermonuclear war tolerable, makes the threat to use it to prevent Communist escalation against our limited victories rational, and makes its use to prevent our own limited losses (in case the remainder of our forces are not up to snuff) possible.

Some *middle marginalists* also favor a strategic doctrine based on a strong counterforce; given Kissinger's stricture that the choice is not between overwhelming counterforce and none at all, most middle marginalists favor some variation. They favor, that is, control rather than the lack of control. Indeed, the unifying theme of the strategic recom-

22 *Ibid.*, p. 125.

mendations of the middle marginal school is control. The middle marginalists are not united on the values they espouse, some have a "balanced" set of objectives including both the avoidance of thermonuclear war and the preservation of freedom, some build and defend arms policies entirely on the basis of preventing thermonuclear war, most take up various positions between these two poles. But in their basic analytical picture of the world, the members of the middle school are close to one another. Their stress on rationality on our part and with hope for rationality on the part of the Soviets, together with their picture of the Soviets being opponents but careful ones, leads to strategic recommendations based on two overlapping concepts, arms control and deterrence. The middle-marginal concept of arms control resembles the main disarmament theme of the anti-war school in its values, but differs in its basic analysis; the middle-marginal concept of deterrence resembles the main "forward strategy" theme of the anti-Communists in its analysis, but differs in its values.

Perhaps the best-known middle-marginal definition of arms control is that of Schelling and Halperin:

We mean to include all the forms of military cooperation between potential enemies in the interest of reducing the likelihood of war, its scope and violence if it occurs, and the political and economic costs of being prepared for it. The essential feature of arms control is the recognition of the common interest, of the possibility of reciprocation and cooperation even between potential enemies with respect to their military establishments. Whether the most promising areas of arms control involve reductions in certain kinds of military force, increases in certain kinds of military force, qualitative changes in weaponry, different modes of deployment, or arrangements superimposed on existing military systems, we prefer to treat as an open question.[23]

This is a very broad statement. Partly by what it says and partly by the vast ground it covers, it is in disagreement with

[23] Thomas C. Schelling and Morton H. Halperin, *Strategy and Arms Control* (New York: Twentieth Century Fund, 1961), p. 2.

the anti-war marginal view of control. The middle-marginal search for "common interest . . . between potential enemies," differs from the reasoning of the anti-war school which treats the United States and the Soviet Union as potential *friends* divided by an illusory or shrinking enmity. There is no purely logical incompatibility between potential enmity and potential friendship, but the semantic implications as to whether antagonism or reconciliation is the "normal" state are vital to the differences in recommendations of the two schools.

The primary difference in arms-control recommendations comes over the distinction between "reductions in certain kinds of military force," and the other three categories of controls Schelling and Halperin consider coequal. The anti-war marginalists, basing their analysis on the belief that weapons and irrationality cause war, direct their major recommendations toward disarmament—reduction of the number of weapons. They do not consider the other categories nearly as important, except perhaps for short-run balanced deterrence. But the arms-control recommendations of the middle marginalists are based on preventing war by the potential rational management of weapons. Those in the middle even have some doubt about the over-all efficacy of substantial disarmament, since this in itself may subvert the stability they consider the most important goal attainable between enemies. James King argues, for example, that:

. . . there are ample grounds for caution in approaching the problem of numbers. National armaments may be reduced so low that the resulting temptation to evade the controls may heighten the likelihood of war. Thus, dependence on the controls mounts as the strength of the deterrent forces declines. For example, if the level were set at ten missiles, the addition of ten or fifteen clandestine missiles could give one side an overwhelming advantage and tempt it to initiate war. At higher levels, because successful evasion is more difficult, perfection need not be asked of the controls.[24]

[24] James E. King, Jr., "Arms Control and United States Security," in The American Assembly, *Arms Control: Issues for the Public*, pp. 99–100. Copyright © 1961. By permission of Prentice-Hall, Inc., publisher.

Other middle marginalists would weight more heavily the importance of disarmament as against the other categories of control. In any case, what unites the middle-marginal "arms controllers," as compared to the anti-war "disarmers," is less a uniform belief in high levels of weapons to ensure stability than a belief in the necessity of looking at the specific military effects of any measure in any category of control and weighing these specific effects in determining policy. Under the heading of "The Problem of Evaluation" of arms-control measures, Donald Brennan writes:

From the point of view of the United States (or any other country), any specific arms-control measure or program that has been proposed has two basic aspects: it may improve some component of our security, either in the short or the long term, and it may degrade some other—again either in the short or the long term. Both the hazards it may protect us against or reduce and the hazards it may introduce are often subtle, complicated and difficult to understand. Indeed, they may not be at all apparent when the measure is first considered, and may never be completely understood. The problem of deciding whether or not the proposed measure is "actually desirable" is one of deciding whether the hazards reduced do or do not outweigh the hazards introduced.[25]

This mode of evaluation differs from that used by many anti-war marginalists who analyze the general concept of disarmament, find it desirable, and then assess specific measures by their contribution to this ultimate goal.

The basic difference in mode of evaluation depends in part on the different time values of the two schools. Brennan mentions the long term coequally with the short, but in fact, as has been pointed out, middle marginalists are concerned mainly with the short term. Middle-marginal arms controllers reject the evaluation of proposals by their contribution

25 Donald G. Brennan, "Setting and Goals of Arms Control," in The American Assembly, *Arms Control: Issues for the Public*, p. 32. Copyright © 1961. By permission of Prentice-Hall, Inc., publisher.

to an "ultimate" solution such as disarmament because they reject the idea of ultimate solution. As put by Hedley Bull:

I do not think of security as some future state or condition, some metaphysical plateau which we have not yet reached but towards which we are striving. International security is something we have and have had throughout the history of modern international society, in greater or lesser degree. The promotion of international security is a matter of preserving and extending something with which we are familiar, rather than of manufacturing, out of nothing, some novel device. At the present time it is a matter of restoring, or attempting to recapture, something, for much of it is beyond recapture, of the security which modern weapons, and the continued existence alongside of them of political conflicts bitter enough to promise the use of them, have deprived us; and, in the first instance, a matter of preserving such security as we have now, by arresting or stabilizing its tendency to rapid decline.[26]

This is the short-run "buying-time" point of view, and although longer-run solutions and plans exist, in practice, the Brennan method of evaluation subordinates them in most cases of conflict.

As a result, then, of these general views—the value put on avoiding thermonuclear war, the belief in rationality, the relative deemphasis of disarmament *per se,* the stress on specific evaluation, and the emphasis on the short run—the middle marginalists come to specific proposals for arms controls, which are in the main *ad hoc,* geared to particular times and particular problems. Nonetheless, Schelling and Halperin provide a list of the *sorts* of proposals middle marginalists are interested in. They include measures to:

reduce the possibility of surprise attack (e.g., maintain open skies)
make both sides less vulnerable to surprise (e.g., unilateral or bilateral emphasis on weapons for retaliation)

26 Hedley Bull, *The Control of the Arms Race* (New York: Praeger, 1961), p. 26.

reduce the danger of accidental war (e.g., arrangements to improve command and control in order to avoid making wrong decisions on the basis of wrong information)

reduce the incidence of false alarm (e.g., exchange of warning facilities)

reduce capabilities for destruction if war starts (e.g., reduction of stockpiles of nuclear weapons or delivery systems)

reduce collateral damage (e.g., agreement to stress weapons with high accuracy and low yield)

control the course of a war which has started (e.g., prewar preparation of intrawar communication between the sides)

reduce the dangers, such as preemption, stemming from crises (e.g., facilities for quick communication and negotiation in time of stress)

prevent local wars which might escalate (e.g., arms embargoes)

keep local wars from escalating (e.g., prewar discussion by the United States and the Soviet Union of the conditions of local war)

slow down the technological arms race (e.g., implicit or explicit agreement not to produce certain types of weapons)

decrease uncertainty which might lead to wrong short- or long-run decisions (e.g., exchange of information)

prevent the spread of weapons (e.g., agreement not to share certain classes of weapons with other countries).[27]

This is neither a comprehensive program nor an all-inclusive list. It is not a comprehensive program because it is not a program. The individual ideas may not all be acceptable to the Russians; they may not all be acceptable to

[27] Schelling and Halperin, pp. 9–39.

us. Some of them may well clash with others. The middle marginalists typically do not endorse comprehensive programs based on a single doctrine, but their rationale rather leads them to lists of individual measures, each of which they feel will reduce the danger of war in the short run. And as for the comprehensive listing, this one is typical but not inclusive. The focus on short-run war prevention and melioration is typical of almost all middle-marginal arms-control recommendation; other analysts, however, pay somewhat more attention than this to the long run, and endorse more of the disarmament measures of the anti-war marginalists, *so long as they do not clash with short-run stability.*

One thing which is particularly noticeable about the Schelling-Halperin list, however, is that it draws little distinction among those measures dependent on agreements between the sides which, although they need not be formal, must be explicit (exchange of warning facilities, increased crisis communication); those which can be done on the basis of implicit agreement, by each side watching the other and acting accordingly (not sharing weapons with other countries); and those which can be done on the basis of general agreement not to take every warlike measure within one's power (limitation of types of weapon production). The middle marginalists, although most of them tend to subscribe to the desirability of continued explicit negotiations with the Soviets for purposes of exploring changes in attitude if nothing else, place little faith in the success of this technique. Like the Osgood group, they have their greatest belief in bargaining by reciprocation in unilateral steps. But unlike Osgood, the substance of middle marginalism is based on the channeling of real conflicts of interest away from war, rather than the dissolution of illusory conflicts. And therefore, middle-marginal unilateralism is a subtopic not only of arms control but of deterrence. Deterrent actions are unilateral ones designed to persuade an opponent by threat of force to refrain from doing what we do not want him to do. Much of what we do not want him to do is to start a war and this is where the overlap between arms control and deterrence comes. Deterring an enemy from taking some action we wish him not to take cannot be *defined* as arms control because an essential element in all definitions of control is some sort of *self*-restraint. But deterrent measures designed not only to fulfill their primary purpose of discouraging enemy actions, but also to assure an enemy that *we* do not intend to take similar actions, do properly fall under the arms-control definition. By the voluntary sacrifice of military capabilities which would assist us to start a war, to win it, or to escalate if losing, we emphasize our own preference for stability over military and political victory, and we thus engage in self-restraining arms control. And by doing this unilaterally, we try to encourage the Russians to reciprocate, in a manner not very different from Osgood's.

This division of deterrence, between stability-oriented "arms-control" measures which restrain both sides, and other measures designed to prevent certain Soviet actions without giving up any related capability on our part, is a key distinction in the marginalist debate. *The anti-war marginalists* are interested in short-run deterrence, but almost entirely in that portion of deterrence which falls under the heading of arms control—reassuring the Soviets while deterring them from acting against us. The *anti-Communists* are interested in arms control, but almost entirely in controls over actions which we would probably be afraid to take anyhow. The *middle* marginalists, as has been seen, are interested in arms controls within and without the category of deterrence; they are also interested in deterrence measures among and beyond those which can be categorized as arms controls.

The mixture of arms control and nonarms-control deterrent measures recommended by a particular middle marginalist depends on three factors: the relative *values* he assigns to stabilized peace between the United States and the Soviet Union on the one hand, and to American protection for the peace and freedom of the rest of the world (primarily Europe) on the other; the feasibility and credibility, according to his *analysis,* of United States use of strategic thermonuclear threats for the protection of Europe; and the other alternatives he believes *analytically* to be available for the protection of Europe. Based on these three factors, middle marginalists disagree over two closely intertwined issues of deterrent policy: the extent to which we should design our strategic forces and tactics for fighting and winning a thermonuclear war if it starts, as compared to designing them purely for the purpose of deterring the Russians from starting it by attacking us; and the extent to which *we* should be prepared to start such a war (i.e., to strike the Soviet homeland without their previously having struck ours) in order to deter the Russians from attacks on Europe.

Those who put the greatest relative value on United States-Soviet Union stability, who have the greatest doubts about the feasibility of an American war-fighting capability, and who possess the greatest confidence in nonstrategic alternatives for the protection of Europe, tend to emphasize the arms control aspects of thermonuclear deterrence; they stress forces and tactics designed to deter war over those with a substantial ability to fight a nuclear war and they deemphasize the possibility of our having to strike first. Those who are relatively more concerned with Europe, who have greater faith in our ability to create a capability to fight a thermonuclear war, and who doubt that conventional alternatives for protecting Europe will be adopted (even if physically possible), tend to emphasize a less self-restrained form of deterrence; they want to deter attack on ourselves but they want to be able to fight well and win if deterrence fails, and they want to deter Soviet attack on Europe by being able to threaten credibly and if needs be execute a first strike against the Soviet Union. They argue that by deterring Soviet aggression, this strategy will make thermonuclear war *less* likely over the long run.

The middle-marginal debate over the first issue, the design of forces and tactics, appears similar to the disagreement between Waskow and Osgood over the balance of terror versus the separation of military targets from populations, but in practice it is considerably subtler than either that disagreement or the disagreement of almost all middle marginalists with both Waskow and Osgood. To begin with, as has been pointed out, middle marginalists favor control rather than lack of control. Few of even the most arms-control-oriented would endorse a Waskow system of terror, by which we would have no other option than to strike out blindly and kill as many Russians as possible if we were to strike at all. Contrariwise, they feel that a high degree of control over our forces is essential no matter what strategic posture we adopt. No matter what their disagreement over the answers as to ultimate strategy, they agree that the debate which explores all of the options is essential to the process of continuing strategic determination. Few middle marginalists would disagree with Schelling's argument that:

One of the revolutionary characteristics of modern strategy is that decisions are "canned" in advance much more than they were for earlier wars. There is not much time for adaptation, new indoctrination, ironing out misunderstandings, and changing plans. The options that have been anticipated are programmed into the weapons systems; those that have not been anticipated may be physically unavailable.

Decisions that depend on unexpected information, and that have to be made quickly, just cannot be made if the required information cannot be obtained. Decisions that require coordination and planning cannot be made if the procedure and organization have not been designed in advance, if some plans have not been drawn up, communicated, and embodied in operational procedures.

To identify possible situations and strategies in advance not only helps with respect to those situations and strategies; it also helps in emphasizing the need for flexibility, for adaptability, for communication systems and planning systems and weapon systems that can meet unexpected situations, can improvise, and can react to surprise.[28]

28 Thomas C. Schelling, "Comment," in *Limited Strategic War*, eds. Klaus Knorr and Thornton Read (New York: Praeger, 1962), pp. 257–258.

And this differs fundamentally from the desire of the anti-war marginalists to freeze thermonuclear strategy into a single-purpose mold.

Furthermore, virtually all middle marginalists would agree that even for deterrence of attack on the United States (particularly, in fact, for deterrence of attack on the United States), it is necessary to have strategic forces which are large and well-protected enough that a substantial number of deliverable weapons will survive a Soviet first strike.[29] And most of those in the middle disagree with the anti-war marginalists over civil defense. They argue on grounds similar to Schelling's that even though we think we can avoid thermonuclear war, it is necessary to have facilities "physically available" to protect population if the unexpected situation occurs. This civil defense recommendation is similar to that of the anti-Communist marginalists; the reasoning, however, is quite different from that which makes civil defense a fundamental part of our national strategy.

These three items of middle-marginal consensus—force control, force protection, and defenses for "insurance"—are the foundation upon which the major differences of opinion within the school are built. Beyond these, middle marginalists are divided over the questions of the design and the objectives of our strategic forces and tactics. Those middle marginalists most concerned with the arms-control aspects of deterrence oppose going beyond the basic concepts of force control, force protection, and contingency planning, to maintain over the years a force designed to enable the United States to mount a "counterforce" thermonuclear attack against Soviet weapons which is so large and well planned that it can disarm them and prevent their retaliation against *us*. King, for example, favors holding back from building the largest and strongest force of which we might be capable.

---

[29] This middle-marginal consensus is obvious today. It was not obvious, and indeed did not exist, until Albert Wohlstetter wrote, in January 1959, "The Delicate Balance of Terror" (*Foreign Affairs*, 37:211–234), in which he argued that deterrence was not automatic, but had to be carefully designed.

One possibility, worthy of consideration once our deterrent force is reasonably secure, is that we should continue to engage vigorously in research and development aimed at the design of a national counterforce posture, but moderate our expenditure on actual production of the components unless it seems certain that the Russians are going beyond us. That is, we would provide ourselves with the counterforce considered necessary for the stability of the deterrent, but also try to make it evident to the Russians that unless they set the pace we would not attempt to build counterforce capable of penetrating their deterrent.

. . . The choice is between (1) striving for a superiority that may well be beyond our reach, knowing that in the process we shall be pitting our energies against the trend to improved stability, thereby seeking to perpetuate mutual insecurity at risk of war, and (2) an alternative which, though hardly guaranteed, allows us to exploit rather than oppose the stabilizing forces. If we choose the former, arms control can hardly rise above the level of propaganda; if the latter, it may prove an invaluable safeguard.[30]

In stressing stability, King does not oppose a "counterforce" strategy defined simply as one which aims our weapons primarily at enemy weapons rather than population, but rather the "counterforce" he wants to hold back on is one so strong that it allows us to win by disarming the enemy. Counterforce as a philosophy of targeting has some middle-marginal opponents who fear that unless we deliberately aim at least some weapons at enemy populations, deterrence of Soviet attack on ourselves may be too weak, but most middle marginalists would agree that, once thermonuclear weapons are fired, they are best fired primarily at military targets.

The more important debate among middle marginalists, then, is over the use of counterforce to achieve a war-winning superiority. King's argument is that stability can be achieved only by self-limitation of the military objectives to be achieved in thermonuclear war; if both sides were to strive for superiority the result would be a highly destabilizing arms race.

30 James E. King, Jr., "Arms Control and United States Security," in The American Assembly, *Arms Control: Issues for the Public*, pp. 93–94. Copyright © 1961. By permission of Prentice-Hall, Inc., publisher.

The opposing view was put succinctly some time ago by Air Force Brigadier General S. F. Giffin:

The best way of discouraging an implacable enemy from war—any kind of war—is to be in a position to win it, to survive handily, and to act with the confidence of this position. If war is then not prevented, this is still the position to be in; and from the military or, indeed, any rational point of view, no other position is acceptable. Under circumstances which now exist or can be foreseen, the military ideal of providing complete protection for the population and capital plant of the home base seems certain of compromise, but a system of thought can and must be accepted which envisages the attainment of victory in any kind of war, that is, a situation in which the enemy alone is rendered unable or unwilling to continue organized prosecution of the war.[31]

Aside from the fact that "winning" is now more frequently termed "prevailing," the point of view is still very common among middle marginalists—one deters by being able to win; therefore not only for the purpose of being able to deter "lesser" Soviet aggression by maintaining a credible first-strike threat, but even in order best to deter Soviet attack against ourselves, it is important to be able to win a thermonuclear war.

The middle-marginal argument over whether we should strive for strategic superiority (or, put into more current terms, how hard we should strive to retain the superiority we now have), then, depends on the answers the calculus of deterrence provides to the problems of preventing Soviet aggression at various levels. It depends also on the analysis of the feasibility of retaining superiority; for those middle marginalists who do not accept the dominant answer that superiority best promotes both the values of peace and freedom, it depends on the relative weights assigned to these values. In any case, the middle marginalists all agree on the need for

[31] S. F. Giffin, "Relationships Among Military Forces," *Air University Quarterly Review*, 9:32 (Winter 1957–1958).

control in thermonuclear warfare, but disagree whether this control should be used in the context of stable mutual deterrence or should be pushed toward an attempt to achieve superiority over the Soviets. Those middle-marginalists who want to try for superiority are close to the anti-Communist marginalists in their recommendation, but in the use to be made of this superiority there is explicit divergence between the middle and the anti-Communist marginalists (although implicitly the two sides are actually rather close).

The divergence is over the other one of the dual issues of deterrence—the question of a United States thermonuclear strike against the Soviet Union before we have been struck (a more precise description of what is commonly known as an American first strike)—for which military superiority is a desirable attribute. As has been noted, the anti-Communists eschew the first strike. Their prize strategy is to be able to win at any level of violence, including a thermonuclear force which can "win strike second." Many middle marginalists doubt the achievement of such a spectrum of American capabilities, and they thus want to be able to "win strike first" as well, which seems very likely to be the recommendation of the anti-Communists given the failure of an all-levels capability. The middle-marginal argument in favor of maintaining the capability for a first strike is put by Kahn:

If the balance of terror were totally reliable we would be as likely to be deterred from striking the Soviets as they would be from striking us. We must still be able to fight and survive wars just as long as it is possible to have such a capability. Not only is it prudent to take out insurance against a war occurring unintentionally, but we must also be able to stand up to the threat of fighting or, credibly, to threaten to initiate a war ourselves—unpleasant though this sounds and is. We must at least make it risky for the enemy to force us into situations in which we must choose between fighting and appeasing . . .

Under current [1960] programs the United States may in a few years find itself unwilling to accept a Soviet retaliatory blow, no matter what the provocation. To get into such a situation would be equivalent to disowning our alliance obligations by signing what would amount to a nonaggression treaty with the Soviets—a nonaggression treaty with almost 200 million American hostages to guarantee performance.[32]

Kahn, at the time he wrote this, seemed interested in using civil defense and other devices to make it quite "credible" to the Russians that we would strike first if the situation called for it. Since then he has introduced the lesser concept of the "Not Incredible First Strike,"[33] which may suffice to deter the easily frightened Russians pictured by the Soviet-ologists as being scared enough of thermonuclear war that a small threat will do; and he has stressed the concept of civil defense as insurance which is more common among middle marginalists than that of civil defense as an essential portion of American deterrent strategy.[34]

Kahn's "not incredible" position is the typical one held by most of the middle marginalists who want to preserve the ability to strike first. For two reasons, almost all middle marginalists (as well as the anti-Communists) want to preserve at least some *slight* American first-strike capability: they believe that a preemptive situation might arise in which the choice is between striking first and striking second, rather than between peace and war; and they want it to remain credible that we will strike first in order to protect Western Europe at least against Soviet blackmail based on threatened use of thermonuclear weapons. Out of this large group who want to maintain a credible capability to oppose the most extreme Soviet threats, however, a somewhat smaller number of middle marginalists wish to preserve in addition a credible possibility that we will, as necessary, use strategic nuclear force

[32] Herman Kahn, *On Thermonuclear War* (Princeton: Princeton University Press, 1961), p. 559.

[33] Herman Kahn, *Thinking About the Unthinkable* (New York: Horizon, 1962), p. 244. Copyright © 1962 by Herman Kahn.

[34] See, for example, his contribution to "A Debate on the Question of Civil Defense," *Commentary*, January 1962.

to deter or defeat a *nonnuclear* Soviet threat to Europe. They feel that the spectrum of capabilities for beating the Russians at any level of violence is not and will not be available, and they are willing to prevent the less violent Soviet attack by making use of a more violent type of Western opposition.

The division between the middle marginalists who want to use thermonuclear deterrence against nonnuclear attack on Europe and those who oppose this is closely related to the division between the mutual deterrence stabilizers and the seekers of stability through superiority. Those who emphasize the arms-control aspects of deterrence oppose both superiority and the first strike (except under the extreme preemption or blackmail conditions postulated above). Most of those who want to go beyond arms control want to use superiority in order to preserve first-strike credibility, although a few superiority advocates argue only in terms of "win strike second." This division between the two types of makers of middle-marginal recommendations (as usual, we divide by designating an arbitrary boundary on what is in reality a continuum of varying recommendations) is an important one. Although the difference is certainly less deep than the gap separating the middle from the other two marginal schools—the controlled-deterrence recommendations typical of the middle are vastly different from the deterrence-as-terror recommendations which characterize the anti-war marginalists; the arms-control recommendations of the middle are drastically different from the political-strategy recommendations of the anti-Communists—the middle is divided over both the method and the objective of deterrence. This division is based in part on differences in the relative values given to stability and the protection of Europe, and in part on differences over analyses. One of the key analyses is of the feasibility and credibility of our doing more with deterrence than merely protecting ourselves; the other relates to the set of alternatives available to keep our European allies from Soviet attack or dominance.

United States Arms Policy in Europe

As is indicated by the discussion of the credible first strike, the strategic recommendations of the middle and anti-Communist marginal schools cannot be fully understood in isolation from their recommendations for American strategy in Europe. The credible first strike is one possible alternative for the protection of Western Europe from the Soviet threat; whether the capability to strike first is endorsed for more than the extreme possibilities of preemptive war or nuclear blackmail depends heavily on what other alternatives are available for opposing the more moderate and more likely Soviet threats.

The *middle marginalists* (the anti-war marginalists' European recommendations are so different from the others that it is useful to maintain the narrative flow on the middle at the cost of reversing the usual order by which we have taken up first the anti-war school) concentrate their recommendations for European strategy on finding ways to counter the various Soviet threats. The middle-marginal values most directly relevant to Europe are three: to prevent the kind of war which might escalate into general thermonuclear war; to preserve West European power as a supplement to our own and an aid to the preservation of our freedom; and (at least for those middle marginalists who espouse freedom as a value), to help preserve the peace and liberty of those whose political systems and cultures are most similar to our own. The proximate objectives based on these are the military prevention of either Soviet attack or Soviet political advance based on the threat of attack, the preservation of NATO (and the ultimate unification of Western Europe), and the tying of Germany into the Alliance and into unified Europe with unbreakable bonds. It is the middle which worries about German history, but, unlike the anti-war schools, feels that Germany must be held to Western democracy by self-interest. And it is the middle whose analysis indicates both that the interests of the Soviet Union center on Western Europe and that *our* interest in the area is the keystone of our very existence. Next only to the strategic thermonuclear balance, our strategy must be centered on the military and political issues in the NATO region.

The Soviet military threat in Europe can manifest itself in four ways: through the possibility of massive nuclear blackmail or attack; through attack using tactical nuclear weapons; through the possibility of nonnuclear attack on Western Europe on a large scale approaching that of World War II; or through smaller, probably nonnuclear, actions in which Soviet forces are used to create pressure, as in Berlin (or even to carry out small military *faits accomplis,* as has also been possible in Berlin). And underlying the need for Western resistance to these threats has been the analysis, quoted above from the Senate Report, of the political meaning to Europe of the military balance: "In a large measure, confidence is the essential although intangible binding force of the non-Communist world—confidence mainly that the United States can and will support resistance to aggression."[35] The need then is for the United States to conceive and execute a continuing military policy in Europe which will have the double purpose of deterring and defeating any of the four Soviet military threats, on the one hand, and maintaining the confidence of our European allies that these threats will be either deterred or defeated, on the other. By doing this we maintain the Western alliance, and by maintaining the alliance we keep the Soviets out of democratic West Europe and the Germans in it.

The binding ties of confidence are dependent mainly on the real capabilities for countering the four real threats— massive nuclear, tactical nuclear, large-scale nonnuclear, and limited *fait accompli.* Of these, the first can be met only with countervailing nuclear force. The threat of nuclear blackmail, "Do what we say, or we will exterminate London, Paris, etc.," can be countered only by the deterrent threat to do likewise to Soviet cities. This may appear to be a very un-

35 See p. 189 in Chapter 9.

likely possibility in any case, but the enormity of even the small possibility makes the middle marginalists believe it necessary to have a credible means of combating the threat— necessary particularly to the European nations which feel threatened. And because it is necessary to them, it is important to the ties of confidence. Slightly more likely, perhaps, is the possibility that the Russians might attack Western Europe using tactical nuclear weapons, and the means of meeting this are also subject to middle-marginal debate. Most important, most difficult, and most controversial among middle marginalists, however, are the two less violent threats, the large-scale and the limited nonnuclear attacks. These seem more likely than the others, and the problems involved in avoiding their escalation (or perhaps preserving the chance of their escalation in order to deter them from starting in the first place) are more complex than the others.

Middle marginalists have offered five strategies, together or in combination, for combating the various Soviet threats to Western Europe. These are: the American first strike against the Soviet homeland in case of Soviet attack on Europe; the creation of a nuclear deterrent force under the command of either NATO or its European members; the creation of "independent" national deterrent forces by those individual European nations capable and desirous of creating them; the use of "tactical" nuclear weapons on the "battle-field," rather than directly against the Soviet homeland; and the use of nonnuclear NATO forces to hold or defeat nonnuclear Soviet attacks of either the massive or the *fait accompli* varieties. The first three strategies—the United States first strike, the NATO deterrent, and the independent national deterrents—are alternatives for countering large-scale nuclear blackmail, and general agreement exists among middle marginalists that one of these strategies is necessary for meeting this threat. There is no consensus, however, on which one, and the debate has been an important one among middle marginalists both in the United States and the other NATO nations.

The rationale of the search for deterrents not dependent upon United States action—either the national or all-European forces—has been a fear on the part of Europeans that the United States would not be willing to risk substantial devastation of its homeland in order to protect Europe. The European fear has been that even if a Kahn "credible first-strike" posture were adopted by the United States, the damage to this country which would still be possible would deter us from using our Strategic Air Command against anything but direct attack upon ourselves; and besides there has been no guarantee that the Kahn recommendations will be adopted. As a result of this and various political factors, Great Britain has developed an independent national nuclear force, France has been doing so, and various European strategists have put forward general arguments for this sort of action on the part of individual NATO nations. These arguments have not been convincing to many American middle marginalists; Americans worry more about nuclear diffusion and less about specific European problems than do Europeans. But European arguments have become part of the American debate—some Americans, not convinced that non-American nuclear forces are needed to deter the Russians, nonetheless feel that they are needed to satisfy the allies and hold the alliance together.

French General Pierre Gallois, the chief European theorist of independent deterrence, puts the military arguments against European dependence upon either American or NATO deterrents:

And how believe that the Strategic Air Command would use its weapons of massive destruction for the sake of a third party, if America thereby risked, in reprisal, a setback of two centuries from the extent of the damages suffered!

Then what becomes of the indispensable credibility of the reprisal against aggression? . . .

Still another formula: instead of depending on the Strategic Air Command the instruments of dissuasion could be mustered under the authority of a NATO command. Consequently the

Atlantic nations could feel that their protection did not derive from an American decision alone. They would at least discuss the conditions under which retaliation would be launched. But, in the case in point, it is less the opinion of the guaranteed nation than that of the potential aggressor which counts. If the latter knew that the functioning of the reprisal forces was subordinate to the agreement of some fifteen governments, he would have much less to fear from these forces than from those the American government possessed in its own right, even when acting for the sake of other nations . . .

The foregoing analysis leads to the national deterrent. Not that it is easy to establish or that it is all-powerful. But it is logical that the nation possessing weapons of dissuasion should take the risk of using them when its very existence is threatened. Nationally wielded, the deterrent imposes at least a certain credibility and a certain fear. It presents the advantage of having a meaning only in the one circumstance in which it can be used: the threat of subjugation, blackmail by thermonuclear annihilation, etc. To be effective it need only represent a quantity of destruction equivalent to the advantages the aggressor would derive from the "absorption" of the nation it threatens.[36]

As this has become the official position of the French, some American middle marginalists have accepted it—more on political than intellectual grounds. But many, Americans and Europeans, have opposed the attempts of the NATO nations to obtain independent deterrents because they have been worried about the Nth-country problem—the increased chances of nuclear war consequent upon the diffusion of control over nuclear weapons. They have been somewhat concerned with the statistical increase in the chances of war which might stem from this diffusion; they have been more concerned about the political effect on world stability of the possibility that the Germans might ultimately gain independent control of nuclear weapons; they have been most concerned that the creation of independent West

[36] Pierre Gallois, *The Balance of Terror* (Boston: Houghton Mifflin, 1961), pp. 191–198.

European deterrents might exert political pressure on the Soviet Union to assist China in gaining a similar capability. And because of these concerns, many middle marginalists have recommended the creation of a deterrent force under the control of NATO itself or some part of it; they feel that this may blunt the drive for independent single-nation deterrents. There has been a variety of proposals. Some have advocated a deterrent under the control of NATO as such;[37] others have argued that this would merely perpetuate and duplicate the problems created by the fact that the United States has had a veto over the use of *all* Western nuclear forces, and that therefore a purely West European force should be created. One specific recommendation of this latter type, presented by Charles McClintock and Dale Hekhuis, is rather typical, but is notable for explicit advocacy of West European community institutions, set up to avoid the problem of many fingers on the trigger and many on the safety catch of the joint deterrent force:

The strategy advocated . . . would involve creating a community deterrent in which a group of European nations would agree in advance to accept the decisions of a supranational institution for developing and employing strategic weapons. Through a community effort, sufficient resources would be available, with some United States aid, to build and maintain an effective deterrent. Also, since strategic decisions would be made by predesignated representatives and would not require the approval of sovereign nations, a community organization could meet a variety of environmental contingencies with speed and flexibility. Furthermore, such an organization would provide a more stable basis, i.e., less error, smaller likelihood of irresponsible employment, etc., for the control of nuclear weapons in Europe than would . . . a fragmented deterrence system in which each

[37] See, for example, Alastair Buchan, *NATO in the 1960's* (New York: Praeger, 1960), particularly pages 70 ff. Buchan later changed conditionally to a position which endorsed continued United States control over the final use of its weapons. See his "The Reform of NATO," *Foreign Affairs*, 40:179 (January 1962).

sovereign nation would possess more or less independent control over its own strategic weapon force.[38]

The grounds for such proposals have shifted in recent years; as Great Britain established her nuclear deterrent and France went ahead inexorably with the process of creating hers, it became obvious that a jointly controlled nuclear force could no longer preclude the initial establishment of individual ones. Rather, some have hoped that a joint force can be created out of the British and French forces.[39] This might both accomplish the deterrent tasks for which SAC is becoming less credible, and help achieve the grand objective of European unity which is dear to middle-marginal hearts.

But most middle marginalists believe that in any case, the *ultimate* guarantor of European integrity against nuclear blackmail must remain the possibility that the American nuclear force, much more powerful than anything likely to be created either jointly or separately by the Europeans, will answer an attack on London or Paris with one on Moscow or Leningrad. And many believe that it would be best if the "credible first strike" by United States thermonuclear forces were to remain the *sole* guarantor. The American first strike has been discussed above as a part of United States strategic policy. Albert Wohlstetter puts it into the context of European strategies, and favors Europe's exclusive dependence upon it. He writes of the other two alternatives:

To sum up the case against national nuclear forces: from the national standpoint of a responsible power, they are costly and of dubious military value. Their political value has been exaggerated, for, as the English have learned, it encourages emulation and is therefore transient. From the standpoint of world stability, wide nuclear diffusion would be gravely disruptive. It would increase the likelihood of the use of nuclear weapons both by accident and by deliberation.

[38] Charles G. McClintock and Dale J. Hekhuis, "European Community Deterrence: Its Organization, Utility and Political Feasibility," *The Journal of Conflict Resolution*, 5:234 (September 1961).

[39] See, for example, Henry A. Kissinger, "The Unsolved Problems of European Defense," *Foreign Affairs*, 40:537-538 (June 1962).

... it seems unlikely that a NATO strike force would provide a deterrent to the Soviets more credible than that of the dubious national strike forces. It is still more doubtful that it would improve the American guarantee . . .

Some proponents of the NATO strike force concede that its military worth would be low, but feel that its political value is high. Its political worth, however, may be negative. First of all, its political effects cannot be divorced from its military content. If, as I have suggested, the alleged merits of a NATO strike force will not bear analysis, this will be evident in time and is bound to trouble our allies. Second, the automatic-decision features in some versions of the proposal have disturbing political implications and would be likely to feed the fires of unilateralism both here and in Europe. Third, the probable refusal of some of our principal NATO partners to join in the project would tend to break the alliance into blocs. Fourth, it may be interpreted as a move toward withdrawal of the American umbrella.[40]

Thus these two alternatives are bad ones for two of the major criteria applied by middle marginalists to deterrent forces— by encouraging nuclear diffusion, they are anti-arms control; by their negative political effects they erode rather than encourage the unity of Western Europe.

On the main criticism of European dependence upon an American first strike, then, the possibility that it may be becoming incredible, Wohlstetter also disagrees:

It is fashionable to say that an American response to a Soviet nuclear attack in Europe is incredible. Is the statement true? What precisely does it mean?

Perhaps the first thing to observe is that it means nothing very precise. To talk in terms of credibility or incredibility suggests that the alternatives are simply Yes or No. But in fact neither our response nor our failure to respond is certain. The real questions center on how likely we would be to respond in circumstances that are worth considering . . .

Sober thought would suggest that the American response is

40 Albert Wohlstetter, "Nuclear Sharing: NATO and the N + 1 Country," *Foreign Affairs*, 39:371–377 (April 1961).

by no means "incredible." The fashionable notion, I believe, is wrong, even if we interpret "incredible" as meaning simply "very unlikely." In any plausible circumstance of thermonuclear attack on Europe we would be likely to reply today, and, if we and our allies choose our policies carefully, this will remain true.[41]

Thus the middle-marginal analytical belief in answers which are neither yes nor no but somewhere in between is extended to the concept of the credibility of an American first strike against the Soviet Union. And thus *the credible-first-strike recommendation which appeared to be anti-arms control when compared to the strategic-policy alternative of second-strike-only, is made to appear pro-arms-control when compared to the European-policy alternative of proliferating fingers on the nuclear trigger.*

Most of the inconsistency between these two ways of looking at the first strike, however, is more apparent than real. The three alternative modes of nuclear deterrence of an attack on Europe—by individual countries, by a community of countries, or by the United States—all relate to deterrence of Soviet actions by the use of direct threats to the Soviet homeland. If such deterrents are used *solely* for the purpose of preventing Soviet thermonuclear blackmail against Western Europe—a possibility which middle marginalists feel must be guarded against, but which middle-marginal Soviet-ologists consider to have only a very small likelihood because of Soviet fear of holocaust—then the first-strike capability called for by Wohlstetter may be at least partially compatible with the emphasis on the arms-control aspects of deterrence suggested by King. Such massive Soviet blackmail would, in itself, upset the stability consequent upon King's recommendations for a *controlled* balanced deterrent. By contrast, Waskow's terror-based deterrent might remain unusable against even the most extreme Soviet threats against Europe.

But to the extent the American first-strike or any of the other alternatives for nuclear deterrence in Europe are opposed to the less violent possibilities for Soviet action, tactical

[41] *Ibid.*, pp. 377–378.

nuclear attack, large-scale nonnuclear attack, or a limited *fait accompli,* their threatened use *does* necessarily subordinate the mutual arms-control aspects of deterrence. In arguing for the American-first-strike alternative, largely on the grounds of opposition to nuclear diffusion, Wohlstetter himself remains consistent in his pro-arms-control orientation. He wants to use his American first-strike capability only against the possibility of a massive Soviet thermonuclear threat against Europe, and be able to meet the lesser threats on their own grounds. He opposes Western initiation of tactical nuclear warfare, but favors retention of tactical nuclear capabilities in Europe to meet attacks in kind.[42] And in relation to nonnuclear attack he argues:

> From [the Russian] standpoint the problem of successful aggression in Europe is to find a level and kind of attack large enough to be useful, but small enough to be well below the threshold risking American nuclear response.
> NATO's problem is to try to make sure the Russians cannot manage a useful attack without making it so large that it would be hard to distinguish from the start of a central war. . . . It is becoming more and more widely accepted among critics of NATO that the most important task for the alliance today is to raise by conventional means the threshold of attack that the Russians would have to launch in order to be successful.[43]

Most of those who would like to maintain the American nuclear capability as the sole guarantor of Europe against the Soviet nuclear capability want to do so specifically for arms-control reasons, such as avoiding nuclear diffusion, and they want, also for arms-control reasons, to limit to nuclear provocations the use of nuclear response, meeting *all* aggression at its own level. Some of those, on the other hand, who favor a more diffused nuclear control, want this in part as an answer to conventional aggression as well as nuclear. This is particularly true of those who recommend independent national deterrents. Gallois' argument is directed specifically at

42 *Ibid.,* p. 383.
43 *Ibid.,* pp. 381–382.

preventing the "absorption" of European nations by the Soviet; since the Soviet has the conventional capability to do this, the national deterrents must guard against this conventional capability as well as the nuclear one.

Many of those who are inclined to favor (or at least not to frown upon) nuclear deterrents outside of the control of the United States, however, agree with Wohlstetter that these deterrents should be reserved for the ultimate cases. Kissinger argues for either the meeting of aggression in kind at every level or the opposition of tactical nuclear weapons to massive Soviet conventional attack, but he prefers both of these to reliance on United States strategic deterrence of Soviet ground attack in Europe. His arguments present some of the dilemmas of both the meeting-aggression-at-its-own-level mode and the tactical nuclear mode of opposing Soviet force:

[The all-levels] course is not beyond the capabilities of NATO. Western Europe alone is superior to the U.S.S.R. in industrial capacity and even in manpower, and the North Atlantic Community as a whole should find it much easier than the Soviet bloc to maintain a full spectrum of deterrent power. The frequently heard argument that NATO must retain its present strategy because its people are not prepared to make the necessary sacrifices for an effective local defense is surely inconsistent with the hope of maintaining the credibility of a counterforce first strike. Why should an aggressor believe that people and leaders who are not prepared to make the comparatively small sacrifices needed to assure a conventional local defense would be willing to face the enormous devastation implied by general nuclear war?

At the same time, a decision to rely on a largely conventional defense is not without its risks. Unless we act with great delicacy and subtlety, it could give rise to the notion that the West considers *any* kind of nuclear war unthinkable regardless of provocation . . .

If NATO is not willing to make the effort required for a conventional defense, its other option would be to rely more heavily on tactical nuclear weapons . . .

In this strategy, the conventional forces should be at least

strong enough to stop the Soviet forces deployed in Germany
and Eastern Europe. This would prevent a sudden *coup de main*.
A decisive Soviet attack would require an advance buildup of
troops. If the West's conventional forces were powerful enough
so that very considerable Soviet reinforcements were required,
many targets for tactical nuclear weapons would be presented . . .
Deterrence would be achieved not by protecting against every
contingency, but by confronting the Soviets with the prospect of
a conflict with incalculable consequences.

The difference between this option and the current strategy
is threefold: (a) Major reliance would be placed on stopping a
Soviet attack without resorting to a counterforce strike. (b) Nuclear weapons would be used not after a pause and when NATO's
conventional forces were on the verge of being overwhelmed.
Rather they would be employed early in the operation, as soon
as it was clear that a massive Soviet attack was under way. (c)
The primary use of nuclear weapons would be in the battle
area.[44]

Kissinger thus presents the arguments for the two "local"
strategies to oppose massive attacks. Lacking a conventional
force in substantial excess of 30 divisions, he reluctantly
favors a tactical nuclear strategy. To these arguments he and
most middle marginalists add that even with a tactical nuclear
strategy enough nonnuclear forces are needed to oppose conventionally a Soviet attempt at *fait accompli* in those cases
where it is not "clear that a massive Soviet attack was under
way."

Middle marginalists thus come to as little agreement on
the question of tactical nuclear versus nonnuclear "local"
forces as on the question of who should control the deterrent. They draw their European military strategies from the
two-course menu which includes American, NATO, and
independent national deterrents on the one hand, and conventional and tactical nuclear local defenses on the other.
The particular items chosen from each category by an individual depend in part on his analyses of what is feasible and
what are the dangers of escalation, but they also depend

[44] Kissinger, pp. 524–526.

heavily upon his value judgments. Those middle marginalists who put the greatest emphasis on the arms-control aspects of deterrence tend to favor the exclusively American deterrent and the most nearly nonnuclear local defense; those American middle marginalists most interested in uniting the Atlantic community want a deterrent posture which will give Europe greater confidence than they believe exclusive American control can provide, and a local defense posture which will rely on nonnuclear forces only if they are large enough to succeed beyond question; and at least some Europeans, also middle marginalists, feel that the only way that *they* can have complete confidence is by self-confidence in national deterrents to guard against "absorption" by the Soviet bloc.

As is indicated by the stress on "confidence," and as has been emphasized throughout, all of these recommendations for military policy in Europe have as much a political object as a purely military one. The political basis is the desire to hold together the free-world position in Europe, and all of the middle-marginal strategies are designed to hold at least until Europe is unified, and the Grand Alliance between a strong Europe and a strong United States becomes clearly superior in power to the Soviet Union. This is the basic political reason for the middle marginalists' desire for strong deterrence and defense in Europe. They are generally in favor of exploratory negotiations with the Russians over European as well as other issues, but they are united on the belief that these negotiations should be based on the "strong" position of being unwilling to give in on any issue without a definite *quid pro quo*. This has both short- and long-run aspects. In the short run, we should avoid the temptation to give in "this once." According to Allen Ferguson, writing in 1962 and using the example of Berlin:

If the Soviets do intend to expand into Western Europe, using force if it is necessary and promising, we can look forward to further pressure on such vulnerable points as Berlin. If we should acquiesce in the engulfing of Berlin, and if the Soviets are aggressive rather than defensive, one would expect that they will undertake to move further. If they are defensive and we were to acquiesce, we should then have bought peace at the price of the freedom of only two million more people plus some reduction in hope for all East Germans. . . .

If we resist in Berlin and in subsequent crises, there is some risk of local fighting, and if local fighting develops, there is some risk that general war will follow. Although these risks do not appear to be great in the sense that there is a high probability that in the next several years there will be general war, they are critically important. . . . It is the purpose of both deterrence and disarmament to keep those risks small.

What I have been trying to suggest is that for the Soviets to dominate the world by 1980 or so, they would do well to have Western Europe not long after 1970. There is evidence and some logic in the proposition that they seek to dominate the world and seek to acquire Western Europe. The United States cannot tolerate the loss to the Bloc of Western Europe. Therefore, the major danger stems from potential Soviet aggression against Western Europe. In my judgment, the danger of a major Russian attack on Europe is not now very great, because of Western military power. It can be kept small, even if the Soviets persist in hostile intent, if we keep the price of Europe high.[45]

He thus parlays the middle-marginal analyses of the carefully hostile Soviets, the importance of Europe, and the uses of military deterrence, together with the value placed on both our freedom and that of Europe, into the military recommendation to "keep the price of Europe high," and the political recommendation to "resist in Berlin."

This middle-marginal position favoring "toughness" in positions on the short-run aspects of negotiations also tends to put many of them into opposition to various anti-war marginalist arguments in favor of looking for a more fundamental *détente* in Europe based on military disengagement. Although some middle-marginal Sovietologists, like Brzezinski and Griffith, are interested in small steps which in some descriptions seem to approach military disengagement,[46] the more ordinary position is opposed to recommendations of

45 Allen R. Ferguson, *Disarmament and Deterrence*, The RAND Corporation, Paper P-2553 (Santa Monica, April 1962), pp. 12–13.
46 See p. 195 in Chapter 9.

this type. The dependence of middle-marginal military and
political policy on NATO, plus the lack of great interest in
trying to loosen the bonds on the East European satellites (on
which, as has been discussed, the middle is in disagreement
with *both* the anti-war and the anti-Communist marginalists)
combine to produce some very strong antidisengagement
positions. Disengagement is not a new idea, and the classical
argument against it written by Dean Acheson in 1958 still
gives a good description of the typical (if not universal)
middle-marginal position:

First, let us consider the idea that something called disengagement can be brought about by removing American, British,
Canadian and Russian troops from some area in Europe. What
disengagement does this bring about? Very little, as one sees if
one pauses to consider the realities. Compare the confrontation
which takes place between the United States and the Soviet Union
in Germany with that which occurs along the DEW line—that system of early warning stations which stretches from Alaska, across
the Arctic regions, and far out into the Atlantic . . . they represent
a contact which no action in Germany can disengage. There is
confrontation in every part of the world where the area of the
open and free world system may be reduced by Soviet military,
economic or political penetration. No action in Germany will
produce disengagement here. The word is a mere conception,
which confuses and does not represent any reality.

So let us turn from it to consider something more capable of
delineation. For instance, exactly what is the extent of the mutual
withdrawal about which we are asked to negotiate? . . . there can
be little doubt, I believe, that, once a withdrawal begins, it will
be complete, so far as United States, British and Canadian troops
are concerned. . . . If withdrawal is represented as advantageous
for Germans, it would seem equally advantageous to Frenchmen,
Icelanders, Moroccans, Saudi Arabians, and the rest would quickly
follow. And, once the idea caught hold, Americans would, of
course, join in the general demand. . . .

We must think of what we purchase for this vast price. What
would Russian withdrawal from Germany or the heart of Europe
amount to? Is it possible to believe that the Soviet government,
whatever it may say or whatever agreement it may sign, would,

or could, contemplate withdrawing its forces behind, say, the River Bug, and keeping them there? . . . if its physical force were permanently removed from Eastern Europe, who can believe that even one of the Communist regimes would survive? Therefore, wherever Soviet forces might be garrisoned, the expectation and threat of their return must continue to be ever present (at most it would require from twelve to eighteen hours). . . .

At this point in our discussion we must examine the conception of the neutralization of Germany; . . . It is necessary, we are told, that Germany should not be allowed to be free to choose its own course after unification. It must accept limitations upon its military forces and its military alignment. In other words, its national life will be conducted under far greater limitations than those in which other sovereign people live. The possibility that any such situation could endure seems to me quite fantastic.

. . . it would not be long, I fear, before there would be an accommodation of some sort or another between an abandoned Germany and the great Power to the East. Under this accommodation, a sort of new Ribbentrop-Molotov agreement, the rest of the free world would be faced with what has twice been so intolerable as to provoke world war—the unification of the European land mass (this time the Eurasian land mass) under a power hostile to national independence and individual freedom.[47] Disengagement thus goes in precisely the opposite direction to the unified West-*cum*-Germany foreign policy upon which the middle-marginal structure of recommendation is based.

The *anti-Communist marginalists,* of course, are even less interested in disengagement than the middle marginalists, at least some of whom sometimes flirt with the idea. They too want to free Eastern European satellites—this is one of the important and distinguishing features of their policy—but their recommendations for this purpose follow more the lines of Bjelajac's analysis of the uses of guerrilla forces within the Communist area. Frank Barnett recommends, for example:

. . . the creation of an American *fourth weapon,* coequal with the Army, Navy and Air Force. Its purpose would be to offset the current Soviet advantage in non-military weapons systems which may enable them—under the umbrella of nuclear terror—to seize

[47] Dean Acheson, "The Illusion of Disengagement," *Foreign Affairs,* 36:375–377 (April 1958).

Asia, the Middle East, and Africa piecemeal by *coup d'états,* precinct politics, fifth columns and popular fronts. . . .

An American "fourth weapon" might consist of the following components and activities:

1. A separate Cabinet office. . . .
2. A joint Congressional Committee on Cold War strategy. . . .
3. An Assistant Secretary for Non-Military Defense in the Pentagon. . . .
4. A career service for officers who elect to become specialists in the propaganda and psychological warfare fields. . . .
5. The creation of foreign legions composed of Russians, Poles, Hungarians, Koreans, Chinese, Ukrainians, and others who have fled from behind the Iron Curtain. . . .
6. The establishment of . . . a West Point of political warfare.[48]

The anti-Communist marginalists' recommendations for subverting the Soviet satellites in order to keep the Russians off balance and ultimately to liberate Eastern Europe are unique among marginalists. (It is worth noting, in this connection, that Strausz-Hupé, Kintner, and Possony nonetheless explicitly, if tentatively, reject a strategy based upon "wars of liberation."[49]) For their recommendations on American arms policy in Western Europe, however, the anti-Communist marginalists merely choose the "toughest" items from the middle-marginal menu. Unlike most American middle marginalists, the anti-Communists look favorably upon United States encouragement to independent national nuclear deterrents for NATO nations. The editors of *Orbis* write:

The knowledge that the national forces in any given country have at hand nuclear delivery systems for their own defense might make the Soviets hesitate before launching an attack against them. . . .

If the multiple balance could be restored in the new form of independent nuclear power centers, a new dimension of risk

[48] Frank Rockwell Barnett, "Disengagement or Commitment," *Orbis,* 2:432–433 (Winter 1959).

[49] *A Forward Strategy for America,* pp. 31–32. Copyright © 1961 by Robert Strausz-Hupé, William Kintner, and Stefan T. Possony.

might be introduced into Soviet calculations. The Soviets, in planning their gambits, might be forced to calculate the threshold of survival not only of the U.S., but of the countries immediately involved.

. . . What the Atlantic Alliance needs is the capability to meet the *full* range of communist military challenges, with or without resort to nuclear weapons. But unlocking our nuclear vaults to selected countries in NATO would mean a giant step toward this objective.[50]

The anti-Communists thus want to ensure the strongest deterrent action against Soviet nuclear blackmail—action taken by the nations to be blackmailed. This is part of the context in which they feel that the United States strategy need not stress the "credible first strike," but can rather depend upon "win strike second." In context, it is also obvious that the anti-Communists do not perceive independent national deterrents as being useful *only* against nuclear blackmail; they would expect the nations holding the power to deter their defeat by Soviet conventional forces as well. For local defense in Europe, however, the anti-Communist marginalists have two more strings to their bow. For psychological-political reasons, they recommend a strong nonnuclear capability. According to *A Forward Strategy:* ". . . it stands to reason that it would be desirable on political, psychological and military grounds to shift the onus for initiating the use of nuclear weapons to the communists. By maintaining a sizable nonnuclear military capability we can force the Soviets to use *their* nuclear weapons *first* if they choose to fight to achieve their objectives."[51] But, unlike those middle marginalists who favor a nonnuclear ground strategy for Europe, the anti-Communists do not recommend, even if we build our nonnuclear forces up to preponderant levels, that we reserve our tactical nuclear weapons for reply to Soviet first use:

50 "Reflections on the Quarter," *Orbis*, 4:3–4 (Spring 1960).
51 *A Forward Strategy for America*, p. 142. Copyright © 1961 by Robert Strausz-Hupé, William Kintner, and Stefan T. Possony.

. . . the Free World's defenses need to be strengthened not only by raising additional ready land forces, but also by increasing their tactical superiority through the intelligent and vigorous integration of all new technologies, among which tactical nuclear weapons are most significant.

Even considering world opinion, the United States must calculate the disastrous harm to its international prestige if it were defeated in a limited war with the communists because it feared to resort to nuclear weapons. Although we hope that the onus for initiating nuclear war will fall upon the Kremlin, the communist strategists must be under no misapprehension that we will not use, if necessary, nuclear arms.[52]

The anti-Communist marginalists' recommendations for arms policy in Europe are thus consistent with their recommendations for strategic arms policy. They favor deterrent and fighting capabilities on the continent which would preclude the need for a non-European deterrent to protect Europe. But the protection of Europe is a primary necessity for American policy, and we and the Europeans must utilize a multifaceted, heavily nuclear strategy to ensure the continued achievement of this objective. None of this calls for something basically new and different from the middle-marginal recommendations (as the anti-Communist *strategic* deterrent recommendations differed from the middle recommendations, all of which placed stress on the arms-control aspects of deterrence), but rather for Western Europe, the anti-Communist marginalists recommend a very tough version of middle marginalism.

The *anti-war marginalists,* however, are quite different in their European recommendations from the other two marginal schools. They have, for the most part, no very great interest in any of the military alternatives for the protection of Europe, because they feel that the Soviet military threat to Europe is, if not completely illusory, not very great. They favor none of the nuclear deterrents, American, national, or NATO, nor do they favor any such defenses on the European

52 *Ibid.,* p. 143.

continent. They want, even more than the middle marginalists, to keep any kind of nuclear weapons out of German
hands.

All of this is based on the analytical belief that the Soviet
Union is becoming consolidationist, and that, although if we
made it very easy, they might adventure into Europe, the
basic Soviet goal is to consolidate its East European holdings
and prevent any West German "revanchism." The anti-war
marginalists add to this picture of consolidationist Soviet aims
several other analytical and value factors, all of which tend
in the same direction. Their chief value is in the prevention
of war, and their analytical belief is that any war, particularly in Europe, is bound to escalate out of control. Because
of their value-analytical orientation toward the underdeveloped world, they are, at their most extreme, rather suspicious
of NATO, and, at their most moderate, unwilling to place
the kind of emphasis on the Alliance put by the Europe-
oriented middle marginalists. And most anti-war marginalists
are suspicious of Germany; while they do not adopt the Soviet attitude that Germany is now "revanchist" and aggressive, they feel that on the basis of German history it could
well become so again, and they would like very much to
remove the capability for this happening. And, finally, on
the basis of their libertarian values, the plight of the East
Europeans disturbs them; on the basis of their much more
weighty anti-war values, they certainly do not want to take
any militant action to free them; they are therefore interested
in finding another way out.

The result of all this is a double position—one for the
short run and one for the long. In the short run, the recommendations of the anti-war marginalists go a long way in
quest of compromising any conflict of interest with the Soviets
which may arise in Europe. This, it should be emphasized, is
a search for a real compromise, not the unilateral giving in
to Soviet desires which is characteristic of the anti-war *systemists,* but it nonetheless involves more accommodation and
less "standing up for our rights" than is recommended by

either of the other two marginal schools. And in the long run the anti-war marginalists accompany their desire for strategic disarmament with a search for *détente* in Europe— usually *détente* based on some variety of disengagement or demilitarization in Central Europe with emphasis on Germany.

To use Berlin as the example again, then, the basis of the short-run need for accommodation in this area is described by Jean Daniel: ". . . a firm attitude is dependent on that attitude's being both morally indisputable and popular. Yet everyone, or at least everyone in Europe, knows that even the most anti-Communist public opinion will not risk a nuclear war over the status of Berlin. If in the past there was reluctance to 'dying for Danzig,' it is more certain that no one today wants to be annihilated for Berlin. This is what lends strength to those voices in France and in England which are being raised in favor of a negotiation . . ."[53] This paragraph (which was written before the construction of the Berlin wall) suggests Western weakness such that we would have little choice but to salvage what was possible and bargain on Soviet terms. It has been on these beliefs that many proposals for internationalization of West Berlin, *de facto* recognition of East German sovereignty over the corridors to Berlin, and the like, have been based. And the attitude of refusing to "die for Danzig," is similar to that taken by anti-war marginalists in various European crises since 1945, starting with the guerrilla war in Greece.

As the Berlin crisis has worn on, year after year, however, many individuals in all schools have been inclined to look at it less in short-run terms than as the culmination of the fundamental problem of power relations in Europe. The anti-war marginalists have tended to see this basic problem in terms of Germany almost as much as in terms of the confrontation between the West and the Soviet Union. To many in the anti-war school the real importance of Berlin has been

[53] Jean Daniel, "The Pressures on Khrushchev," *The New Republic*, July 24, 1961, p. 12.

as an illustration of the need to stabilize and consolidate both Eastern and Western positions in Germany. As put by James Warburg:

Both sides have now recognized that the situation in Berlin is "abnormal." The question is: "Can its abnormality be corrected without correcting the abnormality of a partitioned Germany?"

It appears to us that the Western powers must finally face a choice which has all along been inescapable. They must decide which of two things they want most—a German military contribution to NATO or the reunification of the two German states. They cannot have both.

Either choice implies a different sort of solution for the problem of Berlin.

If the Western powers decide that they cannot forego German participation in Western defense, then they must accept the more or less permanent partition of Germany, which implies the recognition of the East German state and acceptance of the *status quo* in Eastern Europe. In this case it would be unrealistic to expect West Berlin to remain as a Western-controlled island of freedom in the heart of the East German state. . . .

The other alternative would be for the Western powers to decide that they want German reunification more than they want a German military contribution to NATO. They would then put forward a proposal under which the two German states would be enabled to find their way to reunification without outside interference of any sort. Obviously this would require the withdrawal of Soviet coercive power from East Germany—an end which could not be attained without a countervailing withdrawal of Anglo-French-American forces perhaps no farther than to the west bank of the Rhine. . . .

The first would undoubtedly be easier to negotiate with the Russians. We are opposed to it . . .[54]

Thus, continued endorsement of both German unification *and* continued German participation in NATO is not an available alternative. The concatenation of the anti-war mar-

[54] James Warburg, "A Reexamination of American Foreign Policy," in *The Liberal Papers*, pp. 67–68. Copyright © 1962 by James Roosevelt.

ginalists' search for compromise in the short run, their belief that the Soviet Union is consolidationist enough to withdraw from East Germany if we withdraw from West, the fear of a remilitarized Germany, and their desire to get some people out from under the Communist heel, leads to a proposal for disengagement—removal of Eastern and Western troops from the heart of Europe.

Indeed, disengagement is *the* single basic anti-war marginal recommendation for Europe. The term "disengagement" covers a multitude of specific proposals and, since the anti-war marginalists intend such disengagement to be conditioned on agreement with the Soviets, there are no unconditional recommendations for unilateral withdrawal involved. Nonetheless, the outline of the anti-war marginal disengagement recommendation on negotiable proposals is fairly clear. They want at best removal, or at worst, severe thinning out, of Western troops in Germany, and Soviet troops in Germany, and if possible in Poland and other satellites. The anti-war marginalists want, in the main, a reunified Germany to come out of disengagement; for some, like Kennan, reunification of Germany in order to prevent a recrudescent German nationalism based on this issue is a chief motivation for disengagement[55] (and in this they differ from the anti-war *systemists,* who would just as soon have disengagement *and* continued German division). And the anti-war marginalists want disengagement to be enforced by the guarantees of a NATO which probably could no longer contain Germany. In general, the proposals are for the demilitarization of the German union, but the anti-war marginalists want the continuation of NATO and a continued American presence in Europe. And in this too they differ from their systemic neighbors who would look with favor on the dissolution of NATO and the removal of American troops from the continent of Europe. Some of the more extreme anti-war marginalists are

[55] See, for example, George F. Kennan, "Disengagement Revisited," *Foreign Affairs,* 37:195–198 (January 1959).

not overjoyed with NATO—in part because of the German
question, in part because of the emphasis on the underdeveloped world. Waskow fears "a NATO-centered foreign policy
in which NATO is defined in heavily military terms. . . .
To most of the world, such a NATO-centered policy would
look disastrously like an alliance marked 'Whites Only.' "[56]
But neither Waskow nor any of the other marginalists propose more than a marginal contraction and a gradual lessening of dependence on NATO.

The point of this stress on disengagement is quite similar
to the point of the anti-war marginal stress on general disarmament in the strategic field. The whole situation is un-
tenable and highly dangerous as it stands; the Soviet Union
need not be considered benign, but it may be consolidationist
enough that there is a real chance *now* to start on the road
toward *détente* and the final solution of the current crop of
world problems—problems which exist, but are not the real
ones of the next decades. For the anti-war marginalists, the
real problems are those having to do with the underdeveloped portions of the globe. Although many of these are not
military, they too have their military aspects.

United States Arms Policy in the Rest of the World

There is general agreement among marginalists, even including the anti-Communists, that in much of the world, the
confrontation of the Western world with the communists is
not a military one. In much of Africa, Ghana, and Guinea,
for example, the competition is sharp, but no marginalist
would recommend our trying to win it by military means.

The *anti-war marginalists,* however, go further than the
rest in deprecating the importance of military conflict and
deploring the Western use of military means in the underdeveloped areas. For them, even in those places where military conflict currently exists, it exists as a factor distorting the

[56] Waskow, p. 119.

real issues. Just as the anti-war marginalists quest after disengagement and *détente* in Europe because they believe that the concentration of American attention on the cold war in Europe distorts our view of the world, they also feel that the use we make of military force in other areas is distorting in itself.

The "rest-of-the-world" arms recommendations of all three schools can be exemplified by their specific recommendations for American policy in Southeast Asia. This has long been the chief region of the underdeveloped world where military conflict between the two world-power blocs has existed. At the time of this writing, the struggle is concentrated in South Vietnam, a shaky-seeming arrangement having been reached in the other Indo-Chinese combat area, Laos. The recommendations of the three schools for what to do now provide excellent illustrations of their continuing arguments over military policy in the "peripheral" areas outside of Europe.

The basic recommendation of the anti-war marginalists is that rather than give military backing to right-wing governments in Southeast Asia, we ought to get out while we can, leaving behind us truly neutral governments. Two value judgments underlie this, the fear of war and the distaste for right-wing dictatorships. And the analytical basis lies first in the belief that United States military involvement in the area will escalate into large-scale war with Communist China; second in the analysis of power-as-a-tool which has it that the real basis of power in these areas is the carrot—the capture of the minds and imaginations of the inhabitants through economic, political, and social devices; and third in a belief in the viability of independent neutralism on the Communist borders. They believe that our military policy reinforces reaction and opposes the inexorable revolutionary forces in Southeast Asia. And if we oppose, we make Communists out of revolutionaries who need not be Communists.

Writing in *The New Republic,* the pseudonymous "Z" attacks both the basis and the makers of American policy in South Vietnam:

Remembering their own earlier commitments they cannot abandon Ngo Dinh Diem. Instead they now tell us that although he is not very good, he is "the only man we've got," and that, in any case, "one doesn't change horses in midstream." At the same time, they begin to point subtly toward the Communist guerrilla wars in Malaya and the Philippines . . . which lasted 12 years and eight years respectively, to prepare the American people for the kind of long "bleeding war" operation which the French had to face in Indochina and Algeria. And they keep forgetting to tell the American people that the wars in the Philippines and Malaya were won for two reasons: (1) because there was no such thing as a Communist "sanctuary" next door—as there is in South Vietnam, with Communist North Vietnam and Communist-saturated Laos; and (2) precisely because both the Philippines and Malaya had the courage to change political horses in midstream. Magsaysay and Tungku Rahman became the leaders of reform administrations in the midst of a bitter guerrilla war and led their peoples to victory.

In South Vietnam, on the other hand, the United States seeks to win the struggle by mechanical means (helicopters and weed-killers) forgetting all over again that a revolutionary war can be won only if the little people in the villages and the hills can be persuaded they have a stake in fighting on our side.[57]

"Z's" implied recommendation appears to be that by getting rid of Diem the West can win with a liberal anti-Communist government like those of Magsaysay and Tungku Rahman. The editors of *The New Republic,* however, in an editorial in the same issue based in part on "Z's" article, go further in their recommendation—they just want to get out: "Though there may be places in the world where the new counter-guerrilla squads now in training can be profitably fielded, Vietnam is not one of them, for the North can literally carry on the war forever. The alternatives before the U.S. appear to be general war involving China, a last-ditch stand in Saigon ending in Communist encirclement, or an active diplomatic effort to couple a settlement in Laos with some form of

[57] "Z," "The War in Vietnam: We Have Not Been Told the Whole Truth," *The New Republic,* March 12, 1962, p. 26. Copyright © 1962 by Harrison-Blaine, Inc.

international guarantee for a neutralized South Vietnam."[58] In their choice of the last alternative, the editors of *The New Republic* go beyond "Z," but the difference in the two recommendations, both based on the analysis of power as a carrot, is much smaller than the difference between both and the recommendations of the other marginal schools.

To the *anti-Communist marginalists,* power is the stick, and the goal is the defeat of the Communists in (almost) whatever way is possible. The Communist threat in Southeast Asia is, like the world-wide threat, a politico-military problem, but politically, the Diem regime is worth defending, and it must be defended by whatever means are at hand. The editors of *America* describe the problem and the regime: "The harsh truth is that there is no easy answer to the devilishly clever Communist assault on South Vietnam. President Diem's government is at the moment the best possible one and by Asian standards it is honest and efficient. The South Vietnamese Army is a fairly good organization—though inadequately equipped . . ."[59] And, in another issue they provide a specific recommendation for going about the defeat of the Communists:

This is the sort of war that cannot be won except by beating the Communists at their own game. Wipe out one Red guerrilla concentration and another takes its place from across the border. Carrying the fight to the enemy's heartland may be regarded by some as a violation of international law. To the hardheaded realist, however, there is only one way to lick the Reds in Southeast Asia. That is by giving the Communists a dose of their own medicine. If tough United States-trained Vietnamese marines are not operating in Laos and North Vietnam, they ought to be—and we hope they will be soon.[60]

"Carrying the fight to the enemy's heartland" is the phrase of a forward strategy, although the heartland meant in this context is North Vietnam, rather than either China or the

58 "Engagement in Saigon," *The New Republic,* March 12, 1962, p. 4.
59 "General Taylor's Mission," *America,* November 18, 1961, p. 236.
60 "Playing the Communist Game," *America,* August 26, 1961, p. 647.

Soviet Union, and the forward strategy is that of the anti-
Communist marginalists, rather than the systemists. In any
case, the need to make victory in the struggle with the Communists superior both to any rules of international law and
to any fear of escalation or war with the Chinese Communists
can be directly deduced from the values of the anti-Communists. The victory is the thing; the "liberation" of North
Vietnam and the deliberate risking of war with China are
systemic recommendations not on the current program of the
anti-Communist marginalists, but the risks which must be
taken if we are to hold what is ours and to maintain what, in
contradiction to "Z's" argument, is the "best possible" government, are the risks we should take.

Because of the fact that the *middle marginalists* have not
yet developed a full-fledged theory of power synthesized from
the anti-war carrot and the anti-Communist stick, different
middle marginalists have produced two rather distinct sorts
of recommendations for American arms policy in Southeast
Asia. As suggested above, the failure to synthesize frequently
causes middle marginalists to fall back on an almost purely
military use of power. Thus, since the Communists are attacking in Southeast Asia, they must be countered militarily.
According to S. L. A. Marshall:

> High policy may still have been right when, under the leader-
> ship of Ambassador Averell Harriman, the decision was taken to
> gamble that a neutralist coalition might gradually tranquilize
> Laos and persuade the Pathet Lao to lay off, at *least* for a
> time. . . . There is no reason why, in such dealings, Harriman
> should be expected to think like a soldier. But someone should
> be doing so.
>
> . . . the scuttling of the faint hope in Laos was speeded by Wash-
> ington attitudinizing and our diplomacy afield. This was unbeliev-
> able obscurantism, for the security of Southern Laos is essential
> to the prospect of successful operations in South Vietnam. Should
> the lower shank of that inland state come under Communist
> control, the alternatives facing the United States will be either to
> ruin its credit in Asia by staging an agonizingly painful with-

drawal, or to mount a massive buildup and fight a difficult war where no decisive purpose can be served. The fact that we are not formally at war with the Viet Cong cannot change the forfeits. Asians know the score. We cannot quit the peninsula without announcing to the world that we are defeated.

Again, it should be emphasized that the real estate under discussion is southern Laos, not the entire country. This is a relatively small land area, not too inaccessible and with friendly borders for the most part, which is politically and geographically related to the problem of holding South Vietnam.[61]

The recommendation to keep control of Southern Laos in order to prosecute the war in South Vietnam is one made by a skilled military tactician looking aghast at the possibility of support to the Viet Cong (South Vietnam Communist) rebels coming from a neighboring Communist-dominated area. Harriman is not a soldier; this is war, and soldiers must think militarily. But this middle-marginal military recommendation is a tactical-logistical one, investigating the military means of succeeding in a certain area, rather than the "hit 'em in the heartland" attitude of the anti-Communists (although the initiating of combat within Communist "sanctuary" areas is not necessarily excluded by all middle marginalists).

The military strand of middle-marginal power analysis tends to ignore any question of the political viability of either a nonneutral Laos or a Diem-dominated South Vietnam— the questions asked by the anti-war marginalists and answered by the anti-Communists that these are "the best possible." The middle-marginal attempts at a synthetic interpretation of power, however, although they still recommend going with Diem, want to go with him on the dual basis of the combating of the military threat *and* the promotion of political and social democracy in South Vietnam. Leo Cherne takes the "synthetic" position:

. . . by our standards South Vietnam is not a democratic country. It is still a long way from becoming one.

[61] S. L. A. Marshall, "The Big River," *The New Leader*, May 28, 1962, p. 5.

Nonetheless, President Ngo [Diem] was as emphatic in his commitment to democratic ideals . . . as he was . . . in 1954. . . .

What will truly determine the future of a free South Vietnam? There are two factors. Within the country it will be the ability of the slow, emerging democratic forces of social improvement to meet the attacks of those who use terror to extend Communist control over free people. Outside the country, it will be the will of the American government and our SEATO allies.

There will be moments when a "neutral" exit from hazard and bloodshed will be urged by some of our allies weary of a struggle without end. But continued strength in South Vietnam to pursue the elusive goals of further economic and social growth while resisting the military thrust from the north will require substantial increases in American aid.[62]

The "two factors" show the attempted middle-marginal synthesis. But when getting down to cases—down to the question of the inevitable conflict of backing Diem against the Communists while pressing him to strive harder for the backing of his own people—the attempted synthesis provides no answers and, at the time of writing, the middle marginalists have come up with no answers. The answer, when and if it comes, will be, like almost all of the middle-marginal answers, the results of a calculus, so much of this and so much of that produce an "optimum" mix. Until then, the tendency will be, as it also is on other questions, to fall back on Marshall's sort of military answer (or perhaps even the stronger military answer of the anti-Communists), because military power is tangible, and the only other tangible solution is that of "Z" and *The New Republic,* which means to the middle marginalists the passive acceptance of immediate "defeat."

SUMMARY

Table 2 summarizes the major recommendations of the three marginal schools of thought. The visual impact of the

[62] Leo Cherne, "Deepening Shadow over Vietnam," *The New York Times Magazine,* April 9, 1961, p. 115.

TABLE 2. Summary of recommendations by marginal schools

	Anti-war	Middle	Anti-Communist
	Agreement			
	The United States must maintain military force and deterrence in the short run			
	The world should agree to controls over force in the long run			
	Disagreement			
Strategic recommendations: Arms control	Short run: stable deterrence Long run: world peace through universal disarmament to be gained by negotiations which may start with unilateral initiatives	Short run: make war less likely and/or terrible by controls over numbers and/or uses of armaments to be gained by unilateral steps and/or tacit or explicit multilateral agreements Long run: a series of short runs	Short run: unilateral control over warfare to make war thinkable as a political tool Long run: agreement with Communists delineating areas of conflict and common interest
Deterrence	Only as a part of short-run stable deterrence	Various mixes of arms control and political deterrence; of controlled counterforce and/or countercity targets; of second-and first-strike	Controlled deterrence as a political weapon; "win strike second" as a shield against enemy escalation
European recommendations	Conventional forces only Short-run accommodations with the Russians Long-run disengagement and *détente*	Choice of: US "credible first-strike" deterrent; national deterrents; multinational deterrent Choice of: tactical nuclear defense; nonnuclear defense *Quid pro quo* negotiations NATO unity	Independent national deterrents Nonnuclear *and* tactical nuclear defense No compromise NATO unity Satellite "liberation"
Other areas	Support democracy and neutralism	Either support anti-Communism militarily or synthesize such support with political support for democracy	Support anti-Communism with whatever means necessary

table, showing the disagreements among the schools to be many times larger than the consensus, is not misleading. In terms of the literature, the consensus must be dug out of obscure passages; the disagreements are obvious on every page. In terms of the impact on national arms policy, the consensus can be assumed offhand by the marginalists who make the policy; the disagreements are what preoccupy the makers of policy in the White House, the Pentagon, the State Department, the Arms Control and Disarmament Agency, and the other governmental institutions where policy is actually determined.

In the *public* debate over arms and disarmament, however, the consensus can no longer be assumed. It is precisely this consensus which is challenged by systemists of the right and the left, and the picture cannot be complete without some consideration of the anticonsensus systemists.

✢　✢　✢　✢　✢

CHAPTER 11

THE SYSTEMISTS

The systemists challenge the marginal consensus. The anti-war systemists base their unconditional recommendations for systemic change on disagreement with the consensus favoring continued use of military deterrence in the short run; the anti-Communist systemists base their unconditional recommendations for systemic change on disagreement with the consensus favoring continued efforts to reach understandings with the Russians over the long run. But the consensus rules. As has been noted, the councils of government, particularly of the executive branch, are made up almost entirely of members of the three marginal schools, and the *direct* impact of systemists upon governmental arms decisions is thus small. Yet the systemists play a role in the arms debate which cannot be ignored. They are much more frequently in the public eye than they are in the sessions of the policy makers. In universities, in the public prints, and in volunteer organizations on both extremes, the systemists put forth their views challenging the marginal consensus. While these views are still outweighed quantitatively by those of the marginalists, in public as well as in the policy process, they are not over-whelmed in the public debate. They form an important segment of American "elite" public opinion (and perhaps an even more important one in other countries) and even the debates among marginalists can be fully understood only in the light of the systemic arguments.

But the public impact and the importance to the arms debate of the two opposing groups of systemists is not equal.

In the following discussion primary attention is paid to the anti-war systemists, with the anti-Communists discussed mainly in terms of their similarities to and differences from the others. In spite of the fact that the anti-Communist systemists probably have more political power in the United States than the anti-war school, paradoxically, the ideas of the latter on arms policy have more influence on this policy. For one thing, much of the political energy of the systemic right is dissipated in fighting the menaces of internal Communism, the First through Ninth and Thirteenth through Sixteenth Amendments to the Constitution, the Supreme Court, fluoridation of water, and other matters which have little to do with the making of national security policy. Although the John Birch Society viewpoint that the external Soviet threat is a bugaboo conjured up by the internal Communists to divert us from the real danger and to bankrupt us is extreme even among extremists, this sort of belief in relative menaces does pervade much of the thinking of those who might otherwise be members of the systemic anti-Communist school of arms policy. In contrast, the "natural" members of the systemic anti-war school have only one other field of policy which holds their attention as much as arms policy—that of race relations. Though the fight against segregation dissipates some energy which might otherwise be devoted to arms policy, there is no loss of intellectual vigor from any conflict between the two objectives.[1]

But the major reason for the greater influence of the systemic anti-war group is that, unlike the anti-Communists, it has a great impact on the intellectual community from which many of those who actually make policy also come. In suggesting that the ideas of the systemic schools, left and right, are similar to one another, there is no attempt to state that sociologically these groups are in any way the same. The dif-

[1] It is, of course, not necessary to be a pacifist in order to be antisegregation. It is probably the case that anyone with systemic anti-war views in the United States is also strongly antisegregation. The reverse is not true— the antisegregation group being much larger than the pacifist one.

ference between the two radical groups is too obvious to require much elucidation. The members of the systemic anti-war school write books read and discussed within the general community to which the decision makers on arms policy belong; contribute articles to magazines and journals of a similar nature; read and write letters to the same newspapers; and in almost every way bear a close intellectual relationship to many of those who make national policy. This may be more the case under the Kennedy administration than under Eisenhower, but only by degrees. Further, the writers of the systemic anti-war school have the facility of pricking the consciences of the decision makers. Those governmental officials who are in the anti-war marginal school have value systems which are quite close to those of the anti-war systemists. Even more important, however, the much larger number of decision makers inclined toward the "analytical" pole of middle marginalism—those who present their arms recommendations almost entirely in terms of the effects of these recommendations on peace and war—also possess rather similar values. For all of these reasons, the ideas of the systemic anti-war group do have an influence on policy makers, either by conviction or by making those who disagree feel that they must disagree explicitly. And through the policy makers, these ideas do affect arms policy. This is much less true of the ideas on arms policy of the systemic anti-Communists.

THE ANTI-WAR SYSTEMISTS

The five schools of arms policy are defined by the recommendations they make. For the members of the systemic anti-war school these recommendations are unconditional ones for drastic moves away from military strength and deterrence and toward disarmament and international *détente*. The anti-war marginalists, too, want to move in this direction, but they want to move gradually, with each move conditional on the success of the previous one, not abandoning deterrence until we have something better. The *systemists*, however, are unwilling to wait or to condition their recommendations. Their attitude toward the marginalist consensus is expressed by Paul Goodman:

The general class of falsely practical behavior is choosing the lesser of two evils; and there is current an abominable doctrine that *only* such choices indicate that a man is tough-minded and serious, rather than utopian and dilettantish. . . . Let us be clear on what is involved here. Choosing the Lesser Evil does not mean accepting half a loaf, or one slice, or even the promise of a crumb tomorrow; it means swallowing a milder rat poison rather than a more virulent rat poison . . . the *ne plus ultra* of Choosing the Lesser Evil is accepting Deterrence as a policy, even though this policy is likely to produce the maximum calamity, and even though the first stroke of unfinished business in this area would be to call for a national and world-wide mourning for Hiroshima.

. . . it is a mistake for peace actions to discipline themselves to "respectability" in order to win bourgeois support. . . . Discipline for such a motive takes the heart out of any committed behavior, which one must perform as one is, not as one wishes to appear for public relations. . . .

In part, well-intentioned and radical professors are kept from decisive action by these same decencies, gullibilities, petty ambitions, and embarrassments.
. . . whenever there is an actual event—a "crisis" in Berlin, a resumption of testing—at once the professors start over as if they had not made up their minds, and they bat it around in the terms of the front page of the *Times* . . . They even go so far as to indulge in the speculations of war-game theory, their difference from the RAND Corporation being that the RAND people think we can win whereas our people prove that we must lose. . . . This means research not on how to make our wishes prevail, but on the inaccuracies of Herman Kahn![2]

The systemic anti-war school, like all other schools, contains a variety of individual views, and not all anti-war systemists are as critical as Goodman of those who confine themselves to

2 Paul Goodman, "The Ineffectuality of Some Intelligent People," *Commentary*, June 1962, pp. 479–481.

marginal recommendations. But this is a matter of tactics. Some concur with Goodman in his opposition to self-"discipline"; others feel that it is politically best to try to achieve "respectability" if it can be done without compromise of principle; all anti-war systemists agree, however (by definition), that marginal changes, although desirable, are not enough—that they are merely palliative.

The anti-war systemists make several sorts of recommendations in addition to the ones they share with the marginalists. Some of them are *positive* (do this), some *negative* (stop doing this), and some are of a third type which is called here *indefinite* (this is a good thing for all nations to do). Of the positive recommendations, unilateral disarmament is the most familiar, but by no means the most widely held. Recommendations can be much milder than complete unilateralism and still call for large departures from current bases of policy. The recommendation for unilateral *nuclear* disarmament, as it is put by Stuart Hughes,[3] is more typical of anti-war systemism than is complete unilateral disarmament:

> Some of my friends who are less unilateralist than I am prefer the phrase "unilateral initiatives" to "unilateral disarmament." . . . I am quite ready to settle for the term. Indeed, it may have greater clarity. The trouble with the phrase "unilateral disarmament" is that it suggests an all-or-nothing stance. It seems to convey the impression that we are going to strip right down to our underwear shorts without enticing hesitations along the way. . . .

[3] The subsequent discussion of the systemic anti-war writings of Stuart Hughes provides an example of the need for the caveat that the purpose of this book is to discuss the explicit arguments of various schools of thought on arms policy, rather than to classify individuals. Hughes's writings on arms policy, up to and including his book published in 1962, contained many systemic recommendations, examples of which are quoted below. But as an independent candidate for Senator from Massachusetts in 1962, he deliberately and explicitly confined himself to the making of marginal policy recommendations, on the ground that no more than marginal change was possible within the American political system and within the purview of the office for which he was campaigning. Were it important to categorize Stuart Hughes, this would present some problems. Since the task being attempted, however, is to describe certain systemic anti-war viewpoints, his prepolitical writings stand in any case as excellent and coherent examples of these.

Unilateralism as I conceive it necessarily proceeds by stages—
with pauses to give our potential adversaries the opportunity to
respond in kind. . . .

Yet the logic of the unilateralist position lies ultimately in the
complete renunciation of nuclear weapons. Nor will it do to hold
on to these weapons while saying we will not use them. . . . This
is too ambiguous. . . . In short, I believe that we and our allies
should eventually restrict our defense to conventional weapons
alone.

I well know the awful risks that such a decision would involve.
. . . In this world of ghastly insecurity, we would rather take our
chances on nuclear defenselessness and trust to the more primitive
devices by which free men in earlier ages have safeguarded their
liberty.[4]

Hughes favors using the "unilateral initiatives" program to
"entice" our potential adversaries, yet he is clear that, succeed or not in enticement, he wants to take the "awful
risk" of nuclear disarmament. He does not expect this to result in Soviet domination over either this country or its allies,
but he is willing to face up to the possibility that he may be
wrong. And if this ultimate adversity comes to pass, he is
willing to depend on some variety of civil resistance to Soviet
occupation.[5] These recommendations are in opposition to the
marginalist consensus favoring continuing short-run use of
nuclear deterrence, and they sum up, if cursorily, the major
unconditional strategic recommendations of the anti-war systemists.

Hughes's strategic recommendations are related to, but go
further than, the strategic recommendations of the anti-war
marginalists. Similarly, the typical systemic anti-war recommendation for arms policy in Europe is related to but goes
further than the anti-war marginalists' disengagement
schemes. The disengagement favored by the anti-war mar-

4 H. Stuart Hughes, *An Approach to Peace*, pp. 70–72. Copyright © 1962
by H. Stuart Hughes. This quotation and all subsequent quotations from this
book are reprinted by permission of Atheneum Publishers.
5 *Ibid.*, pp. 76–80.

ginalists is characterized by Warburg's posing of the choice between a disarmed unified Germany or an armed divided one—either solution to be approached by negotiations with the Russians. But Erich Fromm advocates a Germany both disarmed *and* divided:

Because of our obsession with the Russian wish for world domination (and maybe also because of many American-German financial interests) we tend to accept the demands of West Germany and thus we make an over-all settlement with Russia impossible. There is much talk that making concessions to the Soviet Union is a repetition of the appeasement policy toward Hitler. I believe that, if one insists on drawing a present-day analogy to the appeasement policy toward Nazi Germany, it lies in *our present appeasement of Adenauer's Germany.*
. . . Those who were against appeasement, like Churchill, recognized that Hitler would not be satisfied only with expansion toward the East. Today, when our whole foreign policy is based on the idea that we must defend ourselves militarily against the Russian menace, we again appease Germany. . . . Are we really so naïve as to see only the Germany of today, and not to visualize the Germany of tomorrow, which we are helping to bring to life?
As far as the recognition of the mutual status quo in Europe is concerned, my proposition is to accept unequivocally the present status quo, and to curb any further German rearmament.[6]

Unequivocal acceptance of the present *status quo* (Germany divided) in addition to Germany disarmed, goes far beyond Warburg's disengagement and that of Kennan, both of which had as a major condition for disengagement (in Kennan's case, a major objective) the reunification of Germany.

And, as a final example of a positive systemic recommendation—corresponding to but going further than the anti-war marginalists' recommendations for the "rest of the world," beyond Europe—Fred Neal proposes unilateral American withdrawal from some overseas bases, and a general contraction of the global interests of the United States:

[6] Erich Fromm, *May Man Prevail?* (Garden City: Doubleday, 1961), pp. 219–220. Copyright © 1961 by Erich Fromm. Reprinted by permission of Doubleday & Company, Inc. and George Allen & Unwin Ltd.

It is true that for the United States to withdraw its military bases from some of these areas might result in exposing them over the long run to Soviet influence and even Soviet domination, although there is no basis for assuming that withdrawal of American forces in various areas near the Soviet Union would mean that the Russians would necessarily "move in" physically. On the other hand, our reliance on a military posture in many countries tends to interfere with the very domestic political and economic reforms—and our acceptance of them—that constitute the basic prerequisite for preventing Communist success. . . .

It is often asked, "Suppose we do restrict our global interests? Suppose, for example, we do give up some bases and stop heckling the Russians about Eastern Europe? What do we get in return?" We have become so used to the idea that we have a right to global interests, while the Russians don't, that this is, for many Americans, a natural question. It is important to realize that we cannot expect the Soviet Union to "give up" anything simply because we cease maintaining a position that threatens Soviet vital interests.[7]

Neal specifically excepts unilateral withdrawal from Central Europe, although he believes mutual withdrawal may become negotiable with the Russians. But like the other systemic recommendations discussed above, Neal's proposals for unilateral abandonment of various American bases outside of Central Europe are similar to, but go further than, the recommendations of the anti-war marginalists. The marginalist Osgood, for example, suggests as a step in a hypothetical sequence of reciprocated unilateral acts, the demilitarization of a single American base. But this demilitarization is to take place only after considerable mutual reciprocation has already occurred, leading to a reasonable expectation that this withdrawal from a base might also be reciprocated.[8] Neal wants to demilitarize unilaterally with the explicit expectation of no reciprocation.

[7] Fred Warner Neal, *U.S. Foreign Policy and the Soviet Union* (Santa Barbara: Center for the Study of Democratic Institutions, 1961), p. 51.

[8] Charles E. Osgood, "Reciprocal Initiatives," in *The Liberal Papers*, ed. James Roosevelt (Garden City: Doubleday, 1962), p. 203. Copyright © 1962 by James Roosevelt.

Perhaps even more typical of the systemic anti-war school than such positive recommendations, however, are the negative ones. These are ordinarily more vague—abandon "the war system," drop "the policy of deterrence." In essence they say to the decision maker, "Stop *whatever* it is that you are doing which will lead, push, or drive us into war." Or, in Bertrand Russell's words, "There is no conclusion possible in this march towards insane death except to turn right round and march, instead, towards sanity and life."[9] The negative policy recommendations of the systemic anti-war school can be well exemplified, oddly enough, by a paragraph from someone who has long been a leading anti-systemist and who would probably reject almost all of the positive systemic recommendations of the pacifists. Reinhold Niebuhr, in his foreword to Harrison Brown and James Real's pamphlet, *Community of Fear*, says: "The authors have wisely limited themselves to the task of describing the common danger, and the irrelevance of the old methods of staving it off by overcoming this or that deficiency in the technology of modern weapons. They have purposely not spelled out the details of a fresh approach."[10] "The irrelevance of the old methods," and the concept of the "fresh approach" imply a need for systemic change, and without the details of the approach they imply a recommendation to stop at least using those methods which are irrelevant. This is negative systemism, and because of the difficulties of thinking up fresh positive systemic policies, it is more characteristic of the systemic anti-war school than unilateralism or any other single policy which can be paraphrased as "do something drastic."

There is nothing which is per se illogical about positive or negative systemic recommendations, no matter how extreme. Beyond the negative systemic recommendation, however, lies another refuge for those who feel strongly that something

[9] Bertrand Russell, *Common Sense and Nuclear Warfare* (New York: Simon and Schuster, 1959), pp. 27–28.

[10] Reinhold Niebuhr, "Foreword" to Harrison Brown and James Real, *Community of Fear* (Santa Barbara: Center for the Study of Democratic Institutions, 1960), p. 5.

is very wrong, but can think of little positive to do about it. The *indefinite* recommendation, because it purports to be something which it really is not, can at least be called evasive. An indefinite recommendation is a statement, intended as a policy recommendation, which covers only what should be, rather than what should be done about it. A simple statement of belief that some state of the world would be preferable to the present state is merely a pious hope of the sort we all indulge in at one time or another. But the statement of belief becomes an indefinite recommendation if its maker intends by saying it to make a recommendation. It is an end without a means. It cannot be a true recommendation unless some action is suggested by which some actor or actors to whom the recommendation is made can at least try to achieve the preferred state. A method and someone who at least in principle is capable of using the method are essential.

A desire for a disarmed world under a system of law similar to that obtaining in the Anglo-Saxon world, for instance, is a hope for systemic change, but it is not a recommendation; nor are most of the individuals who share the hope members of a systemic school. But given in answer to a question such as "what should we do in order to stop the trend toward war?" the sentence, "establish world law," is an indefinite recommendation. Norman Cousins' statement, for example, that "the answer must lie in the establishment of an authority which takes away from nations, summarily and completely, not only the machinery of battle that can wage war, but the machinery of decision that can start a war. The United Nations is not yet that kind of authority. The main job of the world is to make it one,"[11] still provides no method on which anyone can act, and thus becomes an indefinite recommendation.

The indefinite recommendation can be backed up in several ways, the commonest of which is exhortation. The hortatory note is not absent from the writings of any school, but it is one of the most familiar among the systemists. Real

11 Norman Cousins, *In Place of Folly* (New York: Harper, 1961), p. 99.

recommendations are frequently worded as ringing appeals, but exhortation is also used as the main instrument in converting a pious hope to an intended recommendation, which, because it lacks answers to the questions how and who, is necessarily indefinite. Cousins' prescription, "The main job of the world is to make" the UN into a powerful authority, provides an example of a hortatory indefinite recommendation. Such exhortations to the American people to adopt a new policy "In Place of Folly" (the title of Cousins' book) abound. Less frequent but equally interesting are hortatory recommendations by American systemists to the Russians, to convince them of their need for a peaceful world. And, because the wish is father to the thought, these appeals telling the Soviets how they should act become exhortations to the people of the United States telling us that we should act as if the Russians will in fact act the way they ought to. Thus, Erich Fromm analyzes the current problems of the U.S.S.R. and concludes: "The Khrushchev regime is—and must be— most interested in the development of its system; the bureaucracy ruling the Soviet Union is expanding and securing the good life for themselves, their children, and eventually for the rest of the population. Khrushchev neither believes in the possibilities for revolution in the West, nor does he want it, nor does he need it for the development of his system. What he needs is peace, a reduction in the armaments burden, and unquestioned control over his system."[12]

Fromm has a strong belief about what Khrushchev "must be" interested in for his own benefit, and "what he needs." And from the indefinite hortatory recommendation to Khrushchev comes the exhortation to the United States to believe in a Soviet Union which acts as Fromm thinks it should—a Soviet Union more peaceful than that pictured by even the most extreme of the professional Sovietologists.

Beyond exhortation, the indefinite recommendation can be reinforced in several ways. One of these is to fill in the details by the use of indefinite subordinate recommendations,

[12] Fromm, p. 137. Copyright © 1961 by Erich Fromm.

perhaps based upon someone else's work. Cousins does this with Grenville Clark and Louis Sohn's book, *World Peace Through World Law*. The book was written largely to give technically sound substance to the sort of hope for world order shared by many individuals in all schools, but Clark and Sohn avoided the pitfall of recommending an action which nobody could try to carry out. Instead, Clark wrote in his Introduction: "A prime motive for this book is that the world is far more likely to make progress toward genuine peace, as distinguished from a precarious armed truce, when a *detailed* plan adequate to the purpose is available, so that the structure and functions of the requisite world institutions may be fully discussed on a world-wide basis."[13] This is not intended as an unconditional recommendation for what we can do, but rather is a highly conditional one for doing something as and when we can do it. But Cousins backs up his initial indefinite recommendation by devoting a chapter to the statement that a UN Charter revision conference should be called, and then by summarizing Clark and Sohn as a recommendation for what should be adopted by this conference, still without saying how to obtain a conference or how to bring such matters into discussion.[14] The Clark-Sohn book is thus converted into an indefinite recommendation to back up Cousins' initial indefinite recommendation for making the UN into a world government.

Indefinite recommendations, however, are frequently backed up by real recommendations. The feature which makes many anti-war recommendations into statements of goals without means is that their implementation requires mutual action by two or more nations, and the statements provide no course of action for the decision makers who control the policy of a single state. But such indefinite recommendations can be made more concrete by unconditional statements of the sort, "We are for this, of course, on a mul-

[13] Grenville Clark and Louis B. Sohn, *World Peace Through World Law* (Cambridge, Mass.: Harvard University Press, 1960), p. xv.
[14] Cousins, chap. X.

tilateral basis, but in any case, do it unilaterally until a multilateral possibility comes along." Such combinations of the indefinite recommendation with the systemic recommendation are common in the field of disarmament. An example is provided by Bertrand Russell:

> The question at issue between my critics and myself arises only if all attempts at negotiation fail . . . The argument proceeds on the hypothesis that, if there is a war between the two blocs, the human race will be exterminated. It further supposes a situation in which one of the two blocs is so fanatical that it prefers the ending of mankind to a rational compromise. In such a situation, I think that the less fanatical bloc, if it had the welfare of mankind in view, would prefer concession to warfare. I should say this equally to both sides.[15]

This in itself is not an extreme statement, hypothesizing a situation which Russell feels will not come to pass, but it is characteristic of the thought of many members of the systemic anti-war school in situations other than the ultimate one. "I should say this equally to both sides," is an indefinite recommendation. "But in any case, concede," is the systemic recommendation which gives force to the other. Were Russell's recommendations all of the "Negotiate!" type, subscribed to by the marginalist consensus, he would not be a systemist at all, but the fact that he backs this up with unilateralism of many types distinguishes his systemism from marginalism.

It is, then, the indefinite recommendations as well as the positive and negative systemic ones which distinguish the systemic anti-war school from the marginal ones. Of course, not only systemists indulge in the making of indefinite recommendations; members of all schools do it at one time or another. But such recommendations are much more characteristic of systemism because systemism is built on the belief that something is terribly wrong and needs systemic correction; what steps a single sovereign government should take

15 Russell, p. 86.

to correct the situation is a more difficult problem approached only by the most courageous, like Hughes. It seems likely that many members of the marginal anti-war school, such as Osgood, Etzioni, and Waskow, have come to their particular brand of marginal recommendations in part as a reaction to the systemic indefinite recommendation. Such marginalist "unilateral initiatives" recommendations may be subject to criticism on the basis of their content, but the very fact that they have content makes them a portion of the arms debate worthy of consideration.

In any case, the positive and the negative recommendations of the anti-war systemists, like the recommendations of the other schools, stem from trains of logic which bring together values and analyses in order to choose among possible courses of action. The recommendations of the anti-war systemists are ordinarily based on one or both of two related chains of reasoning. One, the ethos of nonviolence, is discussed below, but is characteristic of only a portion of the school. The other reasoning, shared by most of the school including those who have a philosophical belief in nonviolence, is based on po-litical values and analyses which, like the systemic recom-mendations that result from them, resemble but go further than those of the *marginal* anti-war school. The anti-war marginalists' primary value judgment gives greater weight in the arms-policy calculus to peace-keeping than to preven-tion of Communist advance; their most important analytical beliefs are that unintentional war due to the existence of weapons is coming, and that the conflict with the Soviet Union for which the weapons are maintained is shrinking in scope as the Soviets become a conservative "have" power. But the marginalists assign *some* weight to the conflicting value of preventing Communist advance; and their analytical belief is that the Communists are still opportunistic and will take advantage of any substantial unilateral withdrawal of dependence upon weapons and deterrence. And as a result, the anti-war marginalists come to their recommendations through an *optimizing* mechanism of choice which, although it weighs the "peaceful" values and analyses most heavily, nonetheless considers all factors.

The anti-war systemists go further. Their values and analyses lead to a fear of thermonuclear war which enters the choice mechanism with infinite weight compared to the fear of forcible Communist advance. This fear of war is not a personal one—the advocates of nonviolence, for example, are anything but personally fearful—but it is a combination of values and analyses which dominates their beliefs. The infinite relative weight given to this fear may be a literal infinity or it may be an "almost-infinity" of the type defined above, whereby the mechanism of "psychological certainty" allows one to be logically aware of certain other factors and yet act as if they were absolutely nonexistent.[16] Nonetheless, "infinite relative weight" accurately describes the way in which the values and analyses associated with the fear of war enter the recommendation-choosing mechanism of the anti-war systemists. And given such weights, it becomes reasonable to use for these choices a *maximizing* mechanism which concentrates on the single factor of staying out of war, and ignores possible Soviet aggression.

This high-low relationship between the two fears is achieved by anti-war systemists in one of three ways: a fear of war which is so high that it makes no difference what is believed about Communism; a fear of the Communist military threat which is so low that it makes no difference what is believed about war; or a combination of the two. The high fear of war is more typical than the low fear of Communist aggression, but most commonly both are held as the bases for systemic recommendations, each reinforcing the other.

The word "fear," however, is an imprecise one, used here to convey an imprecise concept. Fear of war and fear of Communist aggression are each composed of three elements: an *analysis* of the sureness and the nearness of the danger; an *analytical* picture of what war or Communism looks like; and a *value* weight, based on this picture, placed on the

16 See p. 41.

avoidance of each. Logically, neither a belief in the inexorability of war, an apocalyptic picture of its nature, nor a near-infinite value on its avoidance is by itself necessary for assigning a nearly infinite relative value to peace; nor are their analogs in relationship to Communism necessary for placing the importance of its avoidance near zero. In practice, however, systemic anti-war recommendations are based on all three logical portions of the fear of war, and many systemists add at least one of the elements tending to discount the fear of Communist force.

A succinct example of the three elements in the systemic attitude toward thermonuclear war is provided by W. H. Ferry:

> The other alternative [to unilateral disarmament] is war . . .
> For this alternative, however, one need not do any imagining of what would happen . . . I shall not even use the most frightening data available; that is, I shall not insist on the most drastic consequences, which would be annihilation. Let me just use an estimate which says that a "moderate attack" on the U.S. would kill 60 million at once, seriously injure another 20 million, and destroy about half the homes and 35 percent of the industry of the nation . . . Let stand beside it the 20 to 30 million Russians that we might be able to destroy in retaliation. And beside this let us eliminate from the face of the earth the whole of Great Britain, large parts of West Germany, France, Turkey, and other countries serving as advance missile bases . . . It is no longer acceptable, it can no longer settle anything.
> Yet this is the alternative. It seems to be an impractical, not to say immoral alternative.[17]

The first paragraph presents the analysis of the inexorability of war as the single stark alternative to unilateral disarmament: the second presents the analytical picture of what war looks like; and the third offers the value judgment that such an alternative to disarmament is morally unacceptable. Thus the choice is the absolute one between infinity and any lesser

17 W. H. Ferry, *Disarm to Parley* (Philadelphia: American Friends Service Committee, 1961), pp. 8–9.

number. And this illustrates the difference between the anti-war systemists and the neighboring anti-war marginalists. For some anti-war marginalists, war may be "certain" in C. P. Snow's term, within ten years if nothing is unchanged; but unilateral disarmament or even unilateral nuclear disarmament are not the only ways out—many things can be done. It is the absolutism of both values and analysis which is rejected by marginalists.

Ferry's statement is logically sufficient for the making of systemic recommendations. If war is one of two alternatives and is immoral, we must choose the other, no matter what the result. But some anti-war systemists reinforce their near-infinite fear of war with a near-zero fear of forcible Communist advance. This low fear is not based on all three of the possible elements corresponding to the elements in the great fear of war (i.e., *lack* of inexorability of such Communist advance, *lack* of a grim picture of what Communist domination would look like, and *lack* of a strong distaste for such a picture), but only on the first, the belief that Communist aggression would not be certain, perhaps not even likely, were we to disarm. So far as the analysis of what Communism looks like, and the dislike of what is seen, some few American Communists may attempt to paint a rosy picture of an America or West Europe under Soviet domination (and a few more of Cuba), but the more typical attitude among anti-war systemists is the opposite one of Hughes's.

Our real quarrel with Communism scarcely needs to be defined . . . Our real quarrel is with Communism's tyranny over the mind of man. And I mean this in the widest sense. I mean terror and censorship, arbitrary imprisonment and forced labor, the falsification of history and bare-faced lying in international assemblies—every aspect of conduct and policy that is inhumane and deceitful. I am quite ready to agree with the most militant of anti-Communists that in this sense Communism is indeed a "scourge" or a "poison," a dreadful affliction of contemporary humanity.

I think it most important that anyone who advances views such as mine should formally put these things on record—that he should express his unqualified condemnation of Communist brutality and perversion of the truth and that he should dissociate himself from every effort to apologize for them or explain them away.[18]

He believes that Communism may be becoming more liberal internally, but at a rate of speed which makes the liberalization not very relevant to current policy: ". . . since the death of Stalin such an evolution has been in progress. Admittedly it has been confined to Europe and it has several times been interrupted or reversed, but the net effect over the past decade has been a cumulative shift toward a more tolerable life. In this change lies the still dim but ever more discernible hope for humanity in the next half century."[19] This is a very tough view of Communism, and it is important to note that it is shared by many anti-war systemists, notably those who have been in or on the fringes of the strongly anti-Stalinist American socialist movement. But withal, anti-war systemists reinforce their near-absolute fear of war with a range of varying analyses, all suggesting, more or less strongly, that no matter *how* immoral Communism may be, it is not threatening to expand militarily, and will not do so even if we disarm: that fear of Communist advance can remain low relative to fear of war because aggression by the Soviet Union is neither inexorable nor even very likely.

The least sanguine end of the range of systemic anti-war analyses of possible forcible Communist advance is characterized by the idea that such advance is possible and we must face up to the possibility, but that even with disarmament, it is by no means inevitable. Robert Pickus argues, in a debate with another anti-war systemist, that, "we should make clear that our concern for peace, for example, does not ignore

18 Hughes, *An Approach to Peace*, p. 49. Copyright © 1962 by H. Stuart Hughes.
19 *Ibid.*, p. 50.

the problem of Communist expansion: that we are committed to the defense of democratic values, and that our disagreement lies not in our indifference to the danger of Communist expansion, but in our view of what response to it is most likely to secure a just peace."[20] And Hughes's view is quite similar. He explicitly admits the possibility of Soviet expansion, but he is not quite sure as to either the actual likelihood of such expansion or the deterrent effect on a possible Soviet expansionist drive of the civil resistance forces he suggests as the major defense against such expansionism:

> But where does this leave us in the cold war? Is it really possible to choose to oppose the Russians with one type of action and to refrain from doing so with another? Aren't we engaged in a struggle for national and cultural survival, in which such distinctions may dangerously weaken our resolve?
> I confess that I find questions like these hard to answer. I am puzzled as to how to estimate the Soviet Union's present aims. I agree wholly neither with those who argue that it is no longer an expansionist power nor with the more prevalent view that the Communist rulers of Russia have always and forever aspired to world domination.[21]

Hughes is no Sovietologist, and few Sovietologists make recommendations for systemic changes in the United States policy vis-à-vis the Soviet Union. One who does is Neal, who is much more definite than Hughes that the U.S.S.R. should not be viewed as a militarily expansionistic power:

> There is, indeed, grave reason to believe that the American position on these matters is unrealistic, inflexible, and unimaginative. Basically, our position throughout continues to be conditioned by our assumption of the constant danger of Soviet military aggression. Sometimes this is modified by defining Soviet policy as being committed to use "all possible means" for the expansion of communism and extension of its power. As indi-

20 Robert Pickus, "The Non-Communist Fellow Traveler Problem," *The Liberal Democrat* (Berkeley, California), January 1961, p. 6.

21 Hughes, *An Approach to Peace*, p. 80. Copyright © 1962 by H. Stuart Hughes.

cated above, this thinking is based on distorted evidence or no evidence at all and ignores the strong reasons for considering that the Soviet theory of coexistence is predicated not on making war but on avoiding it.[22]

Although Neal quotes Kennan frequently, this goes well beyond Kennan's statement, cited above, that "the Soviet threat . . . is a combined military and political threat with the accent on the political."[23]

Neal, however, although he makes systemic recommendations, is an advocate of unilateral retreat, but not unilateral disarmament—he recognizes that even the "Soviet theory of coexistence" he describes could break down under too much temptation. The most extreme view on the lack of Soviet aggressive tendencies (extreme, at least, among non-Communist Americans) is exemplified by an individual who *is* a unilateralist, Erich Fromm. Drawing on his expertise as a psychiatrist, Fromm feels that the current American view of Soviet policy is a psychotic symptom. In a statement which goes far beyond the argument of Osgood (a psychologist) that our view of the Russians and theirs of us are growing to resemble one another, he says:

It is easy for people to recognize paranoid thinking in the individual case of a paranoid psychotic. But to recognize paranoid thinking when it is shared by millions of other people and approved by the authorities who lead them, is more difficult. A case in point is the conventional thinking about Russia. Most Americans today think about Russia in a paranoid fashion; namely, they ask what is *possible* rather than what is *probable*. Indeed, it is possible that Khrushchev wants to conquer us by force. It is possible that he makes peace proposals in order to make us unaware of the danger. . . . If we think only of the *possibilities*, then indeed there is no chance for realistic and sensible political action.[24]

22 Neal, pp. 43–44.
23 See p. 113.
24 Fromm, pp. 20–21. Copyright © 1961 by Erich Fromm.

Then, after a thoroughgoing analysis of the Soviets in which he exhorts them to follow their own interests in peace, as seen above, and rejects the hypotheses that the Soviet Union is motivated either by the desire to spread Communism throughout the world (Fromm as a socialist feels that the Soviet Union is not socialist) or by more classical imperialistic motives, he concludes: "To sum up: the cliché of the Soviet offensive against the United States in Berlin, Laos, the Congo, and Cuba is not based on reality but is rather a convenient formula to support further armament and the continuation of the cold war. It corresponds to the Chinese cliché that pictures the United States as seeking world domination by the support of Chiang Kai-shek, by the domination of Southern Korea and Okinawa, by the SEATO pact, etc. All these mutual accusations can not stand up to sober and realistic analysis."[25]

Thus some, but by no means all, anti-war systemists add to their beliefs in the inexorability and terror of war and the near-infinite value of peace, the reinforcing analysis that the weapons of war are protecting us against a threat which does not exist. This is a set of beliefs which is similar in each case to those of the anti-war marginalists, but in almost all cases goes beyond the marginalists' values and analyses to a point where, for purposes of determining arms policy, peace is to all other values as infinity is to any other number. For some individuals such as Hughes, this numerical relationship is based in the main on a heavy value given to peace; Hughes in explicitly recognizing the risks of his recommendations puts it frankly that in his personal judgment these risks must be ignored in the face of the greater risk of thermonuclear holocaust. For some, such as Neal, the relationship is based on a relatively high value on peace and a relatively benign analysis of the motives and methods of the Soviet Union. Others, like Fromm, strive for an absolute version of logical *dominance*—they couple with the near-infinite value placed on peace, an argument that the Soviet military threat is near

25 *Ibid.*, pp. 116–117.

zero and that therefore unilateral disarmament would, by aiding in the political-economic competition with Communism, be far better for *both* the peaceful and the anti-Communist objectives of American foreign policy. Whatever the particular combination of factors, however, they result in the use of a maximizing mechanism for choosing among arms policies, basing the choice entirely on the single criterion of the effectiveness of these policies in achieving and maintaining peace. And the recommendations stemming from this mechanism are basic challenges to the marginalist consensus.

Although it is thus logically possible to support an argument for systemic anti-war recommendations entirely on the basis of values and analysis concerning war and Soviet aggression (and indeed, given the maximizing mechanism which chooses on the single basis of war avoidance, it is logically *impossible* to choose as policy criteria any other values or analyses), the anti-war systemists make several important supporting points. Peace has infinite importance, but other values can be considered *lexicographically* —as in the process of alphabetization, the secondary values are *always* subordinate to the primary, but still are important relative to one another. Like the major themes, these other points are similar to some of the arguments of the anti-war marginalists, but go further. One such has been cited already: Fromm's belief in the inexorability of revived German militarism, as compared to the anti-war marginalist belief in its possible eventual danger. Because of this dislike and fear of Germany, Fromm endorses the idea of disengagement, common among anti-war marginalists, but goes further—advocating neutralization of Germany *and* its continued division. Related to this is another difference of marginal and systemic anti-war opinion which bears heavily on disengagement. As has been pointed out, the analytical issue of the tightness of the Soviet grasp on the Eastern satellites causes an odd disagreement among the marginal schools; the anti-war and anti-Communist marginalists are closer to one another in their hope that this grip can be relaxed than either is to those middle-marginal Sovietologists who see Eastern Europe as being permanently under tight Soviet hegemony. And, to compound the oddity, some of the anti-war systemists are closer to the middle marginalists than to the anti-war marginalists. Neal, for example, claims that ". . . the Soviet Union will under no conditions make any agreements or take any steps deleterious to its hegemony in Eastern Europe or cease to object violently to any indication of interference in this area. On perhaps no other single point is the U.S.S.R. so sensitive. As long as the Soviet Union remains a nation-state, it will see Eastern Europe as . . . non-negotiable."[26] Neal uses this to argue for a cessation of United States propaganda aimed at the satellites, whereas the middle marginalists use it to argue against disengagement, but the analytical similarity is nonetheless quite close.

One final issue on which the anti-war systemists' views are a more extreme version of those of the anti-war marginalists is the question, important to both schools, of militarism in the United States. The anti-war marginalists are worried about the future of military power; the systemists are much more worried and put the case in much stronger terms. According to Fred Cook:

If we really believe in the peace we profess, there can be no room in our policy for the imperialism of the New Militarism. If peace be our aim, the Military's objectives cannot be our objectives; there can be no room for a philosophy that calls for "the preservation and enhancement of our political system rather than the maintenance of peace," for a philosophy that dictates "we cannot tolerate the survival of a political system" inimical to our own. For a Christian people whose ideal has always been that of peace on earth and good will among men, we have bred a strange and powerful and ruthless caste that can look with equanimity upon the slaughter of the world's people by the inconceivable millions.[27]

Cook's quotations are from *A Forward Strategy for America*, which has been characterized above as the Bible of the anti-

26 Neal, p. 32.
27 Fred J. Cook, "Juggernaut: The Warfare State," a special issue of *The Nation*, October 28, 1961, p. 334.

Communist marginalists. Cook does not maintain that Strausz-Hupé and company are currently making American arms policy, although he believes that they have a major effect. But, unlike the anti-war marginalists, he talks about *present* policy making in the United States in terms almost as strong:

The symbol of a vitiated democracy in America today may be found in the simple fact that there is virtually no debate, not even on the most awesome issues that have ever confronted mankind. We wrap our increasingly militaristic society in the folds of the flag and the emotional words of a patriotism that requires no thought. Whether tensions are deliberately fomented, whether troublesome domestic issues are conveniently sidetracked in our preoccupation with foreign military crises—these are matters that hardly ever occur to us, much less concern us. Yet if as the Congressman [unnamed] said, we are going the way of prewar Germany and Japan, we should recognize that the final cataclysm is almost inevitable. For the sober and shocking and little-realized truth is that today it is less possible than ever before to place any kind of effective check upon a dominant Military.[28]

But Cook's statement about looking "with equanimity upon the slaughter of the world's people by the inconceivable millions" also serves as an introduction to the other train of thought which leads to systemic anti-war recommendations. This is the value judgment placed on the Sixth Commandment, interpreted literally. Whereas most of those who make recommendations concerning arms policy base their advice on the desirability of avoiding death through war, a vital part of the creed of many anti-war systemists is not merely the avoidance of death, but the personal and national avoidance of killing. The precept that "thou shalt not kill" is paid some service by all makers of arms recommendations, and it has an effect on policy at least for the anti-war marginalists and for some of the middle marginalists. But for many anti-war systemists—those who advocate nonviolence as a way of life and characterize themselves as religious or philosophical

28 *Ibid.*, p. 282.

pacifists—this becomes the major premise of arms policy. As put by Mulford Sibley:

In the end, rejection of deterrence and adoption of unilateralism depend upon certain propositions about morality. These must be frankly faced and their implications understood.

Among them is the statement attributed by Plato to Socrates that it is better to suffer injustice than to commit it. In the context of the arms race this means that it is better to risk injury and death than to threaten and inflict them. Although we have argued that unilateral initiatives, consistently pursued, would probably lead to competitive disarmament and an extension of international institutions, we have also admitted that these may not be the fruits. Nevertheless, it still is better to disarm and undergo suffering without retaliation in kind than to base policy on the proposition that it is right to wipe out whole cities and destroy millions of human beings. The end result of an arms race is that we both die and kill. If we carry through on unilateral disarmament it is possible that we die, but at least we do not kill. Put in these sharp terms, there can be little doubt about which alternative the moral man must select.[29]

Thus Sibley finds it immoral to kill even to prevent death, and the questions of the numbers killed as against the numbers whose death is prevented are irrelevant. Sibley, however, as he points out, has argued that his recommendation is not only inherently moral, but is also likely to be successful in obtaining certain political objectives. Victor Gollancz, a British advocate of nuclear disarmament, feels that even the practical argument itself is immoral, and he puts his case in terms of the *threat* of the use of nuclear weapons as well as their actual use:

So the following is the case against throwing the bomb in any conceivable or inconceivable circumstances, a case that overrides all possible calculations in the world of so-called practicalities: To throw it would be an utter repudiation of our humanity, a final spurning, eyes open and brain alert, of unity and love. And

[29] Mulford Sibley, *Unilateral Initiatives and Disarmament* (Philadelphia: American Friends Service Committee, 1962), pp. 54–55.

in certain eventualities we contemplate, we have stated explicitly
that we contemplate, throwing it.

To contemplate throwing the bomb, and to manufacture it and
test it and stock it for use if the occasion arises, is a sin very close
indeed to the sin of actually throwing it.[30]

By no means all anti-war systemists take views similar to
these. But, with the exception of those like Gollancz who
find it immoral to think about it, almost all of those who
advocate nonviolence as an absolute principle also subscribe
to the major systemic anti-war reasoning about the values and
analyses of war, Communism, and militarism. (Although not
necessarily the more extreme views on Germany; most advocates of nonviolence find it as difficult to hate Germans as
Russians, and were pacifists during World War II.) To the
extent that they do agree with the *political* reasoning of the
remainder of the anti-war systemists, they can use the maximizing mechanism of choice with either the single principle
of not-killing or the single principle of peace, with no conflict between the two. For those who perceive an analytical
conflict between the two, who find compelling the deterrent
reasoning that killing or the threat to kill may save lives, a
conflict does exist, however. This conflict is resolved by some
in favor of not-killing by the Friends' precept, "Here I stand.
Regardless of relevance or consequence I can do no other."[31]
By others it is resolved in favor of some more complicated
road to peace, and this conflict has converted from pacifism
not only a number of anti-war marginalists, but also some
middle marginalists.

THE ANTI-COMMUNIST SYSTEMISTS

Like the anti-war systemists, the anti-Communist systemists
disagree with the marginalist consensus. The anti-Communist
disagreement, however, is with the consensus that there exists

[30] Victor Gollancz, *The Devil's Repertoire* (London: Gollancz, 1958), p. 125.
[31] *Speak Truth to Power* (Philadelphia: American Friends Service Committee, 1955), p. 68.

some common interest between ourselves and the Communists. Even the marginalist theorists of protracted conflict conceded that both sides had some common interest in setting down rules to avoid the worst varieties of conflict, and that therefore some negotiations delineating legitimate conflict might ultimately be possible. The systemists feel that we are at war with Communism, and that any thought of peace with those who cannot be sincerely interested in peace with us is a contradiction. According to Fred Schwarz, "peace, to the Communist, is total victory. This is it by definition. By definition the Communist or Proletariat class is the peaceful class. There is no action that they can do which is not a peaceful action. If they shoot you it is with a peaceful gun; they put a peaceful bullet in your warlike brain; they give you a peaceful death and they bury you in a peaceful grave."[32] And if peace is impossible, negotiation is impossible. Senator Barry Goldwater applies this belief to arms negotiations in particular:

We must stop lying to ourselves and our friends about disarmament. We must stop advancing the cause of the Soviet Union by playing along with this great Communist-inspired deception. . . .

We must stop negotiating about things that are nonnegotiable, such as the rights of our allies, compromises of our security, treaties like the test ban which can neither be controlled nor enforced. We must not deceive ourselves and our friends into believing that nuclear weapons and modern technology can be negotiated out of existence.

We must stop helping communism, whether by trade, political concessions, technical disclosures, soft talk in the United Nations, recognition of Outer Mongolia, pilgrimages to Moscow, or support for revolutionaries of the Castro type.[33]

And lest there be any doubt about whether Senator Goldwater excludes *arms control* from his proscribed category of

---

[32] Dr. Fred Schwarz, *The Communist Interpretation of Peace* (Long Beach, California: Christian Anti-Communist Crusade, n.d.), p. 12.

[33] Barry M. Goldwater, *Why Not Victory?* (New York: McGraw-Hill, 1962), pp. 162–163.

disarmament, he mentions elsewhere, as a potential danger to the United States, "disarmament, or arms control, as the 87th Congress so cutely termed it."[34]

This is similar to but goes further than the attitude of the anti-Communist marginalists who argue that we should abandon any idea of or negotiations about disarmament but still have an ultimate hope for mutual recognition of the rules of conflict. And as a result of these differences with the marginalist consensus, the anti-Communist systemists come to their systemic recommendations (although, like the anti-war systemists, they share many recommendations with their neighboring marginal school). The anti-Communist systemists make negative recommendations, like Senator Goldwater's "Stop Negotiating!" and they also make indefinite recommendations, although these must be based differently from those of the anti-war systemists. Some members of the anti-war school arrived at recommendations which were characterized as indefinite because they required action of other countries not under the decision-maker's control; some of the anti-Communists' systemic recommendations require action to achieve unachievable military capabilities.

The anti-Communist systemists also make positive systemic recommendations, most of which are variations on the theme "Go to War!" Goldwater argues that we are at war, but concentrates mainly on his negative recommendations and on marginal positive ones for prosecuting this war. Other anti-Communist systemists are bolder. Brent Bozell recommends what is essentially a strategy of political and military warfare:

> Is it extremist to maintain that Communism cannot be successfully resisted merely by attempting to parry its blows? That we must . . . adopt an offensive strategy that is every bit as serious about liberating Communist territory as the Communists are about enslaving ours?

34 *Ibid.*, p. 99.

... The orders [must] go out—
To the Joint Chiefs of Staff: Make the necessary preparations for landing in Havana.[35]
To our commander in Berlin: Tear down the Wall.
To our chief of mission in the Congo: Change sides.

To the Chairman of the Atomic Energy Commission: Schedule testing of every nuclear weapon that could conceivably serve the military purposes of the United States.

To the Chief of the CIA: You are to encourage liberation movements in every nation of the world under Communist domination, including the Soviet Union itself. And you may let it be known that, when, in the future, men offer their lives for the ideals of the West, the West will not stand idly by.[36]

Frank Johnson's recommendations are for a more purely military strategy of limited war:

I. We begin by informing the Kremlin that we intend to win . . .

II. We should not hesitate to employ our military power in limited actions to contract the boundaries of Communism. . . . . Two areas are immediate choices: Cuba and Albania . . . we should be willing to unleash and support Chiang Kai-shek's army in raids against the Chinese mainland. . . .

III. We should employ paramilitary warfare against the Communists on a large scale . . . Eastern Europe should be made into a principal arena for paramilitary warfare . . . East Germany as the most dissatisfied and most geographically accessible satellite, would come in for special attention. We would not do the Soviets the kindness of ruling out intervention by the West German Army in support of a revolt in East Germany, which we might back ourselves if necessary. . . .

IV. The United States should cease immediately to give neutralism its blessing.[37]

[35] This was written well before the missile crisis made an invasion of Cuba seem a much more realistic possibility.

[36] L. Brent Bozell, "To Magnify the West," *National Review*, April 4, 1962, pp. 285–287.

[37] Frank J. Johnson, *No Substitute for Victory* (Chicago: Regnery, 1962), pp. 196–208.

And Major Alexander de Seversky's recommendations are quite different and the most extreme. He writes in italics that "*unless we take leave of our strategic senses, we are not going to fight any limited wars,*"[38] and he therefore opposes preparation for such wars. Rather he favors concentrating all our effort on strategic air power. He wants: "1. Superior offense; 2. Superior defense (*active defense*); 3. Will to survive (civil defense, or *passive* defense),"[39] and he particularly stresses the second—air defense against manned aircraft and ballistic missiles. And lest it be misunderstood that he believes that these thermonuclear forces should be used or will succeed as a deterrent, he writes: "It is clear also that the current balance of terror is transitory in nature and therefore *the side most burdened by the weight of the armament race will be bound to seek relief through war.* We may conclude, therefore, that, barring instantaneous collapse of the Communist state from within, war is inevitable."[40] His solution for achieving any limited ends through American military policy is also thermonuclear: "If we are serious about stopping aggression, it would be better to expand our SAC retaliatory force so that it has the strategic scope and tactical flexibility to crush such aggression anywhere on earth."[41]

All of these sets of recommendations are based, like the recommendations of the systemic anti-war schools, on maximizing mechanisms of choice. The difference between the two systemic schools, of course, is that the anti-Communists want to maximize the avoidance of Communism, rather than the avoidance of war. De Seversky is so extreme that he has no counterpart (at least none I have been able to discover) among the anti-war systemists. He presumably would allow as an exception to the inevitability of thermonuclear war, surrender to the Communists, and his choice is therefore

---

38 Major Alexander P. de Seversky, *America: Too Young to Die!* (New York: McGraw-Hill, 1961), p. 113.
39 *Ibid.*, p. 198.
40 *Ibid.*, p. 196.
41 *Ibid.*, p. 123.

based on a value judgment that of the two alternative inevitable events, he prefers war. Given this judgment, he sets out to maximize the avoidance of Communism by making recommendations for how to win the war. Of all of the makers of recommendations on arms policy, he is the only one who would admit to the validity of the dichotomy "Red or Dead," and even he tempers this with the belief that all-out thermonuclear war need not be quite the equivalent of Dead.

The other systemic anti-Communists, however, correspond more closely to mirror-images of the anti-war systemists. The anti-Communists would answer the "Red or Dead" question, *if put,* "Better dead," just as the anti-war systemists would answer it, if put, "Better Red." But aside from de Seversky, the anti-Communists, like their opposite numbers in the anti-war school, believe that their policies will avoid the ultimate putting of the question. They choose their recommendations by maximizing the avoidance of Communism; like Hughes and the other anti-war systemists, they feel that acting on these recommendations will *probably* also avoid the other evil.

The major value judgment of the systemic anti-Communists, therefore, is that Communism is, compared to war, an absolute evil; their analytical picture of Communism backs this up. And the companion analytical belief is that without the adoption of their policies, Communist victory is inevitable. As put by Senator Goldwater:

There can no longer be any doubt about our situation in today's world: we are at war; not a cold war but a real war—we can call it the Communist war, war of a more deadly nature than any we have fought before. We may well be now engaged in a phase of World War III which if we lose will mean the end of freedom as we know it. But we need not lose this war, either elsewhere in the world or here at home; and it is my hope that the suggestions I will make in this book, in admittedly limited fields, will help point the way to victory. Victory is the key to the whole problem; the only alternative is—obviously—defeat.[42]

42 Goldwater, pp. 22–23.

Some of the subordinate analyses are interesting: de Seversky believes that we are now terribly weaker than the Communists; Johnson that we are far stronger, and that what we must do is call their bluff. On the question of our geographical interests, James Burnham favors a Europe-oriented strategy, but he goes to some trouble to differentiate it from the European strategy of some of the middle marginalists:

... there have been many with a Western strategic outlook among the members of the Union Now, Atlantic Union and similar organizations and in the Council on Foreign Relations. But many, even most, of these persons have been Softs. They assign priority to Western civilization and its family of nations, as against the Afro-Asian neutralists; they support the Western alliance and usually favor some form of Atlantic Common Market or Community. But they have held such views in a strategically passive way. So far as relations with the Soviet Union and the world Communist enterprise go, not a few of them have been peaceful coexistors.[43]

And just as Fred Cook's article saw a takeover of American democratic processes by the militarists, the anti-Communists see these processes being taken over by the antimilitarists. Goldwater writes:

Even though our peril is great, we find a situation developing where military commanders are in danger of being charged with "right-wing political theories" if they have the temerity to call attention to our danger and point out the methods used most successfully by our enemies.
Curiously enough, we find the Defense Department today threatening to crack down on Cold War seminars held by military commanders to increase public awareness "of the danger of the Communist menace."[44]

Sometimes, the militaristic and antimilitaristic bugaboos are the same people and organizations. Cook's article is one of many by members of the anti-war schools which pays its regards to The RAND Corporation ("a government-subsidized

[43] James Burnham, "Western, Yes but Hard," *National Review*, February 13, 1962, p. 94.
[44] Goldwater, p. 183.

'think' agency," he believes helped to break up the test-ban negotiations);[45] Burnham attacks RAND for opposing nuclear diffusion.[46]

But these arguments are subordinate to the major one. The basic argument of the systemic anti-Communists is that Communism is coming; we must do *everything* within our power to combat it. The systemic anti-Communist school of arms policy, then, like the systemic anti-war school, comes to recommendations for drastic changes in current military policy—recommendations in opposition to those of the marginal consensus—on the basis of mechanisms of choice which strive to maximize the probability of avoiding what they consider the supreme danger to the commonweal. The substantive inputs of the two schools are opposites, particularly the definition of what the supreme danger is, and other less important differences exist between them. But the systemists of the anti-Communist school as much of those of the anti-war school reason similarly to Stuart Hughes that: " 'An act of faith'— such is the only solution I can see to the irreducible dilemma in which the strategists of deterrence have left us, with their fear of Soviet blackmail on the one hand and their implication of the necessity of world order on the other."[47] The anti-Communist systemists choose their act of faith to oppose blackmail; the anti-war systemists choose theirs to achieve the world order; the "strategists of deterrence" in the marginal schools disagree with both—they do not find the dilemma "irreducible."

45 Cook, p. 317.
46 James Burnham, "Escalating Downward," *National Review*, July 17, 1962, p. 5.
47 *An Approach to Peace*, pp. 66–67. Copyright 1962 by H. Stuart Hughes.

C H A P T E R   1 2

INTERPRETATIONS, IMPLICATIONS, AND CONCLUSIONS

WHY THE SCHOOLS DIFFER

In the initial discussion of the five schools of arms-policy recommendation, it was suggested that although it is traditional to place conflicting political viewpoints along a simple linear continuum going from "left" to "right," this is not the most accurate characterization of the differences of opinion over arms and disarmament. Rather, arms recommendations are graded here according to *two* criteria: direction of recommended change and size of recommended change. When it comes to the underlying reasons for the differences of recommendation, the matter is even more complicated; not only do two separate factors, values and analyses, enter the logic leading to recommendations, but there is an asymmetry in the ways in which these values and analyses differ among the five schools of thought. The recommendations of the antiwar and middle-marginal schools differ from one another primarily on the basis of divergent analyses; the recommendations of the middle and the anti-Communist marginalists differ primarily on the basis of different values; the systemists differ from the marginalists on the basis of both; and the middle marginalists differ among themselves.

Figure 3 illustrates in a very rough-and-ready intuitive way these relationships. The vertical axis represents values; to the extent that two adjoining schools differ on values, the boxes representing the two are at different vertical levels. Similarly, the horizontal axis represents analyses; disagreements over analysis are shown by horizontal separation. The figure is not quantitative. The only phenomenon illustrated is the existence of value and analytical differences, and no attempt is made to show either comparative sizes of difference, or other matters, such as the similarity of the extremes on certain issues.

The disagreements of the two systemic schools with the others are the simplest to explain and illustrate. The anti-

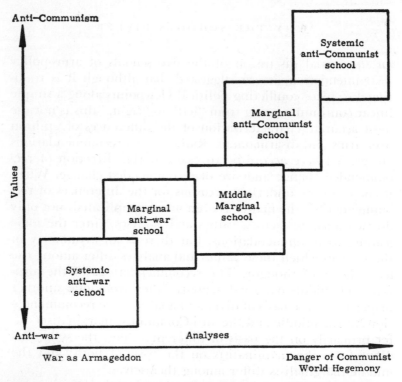

FIGURE 3: The value and the analytical bases for differences of recommendations among the schools of arms policy

war and anti-Communist systemists diverge from their marginalist neighbors on the basis of *both* values and analyses. As has been discussed, the infinite relative fear of war on the one hand and of Communism on the other are sustained both by the analytical concepts of the inevitability of the menace and its grim nature, and the value judgment of distaste for the threat so pictured. Based on these value-analytical "fears," each of the systemic schools has its relative moderates— Hughes and Neal, for example, among the anti-war systemists, and Goldwater among the anti-Communists—and each has its more extreme members, shading off into the two groups whose thinking on arms policy is so irrelevant that it is not discussed here—the Communists on the "left," and the lunatic Internal-Communist-Menace fringe on the "right."

The differences among the three marginal schools are far more important to the making of policy and are also more interesting because they are more complex; the recommendations of the middle marginalists do not differ from those of the anti-war marginalists on the one side and those of the anti-Communists on the other for symmetrical reasons. In the discussion of the relationship of the middle to the anti-war marginalists the distinction between the "analytical" and the "balanced-value" poles of middle-marginal values becomes important. *The so-called "analytical" middle marginalists— those who consider anti-war values to be most relevant to arms policy, whose thinking begins with an analytical picture of the existing world as it appears to them, and whose recommendations based on this picture are for peace through controlled strength—differ very little from the anti-war marginalists on their value judgments concerning the world as they would like it to be.* Both the "analytical" pole of middle marginalism and the anti-war marginalists want arms policy to be used mainly for maintaining the peace. *The major basis of the differences in their recommendations, therefore, lies in different world views—different analytical pictures of the world as it is and can be made to be.* There are, of course, some value differences between the two groups—particularly between the short-run time preferences of the analytical mid-

dle and the longer-run preferences of the anti-war marginalists—but even this is closely related to the different analytical
answers given to the question of whether in trying to achieve
long-run peace, the policies adopted might inadvertently
leave us dead in the short run. In any case, the value differences, although some exist, are minor compared to the
analytical ones. For an optimizing marginalist whose per-
sonal-political value judgments are that arms policy in the
mid-twentieth century should be concerned primarily with
avoiding thermonuclear war, and that the need to defend an
area of freedom against the Communist miiltary threat
should be a major conditioning factor but not a primary
objective, arms recommendations should be based on the
answers given to certain fundamental analytical questions.

Some of these concern war:

If thermonuclear weapons continue to exist in large numbers, is their very existence "certain" (or highly likely) to
start a war through irrationality or accident; or can rationality exert substantial control even over irrationality and accident or the response to accident?

Is deterrence highly likely to result in thermonuclear war
through miscalculation; or can the probability of miscalculation be kept low through the proper use of the "paradoxes of
deterrence"?

Are "limited" wars likely to get out of hand through escalation processes; or can the proper use of deterrence exert substantial control over escalation, too?

Are nuclear wars between the United States and the Soviet
Union likely to become spasms of unlimited mutual destruction; or can control also hold down the death and destruction
once such a war has started?

Is the "arms race" in itself likely to cause war over the
long run; or can a controlled arms race be a relatively stable
one?

Is a fully or partially disarmed condition an inherently
stable and peaceful condition; or can substantial disarmament lead to substantial instability?

Some of the analytical questions concern the Soviet Union:

Is the U.S.S.R. rapidly becoming a consolidationist "have" power aiming primarily at maintaining its current holdings; or are the Russians still looking for opportunities to expand their power?

Is the Soviet Union beginning to concentrate solely on the use of political-economic-social means of achieving its international ends; or is it still willing to use low-risk military means in world affairs?

Is the current major target of Soviet desires the underdeveloped world; or are they still aiming primarily at breaking up the unity of Western Europe?

Can the Soviets be induced to relax their grip on the East European satellites; or is any substantial relaxation a utopian hope which we cannot bring to pass?

Can the peaceful elements within the Soviet Union be best encouraged in their opposition to the more bellicose elements in Russia and China by Western attempts to cooperate; or by Western demonstrations that bellicose Communist policies will not pay off?

And certain other analytical questions are almost as important:

Is deterrence of certain Soviet military actions incompatible with U.S.-U.S.S.R. cooperation on other matters of common interest; or can deterrence and cooperation complement each other?

Is the fulcrum of world power, and therefore of our interest, shifting to the heavily-populated countries of Asia, Africa, and Latin America; or is the core of power still the joining of the wealth of Western Europe to our own?

Is power the carrot; or is the stick equally or more important?

Is the best way to prevent the revival of the dark tendencies of the German past to neutralize, disarm, and unify Germany; or is tying West Germany to a unified Europe more likely to succeed in this objective?

Is the growth of the military power within the United

States a clear future danger; or are the problems which arise minor ones which can be handled on an *ad hoc* basis?

A belief in the analytical validity of the first answers in each pair must lead inevitably to the typical arms recommendations of the marginal anti-war school for disarmament, disengagement, and *détente.* A belief in the analytical validity of the second answers, *by an individual who shares the basic anti-war value system,* should lead to the typical arms recommendations of the middle-marginal arms-control deterrers for arms controls, stabilized deterrence, and strong defense. And someone who accepts the analytical validity of some of the first answers and some of the second will presumably make some of the anti-war recommendations, some of the middle ones, and, where the difference can be split, some recommendations in between.

But the fundamental point to be made is that *the personal choice of a value system which gives heavy primacy to avoiding thermonuclear war cannot by itself determine arms recommendations. "Good will" is not enough; convincing the decision maker that these are the values actually held by the American people is not enough. The selection of one or the other of the alternative answers to each of the analytical questions listed above is not a matter of personal taste; it is a question of right and wrong—accuracy or inaccuracy of analysis —and is, in principle, subject to test.* In practice, of course, even analytical right and wrong are seldom either absolute or demonstrable, and a good test is hard to find. But among those who profess these primarily anti-war values, the debate should be about analytical validity and not about choice of value judgment.

This precept relates in two ways to that portion of the arms debate which is carried on between the anti-war marginalists (or anti-war systemists arguing for marginal changes in policy) and the "analytical" peace-professing middle-marginalists —a dialogue which, in terms of *public* controversy, tends to dominate the current debate. The first implication is critical of the anti-war group; the second is critical of the middle.

The first is based on the fact that the dialogue frequently sounds like one in which the members of the anti-war schools accuse their opponents of lack of morality, and the middle marginalists make counter-accusations of lack of realism. But to the extent that this dialogue is between individuals with roughly similar value systems, the accusation of immorality is almost always invalid. One can make such an accusation against someone who professes the same morality as oneself only if the intention is to say that he is consciously operating on the basis of different values from those that he claims— and this type of accusation is seldom intended, is seldom true of this portion of the arms debate even when it is intended, and is even more seldom at all demonstrable. The faultiness of such accusations is not due entirely to the anti-war marginalists who make them; middle marginalists all too frequently fall into the serious methodological fault of leaving the aims of their recommendations so very implicit that errors of misinterpretation are excusable. (The major *raison d'être* for this study, after all, is that such things must be dug out of most writings on arms policy rather than being exposed by the writers to the view of those who may have a legitimate interest in knowing just what it is that they are after.) Nonetheless, the values exist in all writings on arms policy, and the values of the "analytical" marginalists are similar to those of the anti-war marginalists. Morality should thus not be at question, but rather what should be debatable and debated is whether an individual's arms recommendations best fulfill his professed morality. And this is a question of realism of analysis. The middle marginalists' accusations against the anti-war school of lack of realism may or may not be well taken, but, unlike the countering accusations of immorality, they certainly are debatable.[1]

The second implication of centering the anti-war versus

---

[1] The perceptive follower of the literature will note that, on the basis of further research and thought, this conclusion reverses a statement I made in my "Facts and Morals in the Arms Debate" (*World Politics*, 14, particularly pp. 241–243), where I argued that *both* accusations of lack of morality and lack of realism were poorly taken.

middle-marginal dispute on questions of analysis is based on the fact that the most conclusive way to win a political argument is to demonstrate logical *dominance* —that the policy advocated is best (or at least no worse than any other), not only for certain values, but for all relevant values. In the particular case in point, the middle-marginal recommendations are rather clearly better than the anti-war recommendations for the purpose of stemming Communist advance (except perhaps in the underdeveloped world). To the extent that it can be demonstrated that such a middle-marginal recommendation is *also* better for the cause of peace, it is dominant for the major relevant values, and should be adopted without cavil. As a result, middle marginalists tend to defend their recommendations against the attacks of the anti-war schools on the analytical basis of contribution to peace alone, even in the cases where the differences of opinion are primarily based on different relative values.

There is nothing wrong with this; no matter what the motivating values of a maker of recommendations, if he can prove his recommendations better for the other guy's values, he has won the argument. But sometimes this can be carried to the point of absurdity. It is difficult to see, for example, how a recommendation for a first thermonuclear strike can be defended against pure arms-control deterrence on the basis of peace alone. This is particularly true if the maker of the first-strike recommendation professes time preferences which emphasize the short run, as almost all middle marginalists do. Except in the case of preemption, when the choice is not between peace and war, but between striking first and striking second, it is extremely hard to argue that a first thermonuclear strike is more likely to avoid thermonuclear war than no first strike. *Maybe* a first strike now will avoid war later—maybe not—but a first strike now means the literal certainty of such a war. (Note, however, that this is not true of the creation of a first-strike *force;* whether or not such a force built now will, via deterrence, make war less likely, is a reasonable analytical question.)

Similarly, for a slightly less clear-cut example—it is difficult to see the logic of the recommendation made by some at the time of the building of the Berlin wall, that we should knock it down in the name of peace. Knocking it down appeared to mean a substantial risk of war then; not knocking it down may have meant a substantial longer-run danger of war. Someone whose time preferences are such that he discounts heavily the long run in favor of the short is on swampy ground if he maintains that knocking down the wall could have been defended entirely on the basis of preserving the peace. More generally, the same is true to greater or lesser degree, of many arguments for a "tough" policy as against a marginally "softer" one. Someone who argues on one occasion that the tough policy is necessary for peace in the long run in order to discourage the Soviet Union from ultimately taking the one intolerable step which will force us to go to war, and on another occasion that in the face of all the short-run pitfalls it is unrealistic to design policies against the long-run dangers of a proliferating arms race, had better check his own consistency. *"Tough" policies are readily defensible on the basis of the long view, but arguments for substantial disarmament may be too.* Tough policies are also defensible on the basis of a value system which is not as heavily weighted toward peace as is that of some anti-war marginalists—one very real reason for our refusal to compromise over Berlin has been the freedom of the West Berliners, and some anti-war marginalists have taken the attitude described above by Jean Daniel,[2] that they do not want to die for this cause. And this, then, is a true dispute over values, and not an analytical argument over how best to preserve the peace in Europe.

In fact, as has been pointed out, few middle marginalists are actually at the "analytical" pole which values peace in almost the same way as do the members of the anti-war marginalist school. Many tend this way, but most balance more closely the values placed on avoiding thermonuclear war and

[2] See p. 268 in Chapter 10.

those assigned to the defense of freedom from Communist threats. Some middle marginalists come very close to the anti-war marginalists in placing a relatively heavy value on staying out of thermonuclear war; others enrich the mixture with various quantities of the other relevant values.

If the public debate over arms policy is dominated by the dialogue between the anti-war schools and the middle, the semiprivate intragovernmental debates are to a great extent over different middle-marginal recommendations. The issues debated are mostly those which relate to the mixture of arms-control and political objectives in deterrent policy: How strong a strategic counterforce should we try for? How credible a first strike capability? What is the best way to control Western nuclear deterrence of Soviet threats to Europe? To what threats should we extend the nuclear deterrent portion of Western capabilities? How heavily should the defense of Europe depend on tactical nuclear weapons?

These differences of opinion within the middle-marginal school stem from finely divided compounds of value and analysis. Those who stress arms control favor policies of controlled stability, deemphasis of nuclear deterrence in Europe, and emphasis on conventional defenses in that area. They base these recommendations both on the argument that nuclear diffusion, nuclear deterrence, and nuclear defense are too dangerous (a combination of analysis as to what the risks are and value judgment as to which ones should be taken); and on the argument that they cannot be made credible and therefore are less likely to succeed than alternative policies (an analytical statement). Those who put more emphasis on "prevailing" and on protecting Europe recommend a "winning" counterforce, a credible first-strike capability, a non-American deterrent, and/or a tactical nuclear defense of Europe (no middle marginalist favors *all* of these things). They base these recommendations on the beliefs that it is better to win than to lose and that we have a moral obligation to help protect our allies against Soviet threats (value judgments); and on the belief that some of these "strong" policies can be made credible, whereas the safer ones may deter less successfully *because* they are safer (an analytical argument depending upon the paradoxes of deterrence). Some middle marginalists, like Kissinger, whose value systems assign substantial importance to our obligation to Europe, would prefer the same policies as the arms controllers if they thought that they were politically feasible. Lacking this, they reluctantly advocate such policies as tactical nuclear defense and American recognition of what they believe (analytically) to be the inexorable drive toward a non-American deterrent.

The underlying basis of many of the disputes among middle marginalists is thus as much in differences of value as in differences of analysis. But their explicit arguments on all areas of arms policy tend to be very heavily weighted toward analysis. There are sound reasons for this. Most middle marginalists are searchers after the tangible; because values *are* matters of personal judgment, there is very little to argue about. Better, according to this view, to discuss the concrete; even differing middle-marginal value systems are close enough to one another for such analytical arguments to be meaningful to both sides. If dominance can be demonstrated, then there is no need to worry about the intangible and hard-to-get-hold-of values. This is almost all to the good. Although it is difficult to prove a policy dominant, it is frequently easier to prove another one *dominated*. We may not be able to show what is better than anything else, but we may be able to show that one policy is *worse* on all counts than another, and thus eliminate an alternative. In recent years, such policies as "massive retaliation" in all areas of the world, automatic nuclear reply to Soviet attack in Europe, and unilateral disarmament based on budgetary imperatives have been essentially eliminated from the arms debate (at least among middle marginalists) because they were dominated.

But, as in the case of the attempt to win the debate with the anti-war schools on the basis of dominance, this can be carried too far. Middle marginalists are sometimes puzzled by the fact that recommendations for which they have made strong analytical cases have been rejected. Frequently this may be because those who make the decisions take into account (perhaps must, politically, take into account) values or analytical deductions from values which are considered irrelevant by the middle-marginal maker of arms recommendations. Sometimes the concentration of middle marginalists on analytical argument obscures from them the fact that their values are not universal. If the intragovernmental debates over arms policy are over differences in analysis, it does not follow that the time has come when arms decisions can be purely technical. In one case in point, many middle marginalists argue for greater unification of the services and perhaps a single chief of staff in order to strengthen the top military commands. The case for this in terms of operating efficiency is very strong indeed. But Congress generally seems extremely dubious about the whole thing, on the grounds that strengthening the military may operate against the principle of civilian control, and strengthening the Department of Defense may operate against the principle of Congressional control. These are value judgments (or deductions from first-order judgments) which generally do not enter the calculations upon which the impressive case for centralization is based. It is vital to fight out the analytical issues of arms policy, but it is likely that a substantial residue of difference will always remain, among middle marginalists as well as between them and the other schools of arms policy.

Indeed, even though the anti-Communist marginalists take part in the middle marginalists' technical debate because their general analytical world view is similar to that of the middle, the anti-Communists' recommendations differ because their values differ. The middle and the anti-Communist marginal schools hold in common the analytical views that war is controllable, both in the way it starts and the way it is carried on; that the Soviet Union is and will remain an opponent; that the breakup of NATO is a primary Soviet goal; and that power is primarily a stick. There are analytical differences between the two schools; different colorations on their common analyses—how usable is war as an instrument of national policy, how implacable an opponent is Russia; and divergent pieces of analysis—how likely is the arms race to cause war, how important is the stemming of the Communist tide in the underdeveloped areas, how possible is it to shake the Soviet hold on the satellites.

The basic analytical outlooks of the two schools are nonetheless quite similar. But the recommendations of the anti-Communist marginalists differ from those of the middle about as much as do the recommendations of the anti-war marginalists. The middle wants to use deterrence to decrease the threat of war; the anti-Communists want to use the threat of war to push back the Communists. The middle has a very strong interest in serious efforts at one variety or another of arms control; the anti-Communists endorse one variety, but even this hardly with enthusiasm. Even those middle marginalists who most want to protect Europe want to use nuclear deterrence and/or tactical nuclear defense primarily to hold; the anti-Communists want to use both to threaten as well. The middle marginalists provide a menu of possible alternatives for the protection of Europe; the anti-Communists take from the menu some of everything, with emphasis on the nuclear. The middle marginalists favor a consolidationist strategy based on Western Europe; the anti-Communists want to strengthen Western Europe, but they want a Forward Strategy, pushing eastward.

And, since the basic analyses of the middle and anti-Communist marginalists are the same, the differences of recommendation are founded primarily on differences of value. Indeed, the point is too obvious to be labored. The calculus of risks as estimated analytically by the anti-Communist and the middle marginalists is about the same, but the anti-Communists want to take many of the risks that the middle wishes to avoid. If Strausz-Hupé, Kintner, and Possony say that "the priority objective of any American grand strategy is, by a broad margin, the preservation and enhancement of our political system rather than the maintenance of peace," this is not a testable piece of analysis, but a basic statement of values with which one either agrees or disagrees.

PERSONAL CONCLUSIONS

For myself, I disagree with the Forward Strategists. It has been pointed out to me that in discussing a spectrum of opposing views, one almost always places oneself in the middle. In accord with this precept, I consider myself a middle marginalist (which at this point should surprise nobody), albeit one not very far from the border with anti-war marginalism. My values are such that to me the priority objective of any American grand strategy in the thermonuclear era is to prevent thermonuclear war. If I was once one of the youngest members of the pre-World War II "Fight for Freedom Committee," the change in my beliefs has come not only because I think Communist totalitarianism slightly more tolerable than that of the Nazis, but also because I believe that the creation of thermonuclear weapons means an order-of-magnitude change in the nature of warfare. Even if Fryklund's most optimistic unclassified estimate of 3,000,000 American deaths in a thermonuclear exchange is accurate, 3,000,000 dead in an hour is enough to bother me considerably, as does the additional estimate of 5,000,000 Soviet dead.[3] Not to mention NATO, China, etc. I think that in the long run there may be ways to defeat Communism, but I do not want to do it by nuclear war.

Yet, I am a marginalist. I do not think that no risk of 3,000,000 dead Americans can be tolerable; under some circumstances I would favor taking a substantial risk of a much greater number than that. If I do not believe (analytically) that knocking down the Berlin wall is the best way to keep the peace, and I do not feel that a substantial risk of war should be taken to free the East Berliners, I am willing to

[3] Richard Fryklund, *100 Million Lives* (New York: Macmillan, 1962), p. 14.

contemplate going to war against a direct threat to the freedom of the 2,000,000 West Berliners. And, what should not be surprising but may be—so are some of my anti-war marginalist friends if the issue comes to that.

The analytical question upon which we disagree is how best to avoid its coming to that; how best to preserve the 3,000,000 American lives without an intolerable cost to freedom. Most, but not all, of my analytical beliefs are middle marginal: I believe that rationality can exert substantial control in preventing the outbreak of war and, perhaps more important, I have seen no *better* proposals than those which recommend attempts at rational arms control. Unlike some arms controllers, I place a special emphasis on the disarmament variety of arms control, but unlike the anti-war marginalists, I think that disarmament must be looked at with the arms-controller's calculus or else the long-run cure runs excessive risk of short-run decease through reckless instability. Also, unlike the anti-war marginalists, I am dubious about current efforts toward really substantial disarmament, either through negotiation or through Osgood-type unilateral initiatives. The former, the process of negotiating utopia with the Russians in three easy-to-put-together stages, I believe to be futile and so consuming of the world's attention as well as American intellectual and other resources, that it interferes seriously with a realistic effort to obtain the much more urgent limited arms controls. The latter, the unilateral initiatives program, I find interesting and worthy of further investigation, but I suspect that for the most part there are two kinds of unilateral initiatives—those which have been under way for a number of years, and those which would be dangerous to both peace and freedom. I therefore feel that Osgood (and his followers Etzioni and Waskow to a much greater extent) is standing on very narrow ground. And basically, my fear of the dangers of such unilateral initiatives is based on the analytical belief that the Soviet Union is an expansionistic, opportunistic, and moderately clever opponent. Soviet policy may be becoming consolidationist or liberal, but there seems little sign that it is doing so to an extent significant for our arms policy. I prefer the Brzezinski analysis of encouraging the peaceful elements in the Communist world by denying a pay-off to bellicosity to the arguments that we should try to discover these peaceful elements and cooperate with them.

But like other middle marginalists, I feel myself free to be eclectic. In most debates within the middle-marginal school I find myself on the side of the arms-control stabilizers. I am tempted to favor a countercity strategy as pure deterrence and constantly have to pull myself back analytically to the position that since it probably doesn't take much of any thermonuclear deterrence to deter Soviet attack, countercity deters only slightly better than counterforce, and if we must strike it seems preferable to kill fewer people than more. But I cannot make myself enthusiastic about "prevailing." If it is to be counterforce, let's confine it to one sufficient to deter the worst blackmail threats against Europe (but if we have an overwhelming lead now, as is claimed by Secretary of Defense McNamara, it is far too good a bargaining counter in negotiations with the Soviet Union for us to give it up for free). And I would like to make our European strategy as nonnuclear as possible. Within the limits of the fact that we have no direct control over our European allies and can probably no longer prevent a French independent deterrent, I think that we should encourage them with all our means to think conventionally.

And on some issues I agree with the anti-war marginalists. Although I agree with the arms-control calculus which, by considering the precise implications of each step necessarily gives the short run by far the greatest importance, I am worried about the long run. I theoretically favor substantial (although probably not "complete and general") disarmament; I just don't see now how we get there from here and I do not want to orient our short-run efforts in that direction without a much greater hope for success. Also in the name of the long run, however, I think that *if* the analysis is correct that we can, through a "tough" policy, force the Soviet Union to soften its own, then we ought to start thinking now about the *détente* in Europe which is not yet possible. Brzezinski's policies for encouraging independent tendencies in the Soviet bloc are extremely interesting; in the long run I find disengagement from the strength of a united Western Europe an attractive idea. But in the short run disengagement under Soviet pressure seems dangerous; I *am* worried about the dark German tendencies, and trying to tie Germany to the West with bonds of self-interest seems by far the best of the available policies for controlling them. And finally, the one area where I think the middle analysis is at least as bad as that of the anti-war marginalists is Southeast Asia; the anti-war policy of withdrawal has little appeal, but much of the analysis upon which it is based is compelling. The policy of military backing for unpopular governments has not worked well in the past and I am anxious to view a new middle-marginal synthesis of the concepts of power as the carrot and power as the stick.

I do not claim "truth" for the views I have expressed in the last few pages. I have argued throughout that values cannot be "true" or "false." Were my values different, the analytical views I have expressed would probably be compatible with anti-Communist marginalism. Although I find the analyses of the systemists extremely unconvincing, I recognize that an absolute value placed on either avoiding war or not-killing can reasonably lead to systemic anti-war recommendations. I have considerable respect for those who, recognizing the risks they entail, do make such absolute anti-war recommendations on the basis of pure values, with a minimum of cant about our misunderstanding the Russians. I find anti-Communist systemism so foreign to my way of thinking, however, that I cannot say where absolute values of this sort should lead. And, perhaps because I am so close to the anti-war marginalists and believe that my *values* are about the same but my analyses are right and theirs wrong, it would be difficult to move me closer to that school than the fringes.

THE INTELLECTUAL AND POLITICAL
PROCESSES ON ARMS POLICY

Little reference has been made throughout to ideas directly attributable to those who actually wield or have wielded power. President Eisenhower's farewell address has been alluded to because it has historical significance in the debate over militarism in the United States. Certain moderate anti-war marginalist ideas have been illustrated with quotations from officials of the present administration such as Ambassadors Stevenson and Kennan, and Presidential Advisers Wiesner and Bowles. These were used because to a great extent the field of nonofficial writers with this point of view suddenly became sparsely populated when these gentlemen entered the government. Kennan in particular has created an important subschool of thought (to which I may belong) around his ideas. All of the quotations taken from these officials were from books and articles written before they reentered government.

The reason for this abstinence from the field of official writings is that the presidency, using the term to mean not only the office but the entire executive branch of government, never has had a single point of view. The presidency is in its essence a political compromise. The President is nominated in a convention designed for such compromise, and he is elected to represent the entire electorate including the always-substantial minority voting for his opponent. He picks his subordinates on a basis which lies to a great extent in political compromise, and cannot expect them to be in more than general agreement with his own views or those of each other. And both because his decisions must take account of political factors and because in a government the size of ours he cannot make all the decisions himself, the end results are usually somewhat inconsistent logically.

All this is probably for the best in this best of all possible worlds. It might be nice if the idealized structure pictured here, with all analyses subject to truth tests, and all political values of the electorate synthesized in the elected decision makers, actually described the political structure of arms-policy decision making. In a more realistic vein, it may be both desirable and possible to emphasize the logical factors in arms-policy making as compared to the more purely political factors, such as the necessity to resolve interservice and other intragovernmental rivalries, the lobbying of the "military-industrial complex," the pressures from the Congressional districts to move military installations in (but perhaps to move radioactive fallout away), the need to appease both one's allies and the pickets outside of the White House. The making of arms policy should in principle be different from the making of economic policy, the direct object of which is to balance the welfare of the groups exerting political pressures. In a way arms policy *is* an intellectual problem. Certain value objectives exist, determined by the electorate and the President; how do we best go about fulfilling them?

In fact, it is obvious from the newspaper and magazine writings about the making of policy in the White House, the Pentagon, and the State Department, that the Kennedy administration has moved a long way in precisely this direction. Arms policy *is* freer from sheer political pressures than much other policy, and the administration, led by a strong President and a strong Secretary of Defense, has taken advantage of that fact. But even this could be pushed too far, (although what would be "too far" from the point of view of solving the problems is probably much further than the political limitations will allow). The arms recommendations of the marginalists, particularly the middle marginalists who make most of the arms decisions, are designed to hedge in all directions against their own failure. Nonetheless, man has a finite mind, and analysis, whether by individuals or committees, formal or informal, may not realize all of the possibilities. The makers of arms recommendations strive to give consistent advice, but if the consistent advice has a consistent hole in it, disaster may result. According to General Maxwell Taylor, "during the Lebanon landing in 1958, the United States had an Honest John rocket afloat off Beirut but was not allowed to land it because it could fire an atomic warhead as well as a conventional one."[4] If we had consistently converted all weapons to dual capabilities perhaps we would not have been able to land in Lebanon at all. The fact that the Eisenhower administration had decided on an intellectual basis to depend primarily on big and little nuclear weapons, but was inconsistent about it (perhaps to conciliate General Taylor politically), may have been a very good thing.

The present administration, too, has its inconsistencies and ambiguities. And, although I am bothered when the inconsistent policy is one I oppose, the inconsistency as a hedge may not be a bad thing. Most current American arms policy is derived from the recommendations of the middle-marginal school, with both intellectual and technological lags. Our strategic deterrence is based on the counterforce targeting advised by most middle marginalists and the large forces recommended by those who want to deter nuclearly an attack on Europe as well as one on ourselves.[5] And President Kennedy has been quoted as stating explicitly that "in some circumstances we might have to take the initiative," in thermonuclear war.[6] American policy for deterrence in Europe at the time of writing is consistent with this, being based on asking the Europeans to depend primarily upon the credibility of our first strike,[7] but we are (perhaps inconsistently) clearly moving toward disguised cooperation with the independent national deterrents we oppose. This is being done in response to political, not intellectual, pressure.

[4] Maxwell D. Taylor, *The Uncertain Trumpet* (New York: Harper, 1960), p. 9.

[5] See Secretary of Defense Robert McNamara's commencement speech at the University of Michigan, Ann Arbor, June 16, 1962.

[6] Stewart Alsop, "Kennedy's Grand Strategy," *Saturday Evening Post*, March 7, 1962.

[7] McNamara speech.

But at the same time as these middle-marginal strategic policies are being executed, at least one major anti-war marginal and one major anti-Communist marginal recommendation, both seemingly inconsistent with the basic policies, are being carried out. American arms-control policy has not been based on the little-steps-for-little-feet recommendation of the middle-marginal arms controllers, but on the giant-steps-to-complete-and-general-disarmament favored by the anti-war marginalists. We have been negotiating for a number of years with some sincerity, if little hope of success, over general disarmament in three stages.[8] And American policy for the defense of Europe is neither the nonnuclear policy recommended by many middle marginalists nor the careful tactical nuclear policy proposed by Kissinger, but is rather much closer to the heavy dependence upon tactical nuclear weapons recommended by the anti-Communist marginalists.

For my own part, as I have suggested above in setting forth my own views, I would be happier with a consistent policy based on the recommendations of the middle-marginal arms controllers than with one which, by putting its main dependence upon the policies recommended by the more Europe-oriented middle marginalists, but also drawing important policies from both the anti-war and the anti-Communist marginalists, may in some sense average out at my beliefs. But consistency in any national policy should not be expected and probably should not be desired. What should be desired, and perhaps may be expected, is that the intellectual portion of the political process by which arms policy is made, be thoroughly understood by those who participate in the debate. And what might help this increase of understanding is for the makers of recommendations on arms policy to be much more explicit, to themselves as well as their readers, concerning the separate values and analyses upon which they base their advice. Certainly the values and analyses upon

[8] See my "Disarmament and Arms Control," *The New Leader*, February 19, 1962.

which real policy is dependent can never be sorted out completely neatly and satisfactorily. But marginal moves in the direction of this sort of self-understanding on the part of those who want to contribute to the debate could contribute much to the formulation of policies which best fulfill the values of the American people.

ACKNOWLEDGMENTS

Grateful acknowledgment is made to the following for permission to quote from the works indicated:

American Economic Review: September 1946, Fritz Machlup, "Marginal Analysis and Empirical Research."

Atheneum Publishers: *An Approach to Peace* by H. Stuart Hughes. Copyright © 1962 by H. Stuart Hughes. Reprinted by permission of Atheneum Publishers.

George Braziller, Inc.: *Arms Control, Disarmament, and National Security,* Donald G. Brennan, ed., New York, 1961. Reprinted with the permission of the publisher, George Braziller, Inc.

Mr. Fred J. Cook: "Juggernaut: The Warfare State," *The Nation,* October 28, 1961.

Doubleday & Company, Inc.: Walter Hahn and John Neff, eds., *American Strategy for the Nuclear Age,* 1960.

——— Erich Fromm, *May Man Prevail?.* Copyright © 1961 by Erich Fromm. Reprinted by permission of Doubleday & Company, Inc., and George Allen & Unwin Ltd.

——— James Roosevelt, ed., *The Liberal Papers.* Copyright © 1962 by James Roosevelt. Reprinted by permission of Doubleday & Company, Inc.

Mr. Allen R. Ferguson: *Disarmament and Deterrence,* The RAND Corporation, Paper P-2553, April 1962.

Foreign Affairs: April 1958, Dean Acheson, "The Illusion of Disengagement"; April 1961, Albert Wohlstetter, "Nuclear Sharing: NATO and N + 1 Country"; June 1962, Henry A. Kissinger, "The Unsolved Problems of European Defense."

Mr. Paul Goodman: "The Ineffectuality of Some Intelligent People," *Commentary,* June 1962.

Harper & Row, Publishers: Henry A. Kissinger, *The Necessity for Choice.* Copyright © 1960, 1961 by Henry A. Kissinger. Reprinted with the permission of Harper & Row, Publishers, Incorporated, and with the permission of Chatto & Windus, Limited.

——— Robert Strausz-Hupé, William Kintner, and Stefan T. Possony, *A Forward Strategy for America.* Copyright © 1961 by Robert Strausz-Hupé, William Kintner, and Stefan T. Possony. Reprinted with the permission of Harper & Row, Publishers, Incorporated.

Houghton Mifflin Company: Pierre Gallois, *The Balance of Terror,* Boston, 1961.

Horizon Press: Herman Kahn, *Thinking About the Unthinkable.* Copyright © 1962 by Herman Kahn. Quotations are reprinted by permission of Horizon Press and George Weidenfeld & Nicholson, Limited.

McGraw-Hill Book Company, Inc.: Barry Goldwater, *Why Not Victory?*, New York, 1962.

The Macmillan Company: Richard Fryklund, *100 Million Lives,* New York, 1962.

Orbis, A Quarterly Journal of World Affairs, published by the Foreign Policy Research Institute of the University of Pennsylvania: Fall 1959, Dean Acheson, "The Premises of American Policy"; Summer 1961, "Reflections on the Quarter"; Winter 1962, Herbert Dinerstein, "Soviet Goals and Military Force"; Spring 1962, Robert Strausz-Hupé, "The Sino-Soviet Tangle and U.S. Policy."

The New Republic: March 12, 1962, "The War in Vietnam: We Have Not Been Told the Whole Truth." Copyright © 1962 by Harrison-Blaine, Inc.

Prentice-Hall, Inc.: The American Assembly, *Arms Control: Issues for the Public.* Copyright © 1961. By permission of Prentice-Hall, Inc., publisher.

Public Affairs Press: Raymond Garthoff, *The Soviet Image of Future War,* Washington, 1959.

The Twentieth Century Fund: Thomas C. Schelling and Morton H. Halperin, *Strategy and Arms Control,* New York, 1961.

The World Publishing Company: Ernest Lefever, *Ethics and United States Foreign Policy.* Copyright © 1957 by The World Publishing Company. A Living Age Book, published by Meridian Books, The World Publishing Company. Reprinted by permission of The World Publishing Company.

The Yale Review, copyright © 1959, Yale University Press: Robert Strausz-Hupé, "Nuclear Blackmail and Limited War," Winter 1959.

Quotes from "Rational Defense: Nuclear Displacement" by Charles Osgood are reprinted by permission from the June 1962 *Bulletin of the Atomic Scientists,* published by the Educational Foundation for Nuclear Science, 935 East 60th Street, Chicago 37, Illinois.

INDEX

Acheson, Dean, 204–205, 262–263
Adenauer, Konrad, 123–124
Africa, 142
Agreements, *see* Treaties
Air power, *see* SAC (Strategic Air Command)
Allies, 6, 101. *See also* Europe, France, Germany, Great Britain
Alsop, Stewart, 332n6
America, 274
American Academy of Political and Social Science, 184
American Friends Service Committee, *Disarm to Parley*, 295n17; *Speak Truth to Power*, 305n31
American Strategy for the Nuclear Age (eds. W. F. Hahn and J. C. Neff), 134
Analyses, defined, 3; and probabilities, 9; and recommendations, 12; and values, 13, 21–22, 65, 98–99; statistical, 24–25; and predictions, 25–26; marginalist, 98–103; divergencies among, 312–333
"Analytical futures," 25n7
Anti-Communist marginalism, 48, 61–62, 77–82, 128–153, 217, 329; and "protracted conflict," 77; and freedom, 78; and peace, 78, 80–81; and right wing, 79–80; and power, 80, 136–141; and war, 80–81, 133–135, 144–153; and time, 81–82; and the opponent, 127–136; and Sino-Soviet relations, 129; compared to anti-war marginalism, 130–132, 324–326; and Cuba, 138–139; and world opinion, 139–140; and risk-taking, 140–141; and allies and neutrals, 141–144; and under-developed areas, 141–144; and arms race, 146; and NATO, 148; on military strategy, 229–232; and counterforce, 229–230; and first strike,

230–231; and "win strike second," 229–231; on Europe, 263–266; compared to anti-Communist systemists, 307
Anti-Communist systemism, 47, 50–51, 54, 305–312; compared to anti-war systemism, 48; compared to anti-Communist marginalism, 307
Anti-war marginalism, 48, 61, 70–76, 104–127; and "unilateral initiatives," 61, 71; and peace, 72; and freedom, 72; and power, 72, 75, 117–121; and right wing, 74–75; on imperialism, 74; and Communism, 75; and time, 76; and war, 104–105, 108–109; and deterrence, 105–106; and civil defense, 109; and the opponent, 110–117; and Germany, 113–114, 122–124; and East Europe, 114–115; and allies and neutrals, 121–125; and NATO, 122; and Cuba, 119–121; and United States, 125–127; compared to anti-Communist marginalism, 130–132, 136; on military strategy, 224–229; on disarmament, 234–235; and underdeveloped areas, 271–274; compared to anti-war systemism, 293, 302–303; compared to middle marginalism, 315, 318–319
Anti-war systemism, 47, 267, 281–305; compared to anti-Communist systemism, 48; on Germany, 270, 286–287, 302; and policy makers, 281–282, 305; compared to marginalists, 282–283, 302–303; and disarmament, 284–285, 299; on Europe, 285–287; and nonviolence, 293–305; and maximizing mechanisms, 294; and Communism, 294–298

Appeasement, and "balanced-value" middle marginalists, 86; and "analytical" middle marginalists, 94; and West Germany, 286
Arms control, 5, 219–223, 233–239. *See also* Disarmament
Arms Control, Disarmament, and National Security (ed. D. G. Brennan), 8, 54, 70–71, 84, 95, 106, 171, 197, 217
Arms Control: Issues for the Public (The American Assembly), 135, 165, 221–222, 234–235, 242–243
Arms race, and anti-war marginalists, 106–108; and militarism, 126; and anti-Communist marginalists, 146; and middle marginalists, 173, 316; and stability, 243; and anti-Communist systemists, 309
Arms Reduction, Programs and Issues (ed. D. H. Frisch), 226–227
Asia, and anti-Communist marginalism, 141–143, 274–275; and nuclear deterrence, 148; Southeast, 272–277, 329

Balance of terror, 242n29; and middle marginalism, 165–168, 189; and stabilization, 225; and tactical war, 240–241; and anti-Communist marginalism, 245–246; and anti-Communist systemism, 309
Barnett, A. Doak, 197
Barnett, Frank Rockwell, 263–264
Bay of Pigs, 119–120, 138–139, 201
Berlin, 326–327; and middle marginalism, 193; and war, 249, 260–261; and anti-war marginalism, 268–269; and anti-Communist systemism, 308; and wall, 321
"Better Dead than Red," 38, 310
"Better Red than Dead," 37–38, 40
Bjelajac, Slavko N., 149, 152, 263
Blackmail, nuclear, 133, 150, 312; by U.S.S.R., 165, 246; and civil defense, 230; in West Europe, 249, 254, 256; and NATO, 250; and anti-Communist marginalism, 265
Bowles, Chester, 61, 117–119, 330;

Ideas, People, and Peace, 117–118; *Agenda 1961*, 119
Bozell, L. Brent, 307–308
Brennan, Donald G., 235–236
Brodie, Bernard, *Strategy in the Missile Age*, 7
Brown, Harrison, 6, 107; *Community of Fear*, 7, 107, 288
Brzezinski, Zbigniew, 194–198, 261, 328–329
Buchan, Alastair, *NATO in the 1960s*, 182–183, 253n37; on colonialism, 205–206
Bull, Hedley, *The Control of the Arms Race*, 236
Bulletin of the Atomic Scientists, 118–119, 162, 218–219
Burnham, James, 51, 311–312
"Buying time," 174, 236

Castro, Fidel, 120, 139, 200–202, 306
Chamberlain, Neville, 94
Cherne, Leo, 276–277
China, People's Republic of, and anti-war marginalism, 116–117; and U.S.S.R., 128–129, 196–198; manpower of, 204; and Taiwan, 228; and independent deterrent, 253; and Southeast Asia, 272–273, 275; and anti-Communist systemists, 308
Civil defense, and anti-war marginalism, 73, 109; and middle marginalism, 86–87, 178, 207–208, 242; and anti-Communist marginalism, 147; and balance of terror, 225; and counterforce, 230, 232; and first strike, 246; and anti-Communist systemism, 309
Clark, Grenville, *World Peace Through World Law*, 291
Cold War, 149–150, 207
Colonialism, 74, 122–123, 205–206
Commentary, 283
Common Market, 203–204
Communism, in Southeast Asia, 272–277
    Views of anti-Communist marginalism: 78–79, 128–153, 229–230; on U.S. victory, 81–82, 232; on

Sino-Soviet relations, 128–129; on West Europe, 131, 133, 142–143; on Germany, 131, 133; on East Europe, 131–132; and war, 134–135; compared to anti-war marginalist views, 135–136; on Cuba, 138–139; and world opinion, 139–140; and Asia, 141–143; on subversive groups, 149–150; and domestic threat, 153
Views of anti-Communist systemism: 50, 54, 281, 305–312
Views of anti-war marginalism: 75, 133
Views of anti-war systemism: 294–305; on nonaggressiveness, 294–296, 298–299, 301; on totalitarianism, 296–297; on expansionism, 297–298
Views of middle marginalism: 156–157, 211; "Balanced value," 83, 87–88; "analytical," 83, 92–93
Compromise, 40–43. See also Negotiations, Treaties
Conservatism, 38, 41, 50
Consistency, of analyses, 14, 16, 34
Cook, Fred J., 302–303, 311
Costs, of defense, 182–183
Cotrell, Alvin J., on Communism, 62, 129–130, 151–152. See also Strausz-Hupé, Protracted Conflict
Counterforce, 174–177, 229–230, 328; and melioration of war, 232; and middle marginalism, 232–233, 242–243; and NATO, 258–259
Cousins, Norman, In Place of Folly, 289–291
Cuba, and anti-war marginalism, 119–121; and anti-Communist marginalism, 138–139; and middle marginalism, 200–202; and anti-Communist systemism, 308

Dahl, Robert, Politics, Economics, and Welfare, 29n9
Daniel, Jean, 268, 321
Davis, Saville R., 8
Defense Department, see United States Department of Defense
Democracy, and referendum, 17–18;

promotes marginalism, 21, 58–59; threatened by militarism, 207–208; in South Vietnam, 276–277
Deterrence, mutual, 73, 245, 247; and anti-war marginalism, 73, 239, 266–271; starts war, 105–106; stable, 106, 225–226; and anti-Communist marginalism, 146, 239, 263–266; in Asia, 148; political aspects of, 189–191, 246; and U.S. superiority, 200, 244–245; balanced, 217–219, 256–257; and second strike, 242; in West Europe, 249–254, 256, 258–260; independent, 250–253, 256–258, 265; and anti-war systemism, 282, 288
Views of middle marginalists: 164, 167–168, 170–172, 233, 248–263, 321–322; and "analytical" school, 84; failure of, 158–159; and disarmament, 172–173; and counterforce, 174–175; and limited retaliation, 178–185; unilateral, 238–239, 242–243
Dinerstein, Herbert S., 192
Disarmament, 2, 5, 328–329; unilateral, 51, 54–57, 72, 84, 113, 284–285, 301, 323; and anti-war marginalists, 72, 113, 224–229, 234–235; and middle marginalists, 94, 172–173; multilateral, 228–229; and anti-war systemists, 282, 299, 301; and anti-Communist systemists, 307
Disengagement, 329; and middle marginalists, 262; and anti-war marginalists, 268, 270, 301; and anti-war systemists, 285–286
Dominance, logical, 42–43, 89–91, 300, 320, 323
Dougherty, James E., 62, 129–130. See also Strausz-Hupé, Protracted Conflict
Draper, Theodore, 119–120
Dulles, John Foster, 205

Eisenhower, Dwight D., 18, 143; warns against militarism, 87, 125–126, 208, 330; on nuclear weapons,

119, 166, 332; on Cuba, 120; on
defense costs, 183; on Suez, 205
Elections, 18–19
Ellsberg, Daniel, 41, 99
Emerson, Rupert, 122, 143
Escalation, feared by anti-war marginalists, 73, 105, 109–110; and
middle marginalists, 157, 167–170;
and melioration of war, 231–232;
in Europe, 250; in Southeast Asia,
272, 275
Etzioni, Amitai, 6, 56, 71, 76, 111,
293, 327; *The Hard Way to Peace*,
56, 76, 105, 110–111; on "war by
mistake," 105, 108–110, 160; and
"unilateral initiatives," 228
Europe, and neutral belt, 193, 195;
unification of, 132, 260, 263; and
anti-Communist marginalists, 142–
143; disengagement in, 270–271;
and anti-war systemists, 285–293;
and marginalists, 325, 328
    East Europe: and anti-war mar-
ginalists, 114–115, 267; and anti-
Communist marginalists, 131–132,
140, 263; and middle marginalists,
193, 205–206, 262; and U.S.S.R.,
194–195; and anti-war systemists,
302; and anti-Communist systemists, 308. *See also* German Democratic Republic; Satellites
    West Europe: and anti-Commu-
nist marginalists, 131, 263–266; and
anti-war marginalists, 121–125,
266–271; military forces of, 165,
181–182, 204–205, 249, 251–254;
United States defense of, 166, 195,
239–240, 246, 248, 254, 287; and
NATO, 181–182, 255, 264–266; and
U.S.S.R., 192–193, 249, 256–261,
266, 296; and middle marginalists,
247–263, 317
Experts, military, 102, 126

Facts defined, 22–23
Fascism, 67–68, 75
Federation of American Scientists,
118
Fellner, William, 20, 65n1

Ferguson, Allen R., *Disarmament and
Deterrence*, 260–261
Ferry, W. H., *Disarm to Parley*, 295–
296
Finkelstein, Lawrence S., 94; *Defence,
Disarmament, and World Order*,
89
Finland, 192, 195
First strike, 170–171, 320, 322; by
United States, 165, 176, 240, 246–
248, 250–251, 254, 256–258; "credible," 246, 254–258, 265; Soviet,
175–176; and anti-Communist marginalists, 231, 245, 265; and middle
marginalists, 244–246
Foreign Affairs, 114–115, 117, 164,
172–173, 182, 194–195, 203n57,
242n29, 253n37, 254–255, 262–263,
270
Foreign Policy Research Institute of
the University of Pennsylvania, 62,
77
Fortune, 201
Foster, Richard, 230
France, 251, 254
Freedom, and marginalists, 68, 70;
and anti-war marginalists, 72–73;
and anti-Communist marginalists,
78–79; and "balanced-value" middle marginalists, 86–87; and "analytical" middle marginalists, 90–
92; for satellites, 263
Freund, Gerald, *Germany Between
Two Worlds*, 123
Frisch, David H., 226, 229
Fromm, Erich, 83; *May Man Prevail?*, 6, 286, 299; on Germany, 286,
301; on U.S.S.R., 290, 299–300
Fryklund, Richard, *100 Million Lives*,
166, 174–175, 177, 326; on escalation, 167, 179
Fulbright, J. William, 203

Gallois, Pierre, 257–258; *The Balance
of Terror*, 251–252
Garthoff, Raymond L., *The Soviet
Image of Future War*, 190–191
German Democratic Republic, 114,
269, 308

German Federal Republic, feared by U.S.S.R., 113–114; fear of Nazism in, 123; and nuclear weapons, 267, 270; and anti-war marginalists, 267–271; disengagement in, 270–271; divided and disarmed, 286; and middle marginalists, 317

Germany, 329; reunification of, 124, 206–207; and anti-war marginalists, 125; and anti-Communist marginalists, 144; and "unilateral initiatives," 228; and unified Europe, 248; and disengagement, 262–263; and militarism, 268, 301. *See also* German Democratic Republic; German Federal Republic

Giffin, S. F., 244

Goodman, Paul, 283–284

Goldwater, Barry, 19, 50, 54, 59, 315; *The Conscience of a Conservative*, 50, 54; *Why Not Victory?*, 306–307, 310–311

Gollancz, Victor, *The Devil's Repertoire*, 7, 304–305

Great Britain, and independent deterrent, 251, 254

Griffith, William, 194–195, 261

Hahn, Walter F., 77n11, 151–152

Halle, Louis, 115–116

Halperin, Morton H., 6, 8, 92; *Strategy and Arms Control*, 6, 92, 161; *Arms Control and Inadvertent General War*, 169–170; *A Proposal for a Ban on the Use of Nuclear Weapons*, 179–180

Harriman, Averell, 275–276

Hekhuis, Dale J., 253–254

Hirshleifer, Jack, 207–208

Hitch, Charles J., *The Economics of Defense in the Nuclear Age*, 8

Hook, Sidney, 62, 83, 126–127; *Political Power and Personal Freedom*, 87

Hostages, 231–232, 246

Howard, Michael, *Disengagement in Europe*, 124

Hughes, H. Stuart, 293, 300, 310, 315;

An Approach to Peace, 284–285, 296–298, 312

Humphrey, George, 183

Huntington, Samuel P., 173; *The Soldier and the State*, 8

Iklé, Fred, 162

Imperialism, 74–75, 79–80, 87

Inductive logic, *see* Logic

International law, in Vietnam, 274–275; and anti-war systemism, 289, 291

Jackson, Henry M., 202

John Birch Society, 281

Johnson, Frank L., *No Substitute for Victory*, 308

Johnson, Lyndon, 19

Jordan, Nehemiah, 40–41; *Decision-Making under Uncertainty and Problem-Solving*, 41n17

Journal of Conflict Resolution, 253–254

Kahn, Herman, 84, 283; *On Thermonuclear War*, 7, 89, 91, 165–166, 173–174, 190–191, 202–203, 245–246; *Techniques of Systems Analysis*, 29n10, 42n20; on "buying time," 89–90, 94; on civil defense, 109; *Thinking About the Unthinkable*, 159–160, 164, 246; on escalation, 167; on "credible first strike," 165–166, 251

Kaplan, Morton, *The Strategy of Limited Retaliation*, 177

Kennan, George F., 330; *Russia, the Atom, and the West*, 113; on Communist threat to Europe, 113–114, 121, 299; on satellites, 131; on Germany, 270, 286

Kennedy, John F., 18–19, 106, 140–141, 143; on Cuba, 121, 139, 201; on war, 152, 331–332; on defense costs, 183–184; on United Nations, 205

Khrushchev, Nikita, 112, 115–116, 193, 197–198, 230, 290

King, James E., Jr., 165, 234, 242–243, 256

Kintner, William R., 62; on "systemic revolution," 29n10, 149; and "protracted conflict," 77, 134; on freedom, 78; on war, 80, 135, 137, 145–146, 148; on Communism, 129–132; on psychological offensive, 140; on Asia, 142–143. *See also* Strausz-Hupé, *A Forward Strategy for America;* and *Protracted Conflict*

Kissinger, Henry A., 6, 323, 333; *The Necessity for Choice,* 6, 90–91, 167–168, 176, 178, 206–207, 258–259; on peace, 90–91; on escalation, 167–168; on counterforce, 176, 232; on limited retaliation, 178; on Europe, 182, 206–207, 258–259; on communal deterrents, 254n39

Laos, 273, 275–276

Lefever, Ernest W., 62, 85–86; *Ethics and United States Foreign Policy,* 88, 199; on power, 88, 93, 199–200

Left wing, 209

Lexicographic systems, 39n16, 301

Liberal Democrat, The, 297–298

Liberal Papers, The, 55n10, 72n4, 106, 112, 119, 121–122, 124, 126, 196–197, 227, 269, 287n8

Limited Strategic War, 241

Lindblom, Charles, *Politics, Economics, and Welfare,* 29n9

Lippmann, Walter, *The Communist World and Ours,* 112–113; *The Coming Tests with Russia,* 113–114

Logic, of definitions, 13–14; of value judgments, 14–21; deductive, 22–23; inductive, 24, 34–35

Luce, R. Duncan, *Games and Decisions,* 16n2, 37

McCarthyism, 1–2

McClintock, Charles G., 253–254

Machiavelli, 7

Machlup, Fritz, 30–31

McKean, Roland N., *The Economics of Defense in the Nuclear Age,* 8

McNamara, Robert, 79, 328, 332n5

Mann, Irwin, *Techniques of Systems Analysis,* 29n10, 42n20

Mao Tse-Tung, 197–198

Marginalism, 58–97; recommendations of, 29–30, 51, 60, 210–279; compared to systemists, 30, 51–57, 282–284; and economic theories, 31–32; and value differences, 52, 94–97, 211, 223; on military strategy, 217, 224–247; and negotiations, 220–223; and Europe, 248–271; and Southeast Asia, 271–277. *See also* Anti-Communist marginalism; Anti-war marginalism; Middle marginalism

Marshall, S. L. A., 275–277

Martin, Kingsley, 53

Maximization, 32, 36–40, 59; and middle marginalists, 210; and anti-war systemists, 294, 301; and anti-Communist systemists, 309–310

Middle marginalism, 62–64, 82–97, 154–209, 315–333; and war, 156–185, 232, 235, 316; compared to anti-war marginalism, 158, 168–169, 315; and rationality, 159–163; and escalation, 166–169; and arms race, 173–174; and counterforce, 174–177; and limited retaliation, 177–184; and the opponent, 185–198; and power, 198–203; and allies and neutrals, 203–207; and NATO, 204, 249–250, 258–262; and time, 236, 238; and colonialism, 205–206; and Europe, 204–206, 248–263; and Germany, 206–207; and United States, 207–209; on militarism, 207; and stable deterrence, 244–245, 257–259; and "credible first strike," 251, 254, 256; compared to anti-Communist marginalism, 245; and Southeast Asia, 275–277

"Analytical" middle marginalism: 83–84, 89–95, 315; and logical dominance, 89–91; and time, 89–90, 93–94; and peace, 90, 94; and not-killing, 91; and right wing, 92; and U.S.S.R., 317

"Balanced-value" middle marginalism: 83, 85–89, 205, 315; and peace, 86; and not-killing, 87; and Communism, 87–88; and time, 88–89

Melman, Seymour, *The Peace Race,* 7

Militarism, as threat to United States, 125–126, 207–208, 302–303, 317–318, 330; and anti-Communist marginalists, 153; German, 301; and anti-Communist systemists, 311; and the military, 2, 5, 207–209, 303

Millis, Walter, 72, 106, 119

Mills, C. Wright, 27n8; *The Power Elite,* 10; *The Causes of World War III,* 10

Milnor, J. W., 16n2

"Missile gap," 164, 176

Munich, 94

Murphy, Charles J. V., 201

Myrdal, Gunnar, *An American Dilemma,* 8n15

Nation, The, 72n3, 302

NATO (North Atlantic Treaty Organization), 114, 122, 143; and Germany, 144, 269–270; and anti-Communist marginalism, 148, 264–265, 324; and nuclear weapons, 148, 157–158, 250; and conventional weapons, 151, 181–182, 250, 257; costs of, 183; and middle marginalism, 195, 204, 248–249, 262; and U.S.S.R., 192; and United States, 205; and deterrence, 25, 258–259; as first strike force, 254–255; and anti-war marginalism, 266–267, 270–271

Nazism, 123

Neal, Fred Warner, 315; *U.S. Foreign Policy and the Soviet Union,* 23n6, 286–287, 298–300, 302

Negotiations, 220–223; and anti-war marginalists, 226; failure of, 227, 327; and middle marginalists, 238, 260–261; and anti-Communist systemists, 306. *See also* Treaties

Neutralism, 194, 308

New Leader, The, 83n15, 119–120, 207–208, 275–276, 333n8

New Republic, The, 47–48, 52–53, 115–116, 197–198, 208, 268, 272–274, 277

New Statesman, The, 53

New York Times, The, 107–108, 125–126, 188, 193, 202, 276–277

New Yorker, The, 172

Niebuhr, Reinhold, 288

Nixon, Richard M., 18–19, 152, 183

Nonviolence, 293–294, 304–305

Not-killing, 68, 73, 87, 91, 303–305

"Nth country" war, 252

Nuclear testing, 52–54, 118, 197, 308

Opponent, the, and marginalists, 100; and anti-war marginalists, 110–117; and anti-Communist marginalists, 128–136; and middle marginalists, 185–198. *See also* China; Communism; U.S.S.R.

Optimization, 32–36; and marginalists, 63–64, 210; and anti-war marginalists, 71, 293–294

Orbis, 77, 79n15, 129, 133, 138–139, 143, 147, 149, 192, 204–205, 263–265

Osgood, Charles E., 287, 293, 327; on "unilateral initiatives," 55, 112, 221, 238–239; on U.S.S.R., 111; on nuclear displacement, 218–219; on militarism, 126–127; on peace, 211; on civil defense, 225–227; on balance of terror, 240–241

Peace, and marginalists, 67–68, 70, 211; and anti-war marginalists, 72–73; and anti-Communist marginalists, 80–81; and middle marginalists, 90–91, 239, 320–321; and anti-war systemists, 295, 300–301; and anti-Communist systemists, 306

Pickus, Robert, 297–298

Policy-making process, 3–4, 6–7, 17

Possony, Stefan T., on war strategy, 62, 80, 137, 145–149; on civilian control of the military, 79; on Com-

munism, 130–132, 135; on Asia, 141–143. *See also* Strausz-Hupé, *A Forward Strategy for America*
Power, in marginalist analyses, 68–70, 100–101
Views of anti-war marginalists: 72, 75, 117–121, 273
Views of anti-Communist marginalists: 80, 136–141, 274; military, 137, 140–141; and world opinion, 138–140; as will power, 140
Views of middle marginalists: 88, 198–203, 275, 317; "analytical," 90, 93; compared to anti-Communist marginalists, 205
Predictions, untestable, 24–26
Preemption, *see* War, preemptive
Presidency, 18–20, 330–331
Probabilities, of inductive analysis, 24–25; and optimization, 33–35; and "psychological certainty," 40–41; and values, 98–99; of escalation, 108–109, 168
"Protracted conflict," 77, 80, 134, 148, 152, 217, 221
"Psychological certainty," 40–41, 294
Public Policy, 173

Race relations, 281
Raiffa, Howard, *Games and Decisions*, 16n2, 20n4, 37
RAND Corporation, 261n45, 283, 311–312
Rapoport, Anatol, 71–72
Rationality, 40–43, 145, 327; of middle marginalists, 159–163, 172, 233–234
Real, James, *Community of Fear*, 7, 107
Recommendations, and values, 3, 9, 12–13, 17, 21; divergencies among, 26–30, 45–57, 313–333; unconditional and conditional, defined, 27–28; marginal and systemic, defined, 28–29; optimizing and maximizing, 32, 37
Views of marginalists: 210–279; of anti-war marginalists, 61; of anti-Communist marginalists, 61–

62; of middle marginalists, 62–64; on strategy, 224–247; on Europe, 248–271; on Southeast Asia, 271–277
Views of systemists: of anti-war systemists, 284–292; of anti-Communist systemists, 307–312
Retaliation, massive, 2, 166–168; limited, 174, 177; and first strike, 218–219; and NATO, 251–252
Revolutions, 149, 194
Richardson, Robert C., 147–148
Right wing, and anti-war marginalists, 73–74; and anti-Communist marginalists, 79–80; and middle marginalists, 87, 92, 209
Rockefeller, Nelson, 19, 183
Russell, Bertrand, 37–38, 50–51; *Has Man a Future?*, 37n15; *Common Sense and Nuclear Warfare*, 49, 288, 292

SAC (Strategic Air Command), 251, 254, 309
Satellites, 262–263, 301–302, 317. *See also* East Europe
Schelling, Thomas C., *Strategy and Arms Control*, 6, 92, 161, 233–234, 236–237; *The Strategy of Conflict*, 6, 159, 180–181; and middle marginalism, 63; *The Stability of Total Disarmament*, on war, 32, 91–92, 171, 241–242; on time, 94–95; on NATO, 157–158; on disarmament, 172–173
Schlesinger, Arthur M., Jr., 50; *The Age of Roosevelt*, vol. III, 48
Schumpeter, Joseph, 60–61; *Capitalism, Socialism, and Democracy*, 60n2
Schwarz, Fred, *The Communist Interpretation of Peace*, 306
SEATO (Southeast Asia Treaty Organization), 142, 277
Senate Foreign Relations Committee, *see* United States Senate Committee on Foreign Relations
Seversky, Alexander P. de, 311; *America: Too Young to Die!*, 309
Shulman, Marshall D., 188, 193–194

Sibley, Mulford, *Unilateral Initiatives and Disarmament*, 56–57, 304
Singer, J. David, 71–72
Smith, Margaret Chase, 140–141
Snow, Charles P., 107–108, 296
Snyder, Glenn, *Deterrence and Defense*, 170–171
Sohn, Louis B., 226, 229, 291
Speak Truth to Power (AFSC), 305n31
Stabilization, of nuclear weapons, 224–229; of U.S.-U.S.S.R. relations, 239–240
Stalin, 297
Stanford Research Institute Journal, 230
Stevenson, Adlai, 19, 61, 117, 330
Strausz-Hupé, Robert, *A Forward Strategy for America*, 29n10, 77–80, 130–132, 135, 137, 140–152, 222–223, 229–232, 264–266, 302–303, 325–326; *Protracted Conflict*, 77, 129–131, 142–144; on revolution, 29, 149; on freedom, 78, 211; and U.S. military power, 80, 137, 140, 148; on Communism, 128–133, 135; on satellites, 132, 264; on Asia, 141–143; on rationality, 145; on nuclear blackmail, 150–151; on conventional war, 151–152; and middle marginalists, 155; on "win strike second," 229–230; on first strike, 231
Symington, Stuart, 176n26
Systemism, 72, 280–313; defined, 29–30, 50–52; and political power, 58, 280–282; and "systemic middle-roadism," 47–48; compared to marginalism, 216. *See also* Anti-Communist systemism; Anti-war systemism

Taiwan, 228
Taylor, Maxwell D., *The Uncertain Trumpet*, 331–332
Teller, Edward, 54, 63; *The Legacy of Hiroshima*, 180–181
Time, for marginalists, 69–70, 221–223, 320–321; for anti-war marginalists, 76, 267; for anti-Communist marginalists, 81–82; for middle marginalists, 93–94, 235–236, 238
Tito, Marshal, 115
"Transitivity," 16
Treaties, 179–180, 193, 220–221, 238, 246. *See also* Negotiations
Truman, Harry S., 166

Underdeveloped areas, 88, 112–113, 122, 204–205; and anti-war marginalists, 74–75, 110, 136, 271–274; and anti-Communist marginalists, 80, 82, 136, 140–144, 274; and U.S.S.R., 193–194; and middle marginalists, 317
"Unilateral initiatives," 55–57, 221, 327; and marginalists, 29–30, 71; and anti-war systemists, 29–30, 284–285, 293, 304; and negotiations, 227–228
Union of Socialist Soviet Republics, and anti-war marginalists, 110–116, 136, 267, 270; and "unilateral initiatives," 111–112, 228; threatens Europe, 113, 192–193, 248–250, 256–257, 259–263, 266; fears West Germany, 113–114; and Khrushchev, 114–116; and China, 116–117, 128–129, 196–198; and risk-taking, 133–135, 189–191; and anti-Communist marginalists, 133–136, 185–186; expansionism of, 186–187, 191–192, 298–299, 327–328; and middle marginalists, 185–198, 234–235, 317; and underdeveloped areas, 193–194; and East Europe, 194–195, 302; and negotiations, 220–222, 227–228; and counterforce, 229–230, 243; and U.S. first strike, 245–247; consolidationism of, 267, 270; and anti-war systemists, 290, 298–305
United Nations, 139, 143, 205, 289–291, 306
United States, and marginalists, 101; and anti-war marginalists, 125–127; as moral leader, 140, 203, 231; and anti-Communist marginalists, 153; first strike by, 165–166; De-

partment of Defense, 184, 216, 324; and Cuba, 200–201; and West Europe, 203, 229–231, 248; and middle marginalism, 207–209, 234; and withdrawal, 286–287; and militarism, 302–303
United States Senate Committee on Foreign Relations, 193–194, 249; *United States Foreign Policy in Western Europe*, 151, *U.S.S.R. and Eastern Europe*, 186–189, 195–196
U.S.S.R., see Union of Socialist Soviet Republics
Utility, 15n1, 20, 118–119, 223

Values, defined, 3, 9, 12–21, 27, 33–40; of systemists, 52, 296–302; of marginalists, 52, 65–97, 211; and peace, 67–68, 70; and freedom, 68, 70; and power, 68–70; and time, 69–70; divergencies among, 312–333. *See also* Freedom; Peace; Power; Time
Vietnam, South, 272–277; North, 274

Walker, Edwin, 208
War, "levels" of, 3; limited, 73, 147, 150, 157–158, 167, 177–181, 231, 241, 266, 308–309, 316; melioration of, 73, 80–81, 91, 109, 232; probability of, 73, 108, 160–161, 164, 168; in marginalist analyses, 100; undeterrable, 104, 145–146, 158; "by mistake," 105, 107–108, 160–163, 169–170, 211, 217, 219, 316; "Nth country," 105, 162, 252; in Europe, 110, 166–167, 249, 267; and risk-taking, 133–134, 140–141, 145, 172, 243, 260–261; and "protracted conflict," 134, 148–149; total, 135, 157–158, 167, 176, 181, 187, 190, 316; in Cuba, 139; and irrationality, 145, 159–163, 172, 316; as instrument of policy, 145–146, 152, 163–164, 169–170; and arms race, 146–147; revolutionary, 149, 263–264; guerrilla, 149, 152, 158, 184, 263, 273–274; deterrable, 146, 158, 167–168, 188–189, 240–243; con-

trollable, 147, 174–175, 178–179; conventional, 150–152, 179, 181–182, 240, 249–250, 257–258; tactical nuclear, 148, 179–180, 218–219, 224–226, 241, 243, 250, 257–258, 265–266, 326–327; and "nuclear blackmail," 150; unconventional, 152, 184; by escalation, 157–158, 167, 169, 179, 231–232, 248, 250, 267; and NATO, 157, 181, 257, 267; preemptive, 163–166, 169–171, 176, 219, 230–231, 246–248, 320; by calculation, 164–166; self-generating, 169–171, 185; and counterforce, 174–175, 229–230, 232; and U.S.S.R., 187–190; and balance of terror, 225, 242–243, 246–246; and first strike, 230, 240, 245–247, 254; prevention of, 233–234, 248, 267; in Berlin, 260–261; in Vietnam, 273–277; certainty of, 295–296, 309
Views of anti-Communist marginalists: 133–141, 144–152, 263–266, 324; and risk-taking, 133–134, 140–141, 145, 243, 260–261; and "protracted conflict," 134; total, 135; in Cuba, 139; and irrationality, 145; undeterrable, 145–146; as instrument of policy, 145–146; and deterrence, 146, 240, 243; in Berlin, 260–261
Views of anti-Communist systemists: 307–308
Views of anti-war marginalists: 73, 104, 110, 267–270
Views of anti-war systemists: 294–296
Views of middle marginalists: 156–185, 263–266, 316; of "analytical" school, 83–84, 91; of "balanced-value" school, 86–87; total, 157–158, 167, 176, 181, 316; limited, 157–158, 167, 177–181, 316; and escalation, 157–158, 167, 169, 179; and NATO, 151, 157, 181, 257, 267; guerrilla, 158, 184; and deterrence, 158, 167–168, 240, 243; and counterforce, 174–175; tactical nuclear, 179–180, 241, 243, 250, 257–

258, 265–266; and balance of terror, 240–241, 243, 245–246; on Europe, 249, 267; on Berlin, 260–261
Warburg, James, 121–122, 124, 269, 286
Waskow, Arthur J., 61, 293, 327; *The Limits of Defense*, 74, 109, 126, 172, 217–218, 228–229, 271; on domestic militarism, 74, 126; on time, 76; on balance of terror, 109, 217–218, 225, 240–241, 256; on peace, 211
Weapons, nuclear, 179–181, 218–220, 224–226, 250–259, 265–266; conventional, 181–182, 228–229, 258–259, 265, displacement of, 218–219; inspection of, 225–226; limitation of, 228–229, 238; first strike, 230–231; and counterforce, 242–243; in Europe, 251, 267; diffusion of, 252, 254–255, 257

Whiting, Allen S., 196–197
Wiesner, Jerome, 61, 70–71, 146, 330; on likelihood of war, 73; on mutual deterrence, 106, 217, 225; on disarmament, 229
Willetts, Harry, 135, 221–222
Wilson, Charles, 183
Wilson, Woodrow, 58n1
"Win strike second," 229–231, 245, 247, 265
Wohlstetter, Albert, 164, 242n29, 254–258
Wolk, Herman S., 209
World government, 76, 312
World opinion, 118, 139, 202
World Politics, 8, 23n5, 157–158, 319n1

Zagoria, Donald, *The Sino-Soviet Conflict*, 196

BOOKS PREPARED UNDER THE AUSPICES OF
THE CENTER FOR INTERNATIONAL AFFAIRS,
HARVARD UNIVERSITY

PUBLISHED BY HARVARD UNIVERSITY PRESS

The Soviet Bloc, by Zbigniew K. Brzezinski, 1960 (sponsored jointly with Russian Research Center).
Rift and Revolt in Hungary, by Ferenc A. Váli, 1961.
The Economy of Cyprus, by A. J. Meyer, with Simos Vassiliou, 1962 (jointly with Center for Middle Eastern Studies).
Entrepreneurs of Lebanon, by Yusif A. Sayigh, 1962 (jointly with Center for Middle Eastern Studies).
Communist China 1955–1959, with a foreword by Robert R. Bowie and John K. Fairbank, 1962 (jointly with East Asian Research Center).
In Search of France, by Stanley Hoffmann, Charles P. Kindleberger, Laurence Wylie, Jesse R. Pitts, Jean-Baptiste Duroselle, and François Goguel, 1963.
Somali Nationalism, by Saadia Touval, 1963.
The Dilemma of Mexico's Development, by Raymond Vernon, 1963.
The Arms Debate, by Robert A. Levine, 1963.

AVAILABLE FROM OTHER PUBLISHERS

The Necessity for Choice, by Henry A. Kissinger, 1961. Harper & Brothers.
Strategy and Arms Control, by Thomas C. Schelling and Morton H. Halperin, 1961. Twentieth Century Fund.
United States Manufacturing Investment in Brazil, by Lincoln Gordon and Engelbert L. Grommers, 1962. Harvard Business School.
Limited War in the Nuclear Age, by Morton H. Halperin, 1963. John Wiley & Sons.

OCCASIONAL PAPERS IN INTERNATIONAL AFFAIRS,
PUBLISHED BY CENTER FOR INTERNATIONAL AFFAIRS

1. *A Plan for Planning: The Need for a Better Method of Assisting Underdeveloped Countries on Their Economic Policies,* by Gustav F. Papanek, 1961.

2. *The Flow of Resources from Rich to Poor,* by Alan D. Neale, 1961.
3. *Limited War: An Essay on the Development of the Theory and an Annotated Bibliography,* by Morton H. Halperin, 1962.
4. *Reflections on the Failure of the First West Indian Federation,* by Hugh W. Springer, 1962.
5. *On the Interaction of Opposing Forces under Possible Arms Agreements,* by Glenn A. Kent, 1963.